Hijacking Environmentalism

First published in the UK in 1997 by
Earthscan Publications Ltd

Copyright © Richard Welford, 1997

A catalogue record for this book is available from the British Library

ISBN: 1 85383 398 3 (hardback), 1 85383 399 1 (paperback)

**Typesetting by JS Typesetting, Wellingborough, Northants
Printed and bound in Great Britain by
Biddles Ltd, Guildford and King's Lynn**

Cover design by Andrew Corbett

For a full list of publications, please contact

Earthscan Publications Ltd
120 Pentonville Road
London N1 9JN
Tel: 0171 278 0433
Fax: 0171 278 1142
e-mail: earthinfo@earthscan.co.uk
http://www.earthscan.co.uk

Earthscan is an editorially independent subsidiary of Kogan Page Ltd
and publishes in association with WWF-UK and the International
Institute for Environment and Development

Hijacking Environmentalism

Corporate Responses to Sustainable Development

Richard Welford

with contributions from:
Eloy Casagrande Jr
David Jones
Tarja Ketola
Nick Mayhew
Pall Rikhardsson

Earthscan Publications Limited, London

This we know.
The Earth does not belong to man;
man belongs to the Earth.
This we know.
All things are connected
like the blood which unites one family.
All things are connected.

Whatever befalls the Earth
befalls the sons of the Earth.
Man did not weave the web of life,
he is merely a strand in it.
Whatever he does to the web
he does to himself.

Chief Sealth
Puget Sound, 1854

For Jason

Contents

Part 3 Searching for solutions

Preface

During the past few decades almost every ecosystem and primal culture on Earth has been disrupted, and in many cases totally ruined, by aggressive human beings (mostly men) and the institutional structures which we have created. The massive deforestation, associated species extinction, the replacement of complex animal communities with monocultures of cereal grain or tree plantation, intensive cruel animal farming practices, the poisoning of water supplies, the displacement of many indigenous populations and the murder of protesters who get in the way of 'progress' are all the result of human greed and the organization of the world's resources to serve private capital.

Our world is now caught up in a vicious circle. The more growth there is the more problems appear. The technocrats cannot stop the spiralling monster associated with the large corporation and private capital because they are afraid that if they do, everything will come to a standstill, the system will fall apart and we in the West will be plunged into financial ruin. Of course, the powerful corporate interests in the system, at the root of the crisis, tell us that there is nothing to worry about because they are leading the move towards environmental responsibility. This book demonstrates that this is another corporate lie.

The culture of consumption, materialism and greed which now dominates human behaviour in the West is, of course, a very comfortable one, and one which separates us (for now at least) from the havoc which such a culture brings. Even though we are aware of poverty, hunger, torture, suffering and injustices we do not get too excited about them because they rarely touch us too deeply. In any case as individuals we either feel powerless to do anything about them or feel that it is simply not our responsibility to sort them out. To try to tackle the issues might also put ourselves and our way of life at risk. Such is the extent of our selfishness.

One of the things we must realize is that the growth which we have come to expect and the increasing standards of material living which we have seen over the past decades cannot go on for ever. Infinite growth with a finite pool of resources is impossible. As we exploit our Earth more and more, the consequence is simply further loss of biodiversity, more pollution, increased problems with human health and a widening of the divide which exists between rich and poor.

Awareness of these issues is key. As awareness increases so openness to new ideas expands. The 1990s have seen a growth in awareness and a search by more and more individuals for answers to more and more unsolved issues. Some people are coming to realize the despair which materialism causes, both by those who have consumed but have been left unsatisfied and also amongst those who have been alienated by the inability to consume at all.

There is a recognition that the environmental crisis exists but a great deal of helplessness about what to do about it. On the other hand there are a lot of people (and businesses) who profess to know a lot about environmental issues and claim to have the answers. We must be very wary of those who offer simplistic solutions to complex problems, especially when their wider agendas are unclear.

This book therefore examines the way in which industry has, to date, attempted to deal with the challenge of sustainable development. It argues that progress has been poor because of the lack of a real commitment to all the aspects of that concept. It challenges business to change, to recognize its potential for leadership and to go beyond mere lip-service to the environmental and social crises which are mounting.

The book is divided into three parts. The first, on defining the problem, demonstrates that whilst modernist versions of environmental management have received some attention, the wider ecological, ethical and social aspects of sustainable development have been ignored and usurped. In brief, industry has hijacked the more radical environmental debate taking it out of its traditional discourses and placing it in a liberal-productivist frame of reference. The book shows how senior executives and their business clubs have achieved this by reconstructing the environmental agenda.

In the second part of the book we examine some fundamental underlying tensions between the protection of the environment and the nature of modern businesses. The arguments here show how businesses continue to operate outside of the ecological carrying capacity of the environment. In addition it challenges the sacred tenet of international trade arguing that there remain strong underlying conflicts between sustainable development and free trade. It is also argued that business puts too much emphasis on hierarchical organizational forms which stifle participation (a key aspect of sustainable development) inside the organization.

The final part of the book examines the way forward for the more sustainable business. It presents new models of the sustainable organization which place greater emphasis on issues such as equity and ethics. It calls for an ecological and spiritual awakening amongst business leaders and it ends with a call for more critical research on business activities, abandoning both the restrictive positivist and traditional interpretive paradigms of analysis.

The contributions in this book are best read as a set of related essays. Although there is a structure to the book and I try to move from defining the problem to offering some solutions, each chapter can easily be read and understood in isolation. It also means that the chapters of the book can be read in any order. For the new researcher, for example, starting with the final chapter on research methodology would be a useful way to proceed. Equally the contribution by Tarja Ketola (Chapter 5) mapping out how business operates outside of natural ecological boundaries is a good starting point for people new to this subject area.

Writing this book and collaborating with my co-authors has been one of the most depressing yet enlightening periods of my life. It has left me with bouts of helplessness and depression because I have come to realize just how wrong a system we have created. It is simply ridiculous that we allow businesses to continue to destroy our planet. The bottom line is now simple – people are dying as a result of environmental degradation, people are forced into working for subsistence wages because companies need to increase their profitability, those who resist the progress of capitalism are subjected to torture and even murdered by the state because they have campaigned for human rights. Yet business still operates in concert with the institutions and governments which cause such suffering and people still buy their products. Doing business in countries which abuse human rights and torture citizens means that you accept that practice. Not protesting when your opponents are hanged is tantamount to killing them yourself. To buy the products of such a company is to agree with its actions.

Yet the experience has also made me re-evaluate many of my own values and experiences. We can bring about change through our own actions. Each and every one of us can challenge business to operate more ethically. We can choose the products we buy and reject those which are produced in unreasonable ways. We can come to recognize our spirituality and interconnectedness and feel part of a more mystical process rather than a detached and helpless observer. We must do something however. As Chief Sealth reminded us over 140 years ago, to harm the world around us is to harm ourselves.

As ever, this book would not have been possible without the help and cooperation of many people. As well as the contributors to the book and the staff at Earthscan, I would like to thank a number of people who have given me ideas for parts of the book: Alicia Barcena, Edith Jenkins, Tom

Gladwin, Johannes Brinkmann, Bjarne Ytterhus, Mark Shayler and Sören Bergstrom. I would also like to thank the PhD students and researchers who took part in summer school in Denmark and Sweden in 1994 and 1995 who were a useful sounding boards for some of my ideas. Finally, my love and thanks go to Chris Maddison for everything.

Richard Welford
University of Huddersfield

About the Contributors

Richard Welford is professor of Business Economics at the University of Huddersfield, UK and Director of the Centre for Corporate Environmental Management. He is also visiting professor of Sustainable Management at the Norwegian School of Management in Oslo. This is his sixth book on the subject of corporate environmental management. He undertakes consultancy work and training for selected companies, is an advisor to a number of environmental organizations and is a director of two companies. He is also editor for the leading academic journal, *Business Strategy and the Environment*. His mix of academic and practitioner experience make him one of the leading authorities, worldwide, on corporate environmental management.

Pall Rikhardsson is a researcher and consultant attached to the Aarhus School of Business where he is studying the construction of corporate environmental management. His contribution was written whilst on sabbatical at the Centre for Corporate Environmental Management, University of Huddersfield.

Nick Mayhew is Director of Oikos, a research and communications programme based in London, driving discussion and debate in the business community about the challenge of 'sustainable development'. He specializes in producing entertaining, mixed-media 'lectures' on business and sustainable development issues.

Dr Tarja Ketola is a lecturer in the Department of Management Studies at Brunel University, UK. Her research interests include environmental values, change processes and ecologically sustainable business. Her contribution is based on her PhD awarded by Imperial College, London.

Eloy Casagrande Jr has worked for a number of European and Brazilian NGOs implementing sustainable socio-environmental projects in Brazil. At the time of writing, he was completing his PhD thesis at the Department of Mining Resources Engineering at the University of Nottingham. This relates the concept of sustainable development to the export oriented aluminium industry operating in the Brazilian Amazonian Basin.

David Jones is a researcher at the Centre for Corporate Environmental Management, University of Huddersfield. At the time of writing he was completing his PhD thesis examining culture change strategies for the sustainable organization. He had previously worked for a number of large companies in the UK and Japan.

Figures

Tables

PART 1

Defining the Problem

1

Introduction: What are we Doing to the World?

Richard Welford

There can now be little doubt that the environmental damage caused to the planet over the last few decades has got to a point that it is causing untold damage to humans and to other species. Much of that damage is irreversible and the massive use of non-renewable resources has taken little account of the needs of future generations. The situation is getting worse, impacting on human health, biodiversity and the social infrastructure of many societies. There is now clear evidence of climate change and we are losing the areas of wilderness left on the planet at an alarming rate. Governments have demonstrated little real effort directed at reversing these trends, preferring to leave the task to the voluntary efforts of businesses, pressure groups, other non-governmental organisations and individuals.

We are now faced with a series of very tangible environmental crises. There is a serious water shortage across most of Africa, China, North America and now in parts of Europe. Global food security has declined with carryover grain stocks dropping to their lowest levels in twenty years between 1994 and 1995. Fish catches are in decline and in 1995 there was a shortfall of two million tons of rice (Brown 1995). Over 90 per cent of ancient forests in North America have been destroyed. We lose 25 billion tons of topsoil every year, the equivalent of all the wheat fields in Australia. This type of environmental unsustainability associated with continuously rising demand and a shrinking resource base now spills over into social and economic instability. Events in Rwanda, Somalia, Haiti and even former Yugoslavia have all been exacerbated by battles over access to basic resources. Human health is deteriorating and life expectancy rates in the poorest countries are in decline. The immune system of every unborn child in the world is now adversely and probably irrevocably affected by toxins in food, air and water.

How will we explain to future generations that we were responsible for all this destruction, knew it was happening and then did nothing about it? These critical losses are occurring while the world population is increasing by almost 100 million people per year. Business has to accept a very large share of the responsibility for this devastation and crisis. Businesses are central to a system which is destroying life on Earth and if we continue with this path not one area of wilderness, indigenous culture, endangered species, or uncontaminated water supply will survive the global market economy.

It is important to examine the system which has brought this about. The global economic system and its consequential unsustainable path is founded on the vestiges of modernism. This term has been used to distinguish the contemporary from traditional ways. It originally referred to the new civilization developed in Europe and North America over the last several centuries and fully evident by the early twentieth century. The models of economic development developed there have come to permeate the whole world along with the Western cultural domination which is inevitable in such a process. Modernism therefore saw new machine technologies and modes of industrial production that have led to an unprecedented rise in material living standards. The continuation of this process with an emphasis on output growth is what has become so unsustainable. This modernist Western tradition is therefore characterized by capitalism, a largely secular culture, liberal democracy, individualism, rationalism and humanism (Cahoone 1996). As a package, the modern Western model dominated by the domination of technology, science, industry, free trade, liberal productivism, neo-classical economics and a fixation with growth is certainly unique in human history. The results are easy to see: environmental destruction, anthropocentrism, the dissolution of community, the loss of individuality and diversity, the rise of alienation and the demise of tradition. Even notions of development are now simply equated with economic growth. As Shiva and Bandyopadhyay (1989) point out:

> *The ideology of the dominant pattern of development derives its driving force from a linear theory of progress, from a vision of historical evolution created in eighteenth- and nineteenth-century Western Europe and universalised throughout the world, especially in the post-war development decades. The linearity of history, pre-supposed in this theory of progress, created an ideology of development that equated development with economic growth, economic growth with expansion of the market economy, modernism with consumerism, and non-market economies with backwardness.*

Modernism, the continuation of what exists, translates into 'business as usual'. Business practices and current business education are failing us. They fail to recognize that the future will have to be very different if we are to avoid environmental and social conflict. Business seems content to see the natural system on the planet disintegrating, people starving and social structures falling apart. Business is central to the problem and must be central to the solution. There is no alternative but to change and many businesses would agree with that. The conflict is over the degree of change. To date most businesses who have begun to respond to environmental issues have done so in quite piecemeal and marginal ways. But tinkering with the system will not bring back the extinct species, donations for a prize to underpin a local environmental art competition will not cure the asthma of the painters, periodic environmental audits will not protect an indigenous population, green marketing will not replace slashed rainforests, and printing glossy annual environmental reports on recycled paper will certainly not rehabilitate thousands of square miles of dangerously contaminated land. Change has to be much more radical and much more speedy. Businesses do not like radical departures from what they know and understand. But such change is necessary and, ultimately, inevitable.

Currently, business stands at the edge of a precipice unsure about which way to turn. Its instincts tell it to stand fast and resist the risky path ahead. But it also recognizes that there is no turning back. Inevitably it is faced with an uncertain future and knows deep down that it will have to move forward into the unknown. At the moment however, it is hedging its bets by moving forward in minute steps, groping in the dark and doing everything it can to dictate the road ahead. Thus if the environment is to become centre stage, then business will want to make sure that it is its definition of the environment that we all settle on. Deeper green politics are not consistent with the other aspirations of business which will always be put before the environment.

Since there is very little analysis of what a business really is and what its place in society is (in terms of social responsibility and politics), so there is very little understanding of what it could become. And change is often resisted by shareholders, managers and others who are generally satisfied with the performance of their corporations. So many of us hold shares in large firms in one form or another and all too often pensions are based on profits and the security of our homes dependent on rising share prices. It is not surprising therefore that many people are frightened of 'rocking the boat'. Free-market capitalism is therefore not the great dynamic entity which its proponents espouse but actually creates a good degree of inertia to change. The single-minded emphasis on profit, efficiency, cost reduction and growth dwarfs issues such as employment, protection of the environment, social responsibility and sustainable development.

Businesses have yet to realize that continuation of present forms of industrial activity will simply bring about their own demise. After all, what use is profit accumulation when we are living in a decaying world? The wealthy may be able to build large fences around their property and employ security guards to keep the growing disenchanted out, but there is little they can do to clean up the air around them which is causing asthma in their children. Will industry still be happy with its lot when it has suppressed people's immune systems to such a level that they are allergic to their products, or when their operation has become so efficient that there is no one left in work to purchase their output? When will the business world look at itself honestly and recognize that it is time to change? I suspect only after we have seen a wave of tangible disasters affecting the middle classes in the West. After all, nothing else really counts in the corporate culture.

Business stands at the edge of a massive potential transformation. Whether it grasps its new opportunities will largely dictate the extent to which humankind maintains its well-being. We are in the hands of large corporations who must be persuaded, cajoled or even forced to change. However, as will be demonstrated in further chapters of this book, few businesses have recognized the potential crisis, are committed to change or have any view at all about how to do business better. The reality is that corporations duck and dive, invest in smoke screens, hide behind science and technology and espouse gradualist, marginal solutions to societal pressures. Managers lack vision, are short on creativity, narrow in their outlooks and are driven by a naive model of the economic process. They can never admit this to themselves because that would threaten their very reason for being. Since they are successful, their narrow selfish outlook dictates that the system must be successful.

Many of us, as business educators, must share some of the blame for the inertia in business. It seems that we would rather teach our students how to read a balance sheet, how to forecast growth and how to avoid employment legislation than to know themselves and to understand, appreciate and protect the world around them. Surely, business education should be as much about personal and spiritual education as it is about the functional components of the modern industrial enterprise. I often toy with the idea that we should restructure our universities so that social work educators teach management students and management educators teach social work students. This just might result in a Pareto improvement. At the very least it would open up the minds of our future managers to the social and political ramifications of their actions and make them more sympathetic to the plight of other humans with which they share the world. At the moment they have such short-sighted, blinkered outlooks. Education is central to moving to a more sustainable economy and as a starting point Palmer (1992) lays out some basic requirements:

In an ideal situation, there would be immediate and massive expansion of environmental education at all levels, bearing in mind that education is no short-term process and that time is of the essence to the future of our planet. Such education must take account not only of the practical dimensions of sustainable lifestyles and development issues, but equally of differing values and ethical implications. A holistic understanding of natural systems and the place of human endeavour and concern within these would seem essential to the success of any policies aimed at leading the world in the direction of a sustainable future.

Business can and will have to be different. Hawken (1994) believes that we are on the verge of a transformation which will be brought about through social and biological forces that can no longer be ignored or put aside. This change will be so thorough and sweeping that business, in the future, will be unrecognizable when compared to the commercial institutions of today. That scenario is entirely possible but it is currently blocked by business itself which is risk averse and does not understand the nature of the changes occurring around it. At the moment their myopic planning cannot identify any real reason for change.

The development of capitalism with its emphasis on enterprise and private ownership has separated economics from ecology and created a dominant ideology which sees the monetary side of economics as more important than the real side. It is true that commerce has enriched countries and increased material standards of living but in so doing it has also created powerful individuals, ruling families and a corporate elite. Capitalism has pillaged the natural environment and businesses pick off the opportunities which this has created in a typical predatory manner. There is now, therefore, a dominant corporate culture which believes that natural resources are there for the taking and that environ-mental and social problems will be resolved through growth, scientific advancement, technology transfer via private capital flows, free trade and the odd charitable hand-out. It is undeniable that capitalism has been a great wealth creator because it has unlocked the potential to use basic natural resources and process them into valuable material objects. However, it is also undeniable that, because growth has been so rapid, current wealth is being generated by stealing it from future generations. How will future generations continue the process when there are no resources left? Can this be left to the ubiquitous free market system to sort out?

The free market purists are naive and dangerous people. They seem to have a blind belief in their system which left to its own devices is supposed to achieve the best social and environmental outcome possible. How this is possible, when such people even refuse to define what constitutes social and environmental improvement is puzzling. When Western values and Western life is implicitly seen as being more important than other alternatives, it is difficult to see an outcome which is at all sustainable, either politically or environmentally. The fact is that there are no simple solutions to our problems and that we are a long way off finding any system which can reverse long term environmental degradation and mounting social chaos. But as a starting point businesses can recognize that everything they do has an ethical dimension. Business is only one part (albeit an important part) of a world which is complex, interwoven and cannot be simplified by models of rational economic behaviour. Current business practices seem to be guided by a vague promise that we can continue to increase our standards of living, that the developing world can attain developed world aspirations and that science and technology will come to the rescue and clean up the destruction which we have caused. This is not the case. If we can simply recognize this fact then at least we have a starting point for discussion.

One of the most important lessons we must learn is that the major problems of our time are all interconnected. Individual problems cannot be dealt with in isolation, we must think systemically about the systems and structures which lead to all the problems around us. Take world population, for example. We are not going to be able to stabilize it until we are able to alleviate hunger and poverty. Similarly we are not going to be able to stop the extinction of species until we are able to help the developing world get rid of its huge economic debts. These problems are all interrelated and interlinked and we need to improve our perception of the world in terms of relatedness, interdependence and context.

The emphasis put on science and technology is one of the more damaging aspects of the dominant corporate culture. Reality goes far beyond any scientific framework to a more intuitive awareness of the oneness of all life, the interdependence of its multiple manifestations and its cycles of change and transformation. Moreover, the common Western vision of a mechanized world has created a giant chasm between economic development (normally defined in narrow output growth terms) and the individual's spiritual nature. This is reinforced by the increasing alignment of our institutions with money and markets. The more dominant money has become in our societies, the less room there has been for any sense of spiritual bond that is the foundation of community and a balanced relationship with nature. The world of money and its associated materialistic greed has pushed out the spiritual meaning in our lives to such an extent that you, the reader, may well be thinking now that although my arguments to this point have seemed plausible, to start talking about spirituality in a book about business is crazy. Yet once the concept of the human spirit is truly understood, then consciousness becomes one with the wider cosmos as a whole and it then becomes clear that ecological awareness is truly spiritual.

Conversely, the current narrow vision of business as usual seems to be a world of global products, mass-marketing, free trade, private capital, technology transfer, deforestation, species destruction, chemical-based agriculture, featherless chickens and sick children. Of course, most of this is not an explicit vision but most managers fully (if tacitly) understand the consequences of their decisions and then either ignore them because they are difficult and threaten their egos and value systems, or feel powerless to do anything about them because of the overriding corporate culture which divorces commerce from common sense. Those in charge of our biggest corporations know that they are damaging themselves and their families but continue to do nothing about it. Are those the actions of sane individuals?

When challenged about the impacts of their activities, managers usually respond in two ways. Firstly, they attempt to devalue any challenge to the orthodox capitalist model as being unworkable and unrealistic. Secondly, they hide behind their egos and tell you in school-master-ish tones that there really is no alternative. Perhaps one of the biggest challenges ahead is to change the mindsets and values of key decision makers. But that will not be achieved through expensive management training at existing business schools or even new academies of business. It will only be achieved when managers can come to understand themselves and learn to appreciate nature and diversity, rather than exploit everything around them. That process is far more difficult than organizing yet another three day course on eco-efficiency, costing the equivalent of an annual salary of a Thai sweatshop worker.

Even the internal structures common in business alienate individual workers and remove their powers of self-determination. Modernism has dictated hierarchical management systems rather than more cooperative forms of organization. More contemporary management techniques have done little to improve this. On the face of it, total quality management techniques, for example, call for an increase in teamworking and more responsibility to be given to workers. But very few advocates of total quality management systems ever dare to go so far as to suggest that a logical extension of teamworking would be participation with respect to strategic decision-making and ownership. That would remove power from managers and more senior executives who will always want to hang on to their high salaries, business class trips and company cars.

We should therefore not be surprised to see the deep-seated unwillingness of businesses to change. They find the thought of reconstruction of the capitalist system threatening and difficult to comprehend. There seems to be a fundamental value associated with seeing growth as good. Industry can not imagine that it can survive in a world of adjustment which may require cut backs, decentralization, less rather than more, and free trade being replaced by fair trade. The driving force is more and more profit and the accumulation of ever greater stocks of capital. The basic idea seems to be that the action which yields the greatest financial return to the individual or firm is the one that is most beneficial to society. But we rarely bother to examine just how profits are made or ask if they are justifiable or in the interests of the wider international community which has worked to produce them. Paul Hawken (1994) makes a very perceptive point about corporate profits:

> *The language of commerce sounds specific, but in fact it is not specific enough. If Hawaiians had 138 different ways to describe falling rain, we can assume that rain had a profound importance in their lives. Business, on the other hand, only has two words for profit – gross and net. The extraordinarily complex manner in which a company recovers profit is reduced to a single numerically neat and precise concept. It makes no distinctions as to how the profit was made. It does not factor in whether people or places were exploited, resources depleted, communities enhanced, lives lost, or whether the entire executive suite was in such turmoil as to require stress consultants and outplacement services for the victims. In other words, business does not discern whether the profit is one of quality or mere quantity.*

Business is driven by the imperative to replicate money, to increase efficiency and to cut costs. Since labour has to be paid, the simple consequence of this drive is that employment becomes a source of inefficiency. Thus there is always an incentive to employ fewer people, to pay them less, to shed labour whenever possible and to replace human capital with technological capital. We are therefore moving into a world where fewer and fewer people will be involved in the productive process and therefore the number of people benefiting from the activities of industry will decline. The redundant now end up as disenfranchised and in worst cases become the victims of malnutrition and violence. It is difficult to see how social systems can continue to support growing numbers of unemployed people who in many countries become homeless beggars, criminals, drug addicts and residents of refugee camps. It is little wonder that such people give little consideration for the environment when their main priority is feeding themselves and their families. It is not unlikely that social crisis will be the force for change long before we are forced to respond to environmental devastation.

So far our emphasis has been on business but it is also important to recognize the part which governments have played in bringing about environmental degradation. Many see the use of the power of the institution of government as the only way to halt the damaging processes and activities of industry. But they have not done so to date and, moreover, there is little sign of them challenging industry at the moment. Amongst politicians we have seen a growth in Conservative views of free market capitalism which sees industry as operating most efficiently and most effectively in an unfettered political environment. This liberal productivism implies less regulation not more, the protection of free trade and a very large degree of trust. The argument about the environment reflects that of the dominant corporate ideology: the poor, the developing world, natural resources and the negative impact of pollution will all benefit as business ensures more growth and profitability. Moreover free international trade and economic globalization are enshrined in inter-governmental treaties calling for the removal of trade barriers to the free flow of goods and capital. This is supposed to spur competition, increase economic efficiency, lower consumer prices, increase economic growth and create jobs. Where is the evidence for such claims? Nowhere but in the text books of neo-classical economists.

Governments have created an international environment of deregulation because free markets unrestrained by governments are supposed to result in higher economic growth as measured by gross national output. The primary responsibility of industrial policy seems to be to provide an infrastructure which will help corporations expand their commercial activities. In this respect, governments seek to enforce the rule of law with respect to property rights and contracts – without which the capitalist system comes to a halt. Privatization has been espoused over the last fifteen years and we have seen valuable national assets shifted from the control of governments to the private sector in the name of efficiency. Thus the very role of governments has been to transfer more and more power into the corporate private sector.

Mainstream political parties in the West have, in the post-Communist age shifted towards the more Conservative view of economics and industry. The left talks of the stakeholder society and no longer of vested interests and the living standards of the working classes. They now embrace social democratic principles and democratic capitalism. But mainstream political parties have not embraced green ideas. They have operated on the edges of the environmental debate waiting to see if the green vote will be significant enough for them to respond. They have, therefore consistently lacked any real leadership on environmental issues and their policies have been devoid of any radical green ideas or vision.

The green political agenda (weak as it is) now represents a tension between pressure groups, anti-road protesters and animal rights activists on the one hand, and on the other, the vested interests of the large corporations outlined above. This is a battle ground where politicians have consistently feared to tread. The resulting outcome is that the more powerful business world is allowed to continue its march oblivious to burning rainforests, rare habitats, dangerous waste sites, unsustainable consumption patterns, the legitimization of greed and ultimately people's lives.

More fundamentally however, we must now recognize that politicians and governments no longer have sole control over the management of nations. They may still be able to wage war with their massive stocks of destructive arms when opinion polls desert them, but the management of the economic process has to be done in cooperation with business. Of the 100 biggest economic institutions in the world today, about half are countries and half are companies. Only recently have businesses become major agents in determining how societies and cultures are defined, but they are now expert at it. Indeed, it is business which has created the consumer culture, the fast food culture, and insatiable materialism. It is business which would like to set out its vision of the world's monoculture with its global products, global messages and mass markets. It is even business which supports and sponsors the politicians and political parties which will give it what it wants. Money can buy a lot of votes – one way or another. Thus to look to governments for radical change would be tantamount to expecting the big cats to become vegetarian – it isn't in their nature and they wouldn't understand even if you tried to explain.

Moreover, large corporations have a significant advantage over governments. They are able to cross national boundaries much more easily. The transnational corporations with their massive stock of private capital are much more influential on the global stage than any government or even inter-governmental agency can be. The capital which they use to broker agreements replacing vital natural resources with industrial plant is essentially nomadic. This means that the large corporation is able to change the direction of development of the many countries dependent on its patronage, to suit whatever short term objective seems paramount at any point in time. What development there is in the developing world, for example, is often directed, dependent development and the aspirations of indigenous populations and local environmental concerns are rarely given any real priority. The institutions of government and the inter-governmental agencies which are supposed to protect the greater interest are therefore failing.

Without the necessary institutional controls on business we have seen our once beneficial corporations turned into finance driven institutions who thrive on market tyranny. They move smoothly across national boundaries, colonizing ever more of the planet's valuable living spaces. They destroy wilderness in the name of progress, destroying ecosystems and people's livelihoods. People are displaced, their values ignored and the dominant corporate culture invades traditions, beliefs and long established ritual. The large corporation, the transnational business, is detached from place. It wanders around the world picking off smaller enterprises and influencing sovereign democratic processes. But even productive business is itself threatened by the globalized financial system which it itself helped to create. This system is less interested in the production of real wealth through productive innovation and more interested in the extraction of money. Thus as Korten (1995) points out:

> *The big winners are the corporate raiders who strip sound companies of their assets for short-term gain and the speculators who capitalise on market volatility to extract a private tax from those who are engaged in productive work and investment.*

Why then do we as individual human beings, part of a complex and diverse human race, continue to allow business and the global financial system (often with the help of governments) to get away with the continued destruction of the planet on which we live? There are three main reasons.

Firstly, as individuals we have a lack of power and a lack of will. We are so influenced by the corporate message that 'there is no alternative' that we come to believe it. Moreover, for those in employment, we are so inextricably linked to the destructive process that to challenge it might result in massive personal sacrifice. Standing alone we lack the courage of our convictions. But we have also lost any trust in politicians and governments to truly act in the common interest. After all, governments are now clearly part of the dominant corporate culture and see little reason for change.

Secondly our knowledge, understanding and information about what is really going on is very limited. We have only a piecemeal view of events. There is a need for systemic thinking. Part of our inability to come to terms with the fact that our institutional systems are failing stems from the reliance on television for more and more of our information. Television reduces political discourse to soundbites and we now examine complex issues in fragmented bits and pieces. But academics must also accept much of the blame. We are failing in our duty to advance political debate and retain integrity and independence. Instead of creating discussion and debate amongst a wider audience, we organize intellectual enquiry into narrowly specialized disciplines. In a world of spending cuts we even look towards industry to sponsor our research and spend more time on examining what is, rather than what could be. Thus the dominant corporate culture now even invades the institution of learning and research and the result is further inertia.

Thirdly, as individuals we have lost our interconnectedness. We have got tied up in our own personal aspirations, too often associated with greed and materialism. We are too often simply not aware of what really makes us happy and substitute external things for an emptiness inside. We have lost our spiritual dimension and our closeness with nature. Those of us in the West have got used to our comforts and our selfishness refuses to equate our well-being with other people's suffering. We ignore our obligations to humankind widely defined and care very little about the other species with which we share the planet.

As a starting point for solving the crisis inside us we must broaden our awareness and recognize the systemic nature of all events and activities. Thus systemic thinking calls for a scepticism of simplistic solutions and a distrust of modernist principles. There is a need to seek out the interconnectedness between problems and events. When for example, an oil tanker runs aground causing massive environmental destruction we blame the disaster on the fact that the tanker had a single skin hull rather than a double skin, we blame the pilot or the adverse weather conditions. We rarely ask ourselves why millions of gallons of oil are being transported around the globe in old vessels, crewed by unskilled young men, registered in countries with little respect for maritime law. We do not ask ourselves what kind of consumption patterns, which we take for granted, have resulted in thousands of seabirds, fish, and seals dying to satisfy our greed.

The message here is not one of despair although it is depressing. It is within our means, however, to reclaim the power that we have yielded to the institutions of money and recreate societies that nurture cultural and biological diversity. There are huge opportunities for developing social, intellectual, spiritual, and ecological advancement beyond our present imagination. But first we must challenge the existing order. We may have few tools in order to do this but they can be powerful. As purchasers of products we can boycott those which are excessively environmentally damaging and avoid buying products from companies with abysmal environmental and human rights records. As voters we can challenge conservatism, given sufficient alternatives. As individuals we can lead by example, develop a global consciousness, rediscover the spiritual side of our being and learn to live with and love nature rather than to exploit it.

We are nevertheless left with a fundamental question. The chapters in this book examine key problems and then all attempt to provide some answers to that question. The question is: How do we want our principal economic institution (business) to conduct its commercial activities? It is no longer acceptable that business acts as an out of control marauder. It will have to be tamed and changed. Neither should we leave the more ethical company with all its power. No matter how benevolent a dictator the business may become, it will always have a set of values peculiar to itself. Power vested in a single institution would inevitably destroy the very diversity which is central to a more sustainable world. Nevertheless, the productive activities of business are still important and vital in a move towards addressing the inequity and inequalities in the world and there is a need for cooperation between individuals, enterprises and overarching institutions which serve the whole of humanity and other species.

The business can actually become an important vehicle for change. As employers, businesses can also be educators and as suppliers of goods and services they can influence individuals in a positive way. As large purchasers they can influence the supply chain and as producers they can help to manage our natural resources, find alternatives to damaging processes and put more emphasis on ecologically aware innovation. Businesses should ultimately be the servant of humankind not the other way around. Change will have to be quite radical therefore but change will have to happen. It is clear now that there is really no alternative.

The rest of this book examines many of the topics which I have sketched out in this introductory chapter. I do not ask you to accept all the arguments made above on face value – only to keep an open mind until you have been able to examine the arguments in more detail. Ultimately there may be things which you feel are wrong, naive or even unhelpful. I hope that there will also be aspects of this book which you feel are worthy of consideration. The ultimate message is clear however. It is time for change and without radical change the future path is one towards destruction. We may not be able to prescribe in detail exactly what change will be required. We can, nevertheless describe the failings in the present system and point to some of the remedies. The ultimate message is however, that we had better start thinking about it and talking about it soon!

References

Brown, L (1995) *State of the World*, Earthscan, London

Cahoone, L E (1996) *From Modernism to Postmodernism: An Anthology*, Blackwell, Oxford

Hawken, P (1994) *The Ecology of Commerce: How Business Can Save the Planet*, Weidenfeld and Nicholson, New York

Korten, D C (1995) *When Corporations Rule the World*, Earthscan, London

Palmer, J A (1992) 'Towards a Sustainable Future' in *The Environment in Question* (Edited by D E Cooper and J A Palmer), Routledge, London

Shiva, V and Bandyopadhyay, J (1989) *The Ecologist*, 19, 3

2

From Green to Golden: the Hijacking of Environmentalism

Richard Welford

Discussions relating to the interaction of business and the environment are now well established. Many businesses now have environmental policies, environmental management systems and undertake periodic environmental audits. Industry paints a picture of activity and concern and points to what it sees as considerable achievements in quite a short space of time. The purpose of this chapter is to critically evaluate this corporate environmentalism and the approach taken is to compare the stance taken on the environment by business with the more traditional stance taken by environmentalists.

I begin by sketching out a view of the world which is personal but I know many will agree with it. I do this in order to paint a picture of the way things are and of the path down which we must travel in order to rescue nature and individuals from crisis. It is important to paint this picture because business is a very influential actor within it and we need a backdrop in order to assess the worrying industrial trends which are now emerging. Moreover, it is now simply impossible to disentangle industry from society. A change in society requires a re-evaluation of the way we do business, and business itself has a huge role to play in reversing the environmental chaos and taking its share of the responsibility to create the new.

The dominant ideology of corporate environmentalism is eco-modernism and within that the tool of eco-efficiency. I suggest that this is a limited approach to the concept of sustainable development because it concentrates only on narrow environmental aspects of that concept.

But businesses are pushing this eco-modernist agenda for two reasons. Firstly, it is an agenda not inconsistent with the more traditional priorities which means that radical change within the industrial organization or within society as a whole is not required. Secondly, industrialists often lack the imagination and creativity needed to go beyond this narrow environmental agenda and consider the wider aspects of sustainable development. Our task must be to rescue that debate and reintroduce the radicalism more traditionally associated with environmentalism.

A PICTURE OF THE WORLD AND THOSE WITHIN IT

The model used here is based on the work of Johan Galtung and developed by Rudolf Bahro (1994). Galtung, a Norwegian philosopher and researcher into peace and evolution depicted various styles of social evolution as five colours (blue, red, golden, green and pink) and represented this view of the world in a simple square (see Figure 2.1) with the four corners represented by the first four colours. Developed in the early 1980s this world-schematic represented the Cold War situation rather well. It is worth describing that model before going on to adapt it for the purposes of this chapter.

The four corners represent 'pure principles', considered in each case as an ideal type. Blue represented the West; red was the Soviet; green the sphere of under-development and traditional societies; and yellow (or henceforth golden so as not to imply any racism and in order to stress the links with money) was that of the Japanese and Asia–Pacific rim or so-called 'Tiger' or 'Dragon' economies. In the middle of the square we find the pink, social-democratic model, typified, perhaps, by Swedish politics in the 1980s. We must recognize that Galtung's view was that this square is not an evenly balanced, symmetrical representation (at least in terms of power). He suggested that the centre of gravity lies in the blue corner.

The diagonal running from the blue corner to the red corner has a special significance and is described by Galtung as the diagonal of destruction. This main axis connects the (blue) market-fixation ideology of the West with the (red) state-fixation of the former Soviet sphere. Although even what remains of the communist world has moved decisively towards the blue corner, this diagonal still depicts the fierce argument which exists between socialists, pink pragmatists and the strong (and growing) ideology of blue deregulators. This on-going destructive battle between left and right which has been the scene of

Figure 2.1 Galtung's World – Schematic

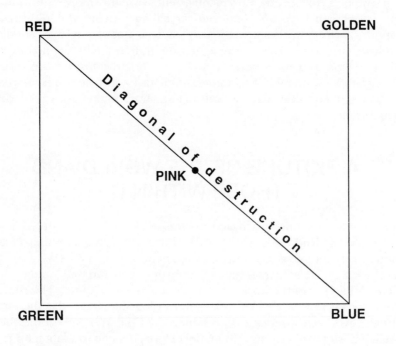

great debate but few solutions is an important characteristic of modern economies and is a point which we will return to.

Given recent events including a new emphasis on deregulation, privatization and the liberalization of international markets, it is clear that the blue corner has had a strong pulling effect which, arguably, has increased over the last fifteen years, even more than Galtung might have originally predicted. But there are now other areas of pull as well and although these may not yet be as strong they are having a significant impact on the shaping of the world. Not least, the economic dominance in the late 1980s and early 1990s of Japan has led many to examine carefully the economic structures and norms which exist within that culture. The golden corner lies off the main diagonal, although in many ways it represents an integration of planning and the free market. But it is a different model as well, based on a different history, culture and value system. It is perhaps less discrete that it was twenty years ago and there is certainly a movement of blue corners and golden corners towards each other. This represents a formidable force against red and green.

Figure 2.2 identifies some of the consequences of various gravitational pulls in more detail. The numbered arrows depict the following trends which we have observed.

Figure 2.2 Competing Gravitational Pulls

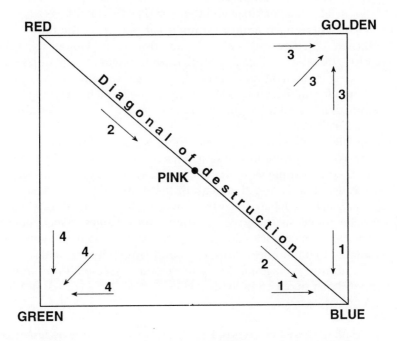

1 The emphasis on free trade, massive private investment by trans-national corporations and Western governmental aid (albeit shrinking) has pulled the underdeveloped world towards the market model. In effect this has drawn developing world countries towards free-market economic policies, liberalization strategies and, at times, deliberate austerity measures imposed on populations in order to reduce indebtedness. This trend has also resulted in developing world populations placing more and more emphasis on consumption and materialism as they strive to emulate living standards in the West. In addition the emphasis on free trade and deregulation which we have seen in the last two decades has also pulled the golden countries into the *laissez-faire* arena.

2 Since the collapse of the Soviet system there has been a rapid move from the red corner towards both pink and blue models. This may have raised and then thwarted many people's expectations but more than anything it has raised new tensions often based around cultural and ethnic differences which were suppressed but not buried by the Soviet regime. This is not an easy or smooth transition and in many countries it has quite literally been a move along the diagonal of destruction.

3 A strong pull towards the golden corner of our model has been created by the economic advancement and success (in economic and financial terms) of Japan and the Asia–Pacific rim. But as suggested above, there is an almost symmetrical pull from the blue corner (arrow 1). The result is a strong and dominant ideology associated with globalization, scale, private (often nomadic) capital, Japanese management styles and working practices, economic growth and deregulation. Bahro (1994) sees this as the trend towards the 'super-industrial breakthrough' – a dangerous and exploitative form of modernism.

4 Finally, we must recognize that there is a green wave and I believe this to be growing in strength. This is an interesting phenomenon created by people who break off from some point on the diagonal because they have had enough of the destructive logic of the plan versus market debate. They look towards alternative values which are to be found in the green corner. These values associated with connectedness, spirituality (as opposed to organized religion), individuality, community, sufficiency and simplicity are seldom to be found on the diagonal. It is a movement growing all the time and based very much on individual responses to the perceived futility of modern society.

As a result of these four trends, I would argue that the line of destruction has actually become less important. Debate between left–right politics is certainly more muted than it was and in many cases, in many countries, it is now difficult to see a clear divide between left and right. More often than not politicians are prepared to throw away ideology in the pursuit of the popular vote. Meanwhile, a new diagonal of tension has emerged between the green and golden corners (Figure 2.3). This is not such a destructive diagonal because there are solutions to be found at the green end of the line. Nevertheless there is great potential for the tension to spill over into conflict. Indeed this is already happening both in terms of struggles over natural resources (the inevitable resource wars) and in terms of resistance in the developing world (particularly amongst indigenous populations) to further transnational interference. The tension revolves around the type of world which we want to see in the future. This is now the centre of the debate even though the left–right battles still exist. It is often represented by a tension between local and global and I have previously typified this as a debate between modernism (a mixture of blue and golden) and a bioregional (green) alternative. Table 2.1 (Welford 1995) summarizes some of the constructs existing at either end of that line of tension.

With an emphasis on the world's resources (both natural and human) we can see the line of tension as also representing a line of exploitation.

Figure 2.3 The Diagonal of Tension between Golden and Green

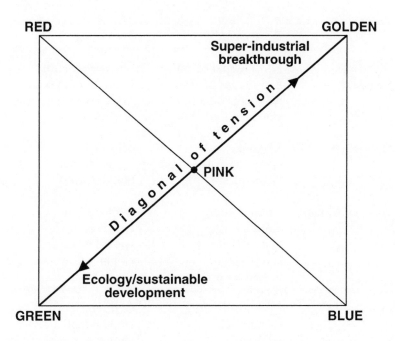

At the green end of the line we live in harmony with nature and with each other. As we move in the opposite direction, towards the golden corner, we see an emphasis on growth, globalization, materialism and consumption which is inevitably exploitative and results in the suppression of nature and the individual in favour of the interests of the corporation and capital. The inevitable consequence of this growth and increase in scale is that the corporation will, indeed, rule the world. Indeed, in so many cases already, corporations are much more powerful than the individual nation state. This is the golden trend.

Returning to Galtung's original model, he pointed out that all five alternatives (blue, red, golden, green and pink) worked badly. Green was, in his view, superior but it often produced poverty and underdevelopment (even in sustainable terms). The pink model was the next best, but it often shared aggression against nature, spirituality and regionalism. Therefore, Galtung defined a zone in his model which he depicted as the rainbow society. This triangle, removed from the extremes of the edges of the model and sitting on the green side of the diagonal of destruction is essentially an open window of opportunity (Figure 2.4). This is an area which I believe many people would wish to inhabit but feel they are prevented from doing so by the modernist constructs which dictate their lives.

Table 2.1 Bioregional Constructs Compared with Modernist Constructs

	Bioregional	*Modernism*
Industrial Organization	Flexible specialization Economies of scope Self-determination Cooperation	Mass production Economies of scale Managerial dominance Hierarchy
Markets	Regional Community-based Specialized	National International Standardized
Economy Aims	Conservation Stability Self-sufficiency Cooperation Sustainability	Exploitation Progress Global markets Competition Growth
Polity	Decentralization Consensus Diversity	Centralization Dominant ideologies Uniformity
Society	Symbiosis Evolution Multi-cultural	Polarization Directed development Mono-cultural

As we shall see below, the rainbow society is not defined by a single ideology, rather it is a mixture of ideas with an overriding acceptance that green is important. This is a society which (unlike the diagonal of destruction) can tolerate differences because it is a society predicated on peace and harmony. It is a society where people are empowered and are able to live more fulfilling lives because the engine of industrialization is secondary to the needs of nature and individuals.

As a personal aside, I find it interesting to note that the colour pink is now more often associated with the gay movement than any balanced form of social democracy. The dynamics of the (quite disparate) gay movement are not untypical of changes we have seen taking place amongst a number of minority groups. Thus we might add another dimension to Galtung's original model, that being, the notion that there are communities often disenfranchised by traditional forms of social evolution. We might depict this as a whole new plane existing under-

Figure 2.4 The Rainbow Society

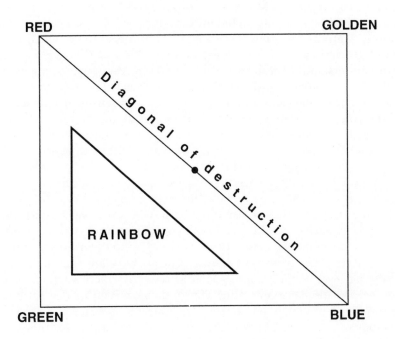

neath Galtung's model because minorities often only inhabit part of any society for part of their time. The point of contact of the two planes and the inevitable point of gravity for minority groups will be found towards the green corner. Here we can find greater emphasis put on individuality, acceptance, love, community (in all shapes and sizes) and caring.

It is also interesting to note that as mainstream society becomes more integrationist, more tolerant and more 'politically correct', minority groups often refuse to accept the overtures of liberals. The gay community although more and more accepted has nevertheless become more ghettoized and often (particularly amongst women) more separatist. So-called 'gay ghettos' (or as I would prefer, islands of communalism) have emerged not because gay men and lesbians are pushed out, but because that is the way they want it. Minority groups find many answers in communities where they can express their individuality. They thrive on self-determination and self-sufficiency. There is a natural movement towards the green corner therefore. As with many forms of social evolution it is the few which lead us all forward to our next stage of development.

Women, too, I believe, often have rather more solutions to the social and environmental crisis which we find ourselves in, than the men who traditionally have the power. Women increasingly espouse values which are different to those of men and seek out greater participation and involvement in society. Moreover, they are powerful in shaping a new society which is less patriarchal and more suited to the needs of all people. Men are so often driven by a disconnected ego which is a singularly destructive force, whilst women, in my experience, have a better understanding of the world around them. Men drive for material well-being, dominance and power whereas women better relate to values associated with sharing, loving and caring. There is a strong female sense of knowing and we must allow this to penetrate the patriarchal ego. Society still undervalues women's contributions and women's aspirations but to give these more prominence would be a positive step forward towards a more sustainable society.

It is a difficult task for men to write about women in a general sense and perhaps we should not try. I can, however, speak more easily of men. I do know that men have created the society in which we live and still run it. They have created the industrial order, the arms of destruction and the environmental crisis. They also hold on to the majority of the benefits resulting from that system. But at the same time men are becoming more feminine in their outlook as they increasingly realize that their creations are generating a life of their own and are now turning against them. Although they toe the corporate line so many men are very unhappy with the super competitive hierarchical lifestyles that they can be forced into. Senior executives find themselves under enormous stress, high rates of alcoholism are common and deep down they are deeply unhappy with their lot. Few manage to find the way out though and so stay and promulgate the suffering in order to justify their own existences. Nevertheless as the cracks occur and become more common, we are seeing the beginnings of a patriarchal unfolding and women increasingly have the power to influence the future. Men are increasingly insecure and often face their own personal crises. Such crises (which I have often faced myself) are in fact incredibly liberating. They give men the opportunity to seek out humility. This is powerful and I recommend it to all men reading this book.

THE DEBATE OVER ENVIRONMENTALISM

Let us now return to the main part of this chapter: an analysis of the interaction between industry and environmentalism. Galtung's model is a useful starting point for an analysis of different forms of environmentalism. Within his rainbow sit many environmentalists and their emphasis on the environment is what binds them together. The rainbow society is what Bahro (1994) calls the 'other republic' or, more accurately, an association of 'other eco-republics' which Greens and Alternatives have been wanting. It is disengaged from the diagonal of destruction although it still has within it a degree of tension between various types of environmentalists.

We can typify these different types of environmentalists by, once again, looking at the corners of the model (see Figure 2.5). Here the edges of the rainbow society are represented by those associated with eco-liberalism, eco-socialism and eco-radicalism.

Eco-liberals are brought together by a belief in pluralist democracy. Their reformist politics associated with pressure group activities is flexible and eclectic. They sit outside of the left–right debate (or above it as some might claim) but according to Pepper (1993) their style of rejection of traditional politics can be seen as somewhat conservative. When it comes to policies, they often try to adapt the existing system advocating eco-taxes, pollution charges and codes of conduct for industry. Of all the disparate groups in the rainbow society it is not surprising therefore that they have been most successful in promoting their views.

Eco-liberals are enthusiastic for, at least, small scale capitalism where the state has a role as regulator and in promoting individual responsibility. Principles of social justice are central and are tied closely to

Figure 2.5 Environmentalism in the Rainbow Society

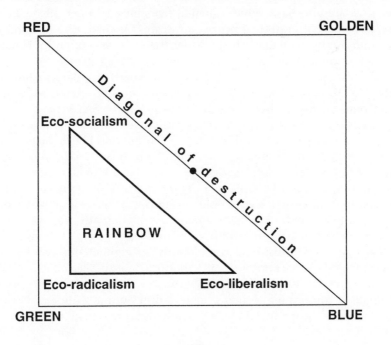

community rather than state. Technology is embraced and should be designed to provide appropriate solutions to environmental improvement and development. Democracy and individual freedom are the cornerstones of the eco-liberal ideology and many would argue that some form of democracy should be extended to all nature's creatures through strong policies on animal rights.

Eco-socialists argue that we should proceed to ecology from social justice, insisting that nature's rights are meaningless without human rights. Central to human being's relationship with nature is production and it is the mode of production which should be changed both in the interests of people and the environment. Eco-socialism would seek to change needs, redefining wealth and ensuring a reasonable material well-being to all. But these needs must be met through socialist production because that is the only way to ensure they do not exceed ecological limits. In an attack on deep green ecologists, eco-socialists would argue that stateless, small scale communes are not viable without complex administrative and social structures necessary to guarantee democratic participation, civil rights and an egalitarian coordination of resources (Frankel 1987).

Eco-socialism defines environmental problems widely. These problems include resource depletion and pollution but also more anthropocentric concerns such as crime, social depravation, unemployment and poverty. Therefore the basic socialist principles of egalitarianism, eliminating capitalism and poverty, resource distribution and democratic control of our lives are also basic environmental principles (Pepper 1993). Eco-socialists may differ in their precise strategies for change but they have in common the need to confront rather than bypass capitalism. Hence the labour movement must be the key force in social change.

Eco-radicals are made up of a range of alternative thinkers including bioregionalists, eco-anarchists, Gaianists and some eco-feminists. What often binds them together are the broad principles of deep ecology. Here considerations for the environment, for sustainable development and for the rights of all people and all species are paramount. The environment mixes with notions of spirituality, communitarianism and harmony. To many it represents an ideal world: the type of world which they want to live in, but the enormous barriers perceived in moving towards this alternative future often lead people to dismiss it as unachievable. Yet on a local scale we can find numerous examples of alternative communities and ways of life consistent with notions of deep ecology. Moreover, we forget that many indigenous populations throughout the world have always led lives which are consistent with sustainable development. These are too often branded as backward because of our Western philosophy dominated by consumption and materialism but anthropologists can often point to the quality of life, happiness and contentment to be found in such communities. Unfortunately globalization and mass communications technology means that the Western value system is quickly permeating such alternative communities.

The bioregional model, in particular, offers a very positive alternative to the golden trend. It is not a single model because the shape of bioregional society and the local economy will be shaped by those people within it rather than dictated by national and transnational organizations. It offers an image of the future that can be regarded as positive and liberating and realistic and energizing. The essence of bioregionalism is to live as close to the land as possible, to decentralize organizations and to live in harmony with nature. Bioregionalism, properly conceived, not merely tolerates but thrives upon the diversities of human behaviour and implicitly increases the fundamental rights of those groups which are traditionally discriminated against. Sale (1974) argues that a bioregion is part of the earth's surface whose rough boundaries are determined by natural order rather than human dictates, distinguishable from other areas by attributes of flora, fauna, water, climate, soils and landforms, and the human settlements and cultures those attributes give rise to. He goes on to suggest that the borders between areas will not be rigid but they will be understood and sensed, or in some way known to the inhabitants, and particularly those rooted in the land. Thus the most fundamental form of bioregionalism parallels the traditional organization of society which we have seen in the past by the North American Indians and at present by some indigenous populations of the developing world.

Bioregionalism's vision is similar to that of the eco-anarchists who advocate small-scale, decentralized commune-ism (Bahro 1986), participatory democracy, a low growth economy, and non-hierarchical living. Such a model has become associated with the 'fourth world movement' encompassing activists living in communes or neighbourhood groups (particularly in the USA) and others who, via theory or practice, push the politics of regional or local separatism.

The eco-radical models put more emphasis on local activity, on local development and on the protection of the environment in a proactive way by all those living in certain areas. They stress the importance of the local economy, smaller scale local businesses, of local employment and the development of local trading networks which are less reliant on traditional forms of mass transportation. Eco-radicalism therefore challenges the common acceptance of the need for large organizations, for large structures and for centralized government and institutions. It is a construct which bonds communities around the common purpose of living in harmony with nature. But it is not an approach which simply translates national cultural domination and suppression into regional control.

Thus one can see that the alliance between eco-liberals, eco-socialists and eco-radicals (and indeed others) within the rainbow society has not always been an easy one. Conflict has often been as common as consensus and many groups have been jealous of the power of the eco-liberals, causing yet more tension. The rainbow society does nevertheless open opportunities for debate centred around a greener vision. It challenges the domination of large-scale capital and seeks to define business in a new way. This is often threatening for industry and for the people who run it because it necessarily implies change and perhaps even discontinuity. The response to such a threat was originally to ignore it or sometimes to attack it. But things have now changed and the response is not to engage it but to change it. Thus we have seen the birth of eco-modernism.

ECO-MODERNISM AND ECO-EFFICIENCY

A characteristic of the last ten years has therefore been that industry, facing pressure from a number of stakeholders, has actively got involved in the environmental debate. This has been difficult because industry is firmly wedded to the system which has caused the environmental crisis in the first place. They have examined the alternatives put forward by various groups within the rainbow society but have generally found them threatening. It is not surprising therefore that they have sought out a discourse on the environment which fits within their other aims and objectives. Eco-modernism therefore represents not a break with what went before but a continuation of it. It adds an environmental dimension to the development path but does not allow that dimension to radically change the path. In some ways it is a conjuring trick or a juggling act where industry espouses the need for environmental action but never really tells the audience what it is hiding backstage. For many of us, seeing is definitely not believing.

Eco-modernism as a philosophy with eco-efficiency as its flagship tool represents a response to concern over the environment by those people and institutions who are committed to the golden trend. As such it represents the hijacking of traditional notions of environmentalism (however disparate) which exist in the rainbow society. Indeed rather than impart any new green values, notions of eco-modernism actually destroys the debate amongst ecologists, completes a spiritual impoverishment and justifies the power of private capital. The tool of eco-efficiency sees no alternative to businesses setting the environmental agenda and businesses controlling the greening of development through the vehicle of technology transfer via private capital.

Accordingly, any model of environmentalism outside of eco-modernism would involve a break with business-as-usual and some sort of discontinuous change. It would challenge the pillars of free trade, scientific and technological domination and the orthodoxy of continuous improvement and economic growth. It is not surprising that alternatives to eco-modernism frighten the corporate establishment and that their response has been to hijack the debate. To my surprise I constantly find people who would, in a traditional sense, be regarded as intelligent, who really believe that eco-modernism represents the best way forward. I am astounded by such false consciousness.

Eco-modernism is typified by the following paragraphs taken from the original Declaration of the Business Council for Sustainable Development (Schmidheiny 1992):

> *Economic growth in all parts of the world is essential to improve the livelihoods of the poor, to sustain growing populations, and eventually to stabilise population levels. New technologies will be needed to permit growth while using energy and other resources more efficiently and producing less pollution.*
>
> *Open and competitive markets, both within and between nations, foster innovation and efficiency and provide opportunities for all to improve their living conditions. But such markets must give the right signals; the prices of goods and services must increasingly recognize and reflect the environmental costs of their production, use, recycling and disposal. This is fundamental, and is best achieved by a synthesis of economic instruments designed to correct distortions and encourage innovation and continuous improvement, regulatory standards to direct performance, and voluntary initiatives by the private sector.*

Thus eco-modernism's frame of reference is certainly the here and now, working within the present institutional framework. It sees as a main instrument for change the use of private capital as essential and emphasizes the role of the free market. Moreover, eco-modernism is actually defined to satisfy the wider interests of business. Schmidheiny (1992, p 99) reflects this when he argues:

> *Companies now have to work with governments to spread environmentally efficient production processes throughout the global business community . . . This will require significant technological, managerial, and organizational changes, new investments, and new product lines . . . it will be increasingly in a company's own interests to develop cleaner products and processes.*

To me such views demonstrate that the sterility of eco-modernism is also one of its key characteristics. Its emphasis on positivism and rationality and its conservative nature means that it denies the existence of spiritual dimensions to the debate which are at the heart of deeper green politics. Moreover, and perhaps more importantly, eco-modernism is wedded to the ideals of maintaining the wealth of the rich (in terms of both individuals and countries). The clear implication of this is that there is always something which will have priority over ecological action. Essentially, ecological action becomes an add-on feature of business-as-usual, and is given emphasis when time and resources allow, or when crisis or public pressure requires a response.

At the centre of eco-modernism we find the search for eco-efficiency. I have never found a very clear definition of what this really means and that in itself reflects the confused and often contradictory thinking of the eco-modernists. The minimalist definition provided by Schmidheiny (1992, p 98) suggests that it is simply 'the ratio of resource inputs and waste outputs to final product'. Thus using traditional business tools of systems and audits, eco-efficiency essentially works on the trade-off between industrial activity and the environment, continuing to do business-as-usual and continuing along the golden path and adding in concern for the environment. Rather than being centre stage, ecological issues are appendages which drop off when the going gets tough. When the airship called business looks like losing height one can be assured that the first thing to be thrown overboard will be the green baggage.

There is a great deal of overlap between models of eco-efficiency and the technological-fix school of thought. This is essentially a defensive school where science and technology are seen as supreme in the defence of traditional notions of capitalism. Industry in the West (and Japan) continues to try to hold on to its domination of the world order by ever increasing its productive capacity through the displacement of labour in favour of capital. This leaves the majority of citizens fighting over an ever shrinking share of the pie whilst a small, powerful, industrial elite seek to maintain their vested interests through marginal adaptions to the demands of the rest of us. Eco-efficiency is such a marginalist smoke-screen. This is the world of industrial imperialism.

Those who advocate eco-efficiency talk about 'ecology' when they really mean 'environmental protection' because they do not perceive there to be any difference. Ecologists know that the scale on which we do things is too massive, complex, unwieldy, exploitative and alienating. This is never considered because the golden trend demands greater scale. Mass demand, mass markets, mass consumption and globalization come to dominate any notion of the greening of industry. Even the population explosion is rarely considered because it does, after all, present new market opportunities. Eco-efficiency must fit within the growth paradigm and actually, it is subtly designed to reinforce it.

The effect of the domination of eco-modernism in our model is quite simple. Essentially it means that the environmental discourse now has eco-modernism within it at the expense of more radical approaches consistent with ecology and sustainable development. Eco-modernism is much closer to the golden corner in our model than it is to the green corner. The eco-modern discourse is therefore outside of the rainbow society however and this represents a flipping over of the triangle as depicted in Figure 2.6. The new triangle has some interesting characteristics. Firstly, some eco-liberals are still involved in the hijacked discourse. Typically, these are now neo-classical economists who see the solution to the environmental problem in the evaluation of environmental costs, internalizing these costs and leaving the market do the rest. Thus monetary values replace the more fundamental societal values of the more radical ecologists. Secondly, some eco-socialists are also part of the discourse, but as the trends of the 1990s have pushed us away from the red corner of our model, so the eco-socialists have lost much of their power as well. The third characteristic is perhaps the most worrying. The traditional diagonal of destruction, which must be seen as one of the

Figure 2.6 Hijacking Environmentalism

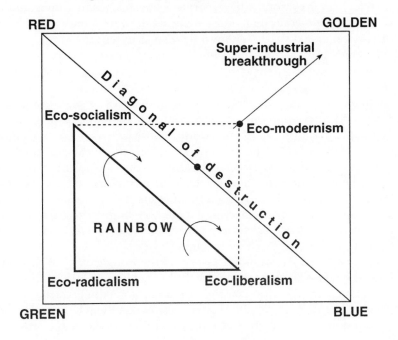

fundamental causes of the environmental crisis, runs straight through the heart of our new triangle. In effect the debates in the lower half of the new triangle are still revolving around the same old left–right arguments. Only as we move further towards the eco-modern corner and towards the golden trend of what Bahro (1994) calls the super-industrial breakthrough do we observe anything different. But this trend is in exactly the opposite direction of a more sustainable development. It represents naked economic growth, scale and world domination. The challenge is simply to reverse this trend.

THE RHETORIC AND REALITY OF ECO-MODERNISM

The eco-modernist approach sees the future as being a product of what went before. Environmentalism, it asserts, must therefore be embedded in what is here and now. The postmodern perspective, which would see the environmental debate more associated with a break from the past, is largely ignored and the usual approach taken to environmental management strategies is therefore largely integrationalist. In other words, corporate environmental management is integrated into (or worse, bolted on to) business as usual. The most significant question therefore revolves around the importance attached to environmentalism. If integration is equivalent to the watering down of more radical forms of environmentalism then it must be seen as a step backwards.

It is increasingly clear that when we discuss environmentalism many of us are essentially speaking very different languages. The rhetoric surrounding eco-modernism lacks any real vision and ignores the complex social and cultural issues which many of us see as central to sustainable development. It lacks any real dialogue and is largely applicable only to the developed world. Those who want to discuss more radical forms of environmentalism are often ignored and sidelined by businesses. In the occasional meetings between businessmen and environmentalists which do take place, the radical in the pack is singled out for derision and is alienated in an attempt to marginalize his/her arguments. Many (particularly academics seeking out research grants) are therefore warned off from this track. It is no wonder that environmentalists often have to hunt in packs.

When industry is under pressure a common strategy is to create forums or clubs amongst themselves to further increase their power and to provide a justification that they are doing something. Such business clubs are created when public restlessness makes them feel lonely. Such clubs are essentially fortresses built to fend off the attacking environmentalists. They become a simple mechanism for reinforcing well established prejudices and ideologies. Well paid secretariats and project managers lunch themselves around the world in the name of consultation and consensus building. But that consensus is usually well defined a long time before any consultation takes place. Such business clubs are therefore very heavy on input but surprisingly light on output.

Industry has its own set of peculiar contradictions. It acknowledges the need for a stakeholder approach and many businesses have included this in their environmental planning. However, it consistently fails to internalize external social impacts and pays only lip-service to the internal social dimensions of employment. Moreover, although the stakeholder approach is heralded, firms fail to be open and transparent in their decision-making processes and rarely provide all the information needed for stakeholders to make a judgement. This has led to scepticism and distrust of businesses.

One of the problems of the rhetoric surrounding the greening of industry is that it is very repetitive. There are surprisingly few new ideas emerging within business. We simply repeat the same old concepts over and over again, often using different words. We go around in circles rather than moving forward towards the real goals of sustainable development. Essentially industry looks backwards; its frame of reference is what went before and business as usual. Managers are constrained in their thinking and often lack any real imagination.

A common characteristic amongst businesses is only to do as much as they perceive to be absolutely necessary. At the same time, what they do is often given an extraordinarily high profile. For example, it is increasingly common for businesses to draw up an environmental policy. As such that is a good starting point but all too often one hears 'that's our policy, we've got one – it shows we are doing something'. The reality is that too often nothing much happens subsequently. Even those companies who produce environmental reports (and they are sometimes produced for very dubious reasons) still operate as if the environment were an add-on to give them a competitive advantage. Too often any environmental strategy exists outside of the day-to-day running of the firm. This add-on rhetoric is dangerous. Those advocating the addition of environmental protection into business as usual fail to recognize the fundamental faults in the system itself and fail to deal with the real challenge facing industry: to do business differently.

Many environmentalists recognize the need for action on the demand side when considering the levels of consumption taking place in the West. But the debate in industry always returns to supply side measures because tackling the demand side means challenging issues such as growth and market share which are sacred tenets to large corporations. Businesses find it almost impossible to conceive of a situation where they are selling less and the emphasis is on ecology and quality rather than growth and quantity.

Managers in the eco-modern firm like simple solutions (and one page documents) and this is what eco-efficiency offers. They claim that they are busy and need fast, practical and cost-effective solutions to the environmental problem. They therefore fail to recognize the enormity of the environmental problem and that there is no single, simple solution to a very complex debate. I find it interesting that seemingly rational managers who claim to care about both the financial and environmental performance of their companies become almost unstable (and often aggressive) when one asks about their social performance as well as environmental performance. They choose either to deliberately ignore their social liabilities or, more often, are clearly unaware of the social dimension of sustainability and are reluctant to engage in any debate. The eco-efficiency fix therefore rules and actually becomes equated with sustainability. Social issues are consistently marginalized.

Environmental managers too often seek out only the technical and scientific solutions to their environmental problems. Eco-efficiency actually encourages this and is therefore welcomed. Again, managers are either unaware of the social and cultural dimensions of their activities or are so scared by such ideas that they dare not even consider them. They simply do not know where to start because they are unaware of the alternatives or are so constrained by a limited corporate culture that they dare not even contemplate anything new.

Because the alternative environmental agenda is diverse and complex and offers no simple solutions, eco-modernists are provided with a stick to beat more radical thinkers. Obstruction through detail is one of the most powerful weapons of the eco-modernists. If one cannot provide them with clear agendas for change, with a detailed (and costed) strategy for implementation then they feel unable to act. They therefore reject alternatives with an air of arrogance and a hidden agenda of conservatism. It is difficult to fight against it and cut down the barriers because the institutionalists are experts when it comes to procedures, protocol and procrastination. What they do not realize because they lack imagination, creativity and vision is that the move towards sustainable development is an uncertain path which involves a good degree of groping in the dark. That path may be dark but we know it is the green path and not the golden one.

Uncertainty over alternatives therefore only adds weight to the more certain strategy of eco-modernism. It supports the culture of continuity of the past rather than change. In the face of this, the cultural arrogance of some industrialists becomes incredible. They rely on telling us the 'way things are' and 'this is the way things are done around here'. They decry beliefs and feelings because they find them dangerous and threatening. They seek to end the normative discourse through aggressive attacks on anyone who does not fit into their model of the economy and society. The frame of reference of such industrialists is, of course, the continuation of business as usual. This is not surprising since this is where they perceive their own interests to lie. They are willing to take on marginal changes to business as usual and therefore tolerate (or even occasionally embrace) eco-modernism, but radical, creative thinking is not on the agenda.

Those who have achieved positions of power and influence often believe that they have done so because they are right and will continue to be right in the opinions which they express. The more powerful they are, the more they simply expect people to listen to and believe their wisdom. Their destructive egos are a major barrier to moving us forward towards a new vision of business.

Academics also have to accept some of the blame for the growing dominance of eco-modernism. We spend too much time analysing what a limited number of companies are doing, using simplistic case study analysis which does little more than map, track and describe. From particular case based situations we try to make generalizations about the greening of industry without any real reference to the social and cultural context of the organization. We are forced into reductionist conclusions which simplify complex relationships, which are necessarily subject to considerable bias both from the researcher's own perspectives and also from the context of established theory and practice. Such a research methodology is bounded, backward looking and may yield spurious results, determined more by discourses created by industry than by real events. Academics (who are supposed to be independent thinkers) must seriously question their own research agendas. They must also question whether the methodology of positivism (which is still dominant) really has much to offer in a complex world.

Finally, we must consider a fundamental question relating to the methodology associated with eco-efficiency itself. If our ultimate aim is to move towards a sustainable development path, we must ask whether the basic concept of efficiency is in fact an appropriate measure of sustainability at all. Efficiency is essentially a neo-classical concept based around optimization. But in the case of the environment we know that to optimize involves an almost impossible trade-off between the many different effects of industrial production. Eco-efficiency turns out to be a complex, messy and inaccurate process often related to assumptions about these different environmental effects. When one adds in the important social dimension of sustainable development into the eco-efficiency function then we reach an impossible position to deal with because it is so complex and uncertain. Such complexity results in businesses leaving the social dimension aside because it would be impossible ever to conceive of a concept associated with social efficiency. Perhaps the concept of efficiency needs to be replaced with consideration of issues such as ethics, equity, equality, empowerment, education and ecology. But we must recognize that there are no simple models to deal with these issues.

THE NEED FOR TURNAROUND

We have already argued that the move towards the golden corner of Galtung's model is a move towards globalization, large scale, domination by corporations and the super-industrial breakthrough. That trend of modernism has not only developed its own form of environmentalism (eco-modernism or eco-efficiency) but has succeeded in moving much of the debate over environmental strategies away from those in the rainbow society. By re-interpreting the demands of environmentalists, the golden trend has tried to provide simple solutions to what is a much more fundamental debate. This type of environmentalism does not move us away from the diagonal of destruction and more insidiously, it does not represent a green alternative but rather a justification of the continuation of modernist madness.

If the super-industrial breakthrough succeeds, the billions of people who live in the developing world would unavoidably strive towards materialist and consumption oriented standards of living. Indeed, growing corporations seeking out larger and larger markets in which to sell their wares would want to encourage this. And who is to suggest that people presently in poverty have no rights to aspire to Western standards of living? This will simply mean, however, that our demand and capacity for damage will increase many-fold. Eco-efficiency strategies might mitigate the environmental impact of that growth but it simply fails to acknowledge that in a world of finite resources with a limited carrying capacity for pollution, growth cannot continue for ever.

The reversal of the golden trend and the move to a rainbow society does not necessarily involve dumping the industrial system in its entirety nor does it necessarily involve dispensing with all industrial capital. To many, the reversal of the golden trend and a move towards a greener society appears to be regressive because it appears to run against traditional notions of growth and development. Indeed it runs contrary to many people's value systems which associate security with consumption and success with materialism. Of course these values are underlined by corporations who constantly strive towards productivism and who are themselves becoming products of a technological determinism which is virtually out of control.

In fact, the move towards the green society is simply a new form of development, consistent with sustainable development and due respect for people and the planet. Technology still exists in the rainbow society and businesses may continue to make profits. But that technology and those businesses are different. Installations, systems and organizations which are too big, complex and often have a life of their own do not exist. What does exist is not backward, it is simply different and it takes courage and creativity to begin to design that future. At the moment though such roads are blocked by powerful corporations, vested interests and individuals too frightened to explore alternatives. It is surprising how many frightened little boys run powerful enterprises.

It is simply surprising how dominant the business-conservative (or business-as-usual) viewpoint has become. Often associated with slogans such as 'there is no alternative', 'that's what it is like in the real world' and 'there is no turning back', this discourse fills me with sadness. Sadness because the people who espouse it often secretly hold rainbow aspirations but dare not come out of the corporate closet, or sad because they actually believe that eco-modernism will provide us with the answers. Such people with limited creative abilities have no right to be running businesses, let alone other people's lives.

CONCLUSIONS

This chapter is not trying to suggest that all the attempts made by industry to improve its environmental performance are bad. It does suggest however, that to date most attempts are inadequate and that eco-modernism has a life outside of other discourses on environmentalism. The concentration on the golden path leaves aside other very valuable models of a society more consistent with sustainable development. Eco-efficiency, moreover, might be seen as a starting point for businesses but not an end in itself. There are great dangers associated with seeing eco-efficiency as a panacea. These include the following considerations:

1   Eco-efficiency can mitigate some direct environmental impacts but it does little to tackle the root causes of the environmental crisis. A reconsideration of consumption patterns, materialism, growth and changing lifestyles are all fundamental to the environmental debate but are not tackled outside the rainbow society.
2   Eco-efficiency and eco-modernism have been created by those committed to the golden path. Such a path is inconsistent with a more sustainable development because its vestiges lie in expansion, globalization, free trade (as opposed to fair trade) and the super-industrial breakthrough.

3   There is a degree of arrogance associated with eco-modernism which could act as a barrier to further development of the environmental agenda. The strive for eco-efficiency is too often seen as an end in itself. The irony here is that environmental action based on models of eco-efficiency may take us a little way along the road towards sustainable development but then may actually block any further progress.

4   Eco-efficiency fails to deal with the social and ethical issues associated with other forms of environmentalism. As such it can only ever been seen as a partial solution.

5   That arrogance and associated power of eco-modernism is now actively preventing the very many other (more radical) debates about alternative ways towards a sustainable future. This is a great loss which we should all regret.

I want to paint a picture of considerable concern but not necessarily one of despair. The concern is associated with my view that eco-modernism, although powerful and growing in popularity, might lead to marginal environmental improvements but lacks the real radicalism needed to bring about sustainable development. But I should also end with a note of optimism. If we can rescue the debate and drag eco-modernism back towards the green corner of Galtung's model, then we can re-establish the alternative discourse about how industry ought to be responding to the environmental crisis. That might be very tough but we must keep raising the issue, keep challenging industry to do more and all work in coalition to re-establish the alternative environmental agenda. We live in a period of rapid change and this is likely to accelerate into the new millennium. Environmental awareness amongst individuals is exploding, increasing numbers of people are looking towards new solutions to the problems in their lives and there is a growing distrust of business activity. Industry will have to respond to that change and although it is now advocating a powerful environmental agenda inconsistent with that change, it will have to come to accept the limitations in eco-modernism and embrace the many radical alternatives to that limited discourse.

References

Bahro, R (1986) *Building the Green Movement*, Heretic Books, London

Bahro, R (1994) *Avoiding Social and Ecological Disaster: The Politics of World Transformation*, English Translation, Gateway Books, Bath

Frankel, B (1987) *The Post Industrial Utopians*, Polity Press, Cambridge

Pepper, D (1993) *Eco-Socialism: From Deep Ecology to Social Justice*, Routledge, London

Sale, K (1974) *Dwellers in the Land: the Bioregional Vision*, Sierra Club, San Francisco

Schmidheiny, S (1992) *Changing Course: A Global Business Perspective on Development and the Environment*, The MIT Press, Cambridge, Massachusetts

Welford, R J (1995) *Environmental Strategy and Sustainable Development: The Corporate Challenge for the 21st Century*, Routledge, London

3

Clouding the Crisis: the Construction of Corporate Environmental Management

Pall Rikhardsson and Richard Welford

We saw in Chapter 2 how businesses have taken the environmental agenda and adjusted and manipulated it to suit their own traditional business objectives. This has had the effect of producing a style of environmentalism more in line with the continuation of growth and the globalization trend than with a move towards sustainable development. We know that this situation has occurred because the whole debate and discussion surrounding the most appropriate corporate environmental management strategies is not neutral. It has been dominated by business and largely constructed by business in an attempt to mitigate the demands of the environmentalists without impacting on the underlying objectives and values of business. We need to examine how this has been achieved before moving on to discuss who has been responsible for the process in Chapter 4.

This chapter therefore examines corporate environmental management from a constructivist perspective and examines the ways in which companies integrate and justify their environmental management practices. In other words, we begin from the premise that corporate environmental management techniques and tools are not neutral but a product of cultures and systems within and outside of firms. We view the emerging practice and methods of corporate environmental management as being based on a certain managerial ideology that accepts only certain forms of solutions and corporate environmental behaviour. We saw in Chapter 2 that this was narrowly defined and often inconsistent with the more radical agendas of environmentalists.

This managerial ideology, we argue, is rooted in a reductionist and positivist way of interpreting the world stressing certainty, quantification and technological development. Inherent in this worldview is a rationality that prefers quantitative arguments, scientific facts and alternatives which can be ranked in a priority order. This ultimately leads to predictable linear solutions to corporate environmental problems. The practice of corporate environmental management is reduced to a matter of choosing the right technology, the right technique or the right tool to solve immediate environmental problems. In other words, when a problem occurs in the workplace, managers will often look towards technical fix solutions rather than examining the underlying tension causing the problem in the first place.

The rational, positivist framework adopted by most managers and their businesses is, however, only one of several alternative modes of explanation and analysis available. Others have developed through time under influences from various philosophers and schools of thought. We identify three alternative approaches which are currently less prevalent in the business world, partly because they lead to fewer straightforward answers, partly because they are more difficult to interpret and partly because they do not lead to the one page solutions which managers like to have on their desk by nine o'clock in the morning.

COMPETING PARADIGMS

An important change in the conduct of science, philosophy and art in the latter half of the 20th century was the movement away from seeing social phenomena in the same way as physical phenomena. This is one aspect of the so-called postmodern trend recently embraced and adopted by a number of academic disciplines. Society is seen as obeying much less clear-cut laws than apply in the physical world such that simple models, broad assumptions and clear predictions become difficult. Thus there is a move towards interpreting social phenomena rather than generalizing, quantifying and classifying them. This is accompanied by a move away from the assumption of value-neutrality and the recognition of interests, conflict and change as a major force in society. Based on these developments there have emerged different ways of interpreting the world.

A useful starting point for our analysis is similar to the approach of Burrell and Morgan (1979) who classify four different paradigms which can be used for explanation and analysis. These are based on the fundamental assumptions adopted by the group or individuals doing the explaining. These assumptions concern firstly, the fundamental nature of social phenomena and secondly, how we interpret the world around us and the society we live in.

The first assumption ranges from an extreme objectivist view to an extreme subjectivist view of social phenomena. The objectivist explanation stresses a world of certainty and predictability such that knowledge exists 'out-there' and only needs to be collected by the researcher who is isolated from the subject of the study. It also has a deterministic view of human nature, whereby human actions are determined by causal laws or some notion of strict rationality, in much the same manner as in the material world. The subjectivistic view, on the other hand, adopts an understanding of social reality as being dependent upon the social actors themselves, implying that knowledge has to be interpreted and that the interpreter is therefore involved or submerged in the subject being interpreted. This approach adopts a voluntary view of human nature, where human action is determined only by humans themselves.

The second assumption about the nature of society ranges from whether the approach taken stresses the status quo (or stability) in society or the aspect of change (often resulting from conflict). The status quo approach is concerned with how things are at the moment, how society is integrated into a cohesive whole and how institutions and individuals deliver this cohesion. The change perspective focuses on how society could be, how it is based on contradictions, how there exists constant change and conflicts between various societal groups and the importance of power relationships.

We thus have two basic assumptions underlying any explanation and analysis, one ranging from objectivism to subjectivism and the other ranging from societal status quo to societal change. By combining these we end up with four possible paradigms as shown in Figure 3.1. On the right hand side we have the traditional positivist paradigm discussed above and an alternative interpretive paradigm. Positivism stresses predictability and the separation of social phenomena and individuals. The interpretive paradigm, on the other hand, places humans in the centre of social phenomena, where the interpretation of facts and knowledge is subjective and in fact created by human actors. Both of these approaches accept society as it currently is, but their ways of exploring particular issues are different. On the left hand side of Figure 3.1 we have more critical approaches. Critical humanism holds the same fundamental assumptions about social phenomena as found in the interpretive paradigm but stresses the need for change and rejects the status quo. The critical structuralist paradigm holds that society is based on certain objective structures that are separate from and independent of the interpretations of individuals. It argues that these structures, resulting from differing amounts of power in society, have to be changed and also rejects the status quo. The direction of change advocated within these

Figure 3.1 Competing Paradigms

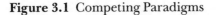

OBJECTIVISM

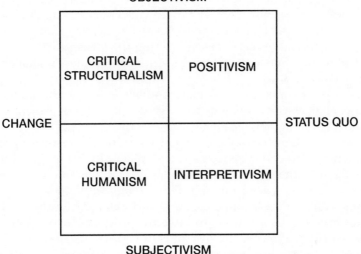

CRITICAL STRUCTURALISM	POSITIVISM
CRITICAL HUMANISM	INTERPRETIVISM

CHANGE .... STATUS QUO

SUBJECTIVISM

more critical paradigms is dependent on the values of the analyst. The critical paradigms have a long Marxist tradition but currently there are other viewpoints developing from which the status quo can be examined. These include feminism, social justice and more radical forms of environmentalism.

Of course, explanations surrounding the causes of the environmental crisis will tend to be interpreted somewhat differently within each paradigm. Positivist explanations tend to favour biological and physical explanations of the environmental crisis stressing the limitations of resources, the growth of population and limits of inhabitable areas. The solutions offered are based on the technological developments and adjustment to processes and systems in society which will eventually solve all environmental problems. This is the approach so often adopted by business, with an emphasis placed on scientific facts and rational argument rather than more all-encompassing approaches which integrate ethics, values and precaution. Moreover, businesses find the positivist approach easy to grasp since it allows them to maintain the status quo until there is scientific evidence that they must change. Any subsequent change can then be technologically driven in a manner completely consistent with eco-modernism.

The interpretive paradigm favours more human centred explanations for our environmental problems. Ultimately such problems stem from the organization of society and its interaction with the natural world. Thus basic concepts such as profit optimization, the undervaluation of the environment, growth, technocentrism, short termism and value neutrality are targets for analysis. The solutions advocated will be based on changing the basic values of society, the culture of organizations and the behaviour of individuals rather than manipulating the physical world with technology. This is a traditional area of activity amongst business researchers interested in re-engineering the business organization to adapt to sustainable development. Although business is challenged to take a more holistic approach to environmental issues, the interpretive paradigm accepts the fundamental values on which the status quo is based. It may seek to mitigate any negative outcomes of present arrangements but it does not challenge the underlying order.

Not so with the critical paradigms. The critical humanist approach to the environmental crisis also sees a problem with ideology, culture and values but rather than calling for adjustment it calls for change. In other words there is a need for radically different ideologies, cultures and values which are not based on the same fundamental values as before. This may include a new approach to the profits made by companies, a re-evaluation of ownership structures, redefining the notion and role of capital, redefining growth and measures of national output and changing corporate ethics and behaviour. This is the stomping ground of many pressure groups.

Critical structuralism on the other hand sees the root of the problem in the type of structures we have created. Indeed, the nature of capitalism with its emphasis on capital accumulation and growth is seen as being wholly inconsistent with sustainable development. Therefore there is a need for some totally new structures within society if environmental problems are to be solved. This might include a radical change in the role and organization of business within society, limits on the transfer of capital, the introduction of new institutions to address environmental issues and a redefinition of international trade arrangements. The system and its structures are to be put under the microscope and, not surprisingly, such calls are derided by business: this is the world of the eco-radicals after all. But some of the most interesting debates are now taking place around this paradigm. However, they are rarely powerful because they are so distant from the dominant discourse of positivism.

One of the central characteristics of both the interpretive and the critical humanist paradigms with respect to the environmental crisis is the idea that there are no absolutes in the social world. Whilst we have to accept the physical absolutes of a finite material world, the way we use this knowledge in a social context is not bound by any natural laws (although some neo-classical economists might just disagree with that). The Western model of economic growth is a good example of the link between the environment and social ideas. Continuing economic growth means increased use of resources, increased production, increased consumption and increased use of environmental waste absorption capacities. Business is often told (and tells us) that continuing economic growth is possible in a finite world through technological development and the human ability to manipulate the material world and harness its powers. This is the traditional positivist argument for increased economic growth. But interpretive and critical humanist arguments would challenge the view that the present scale of environmental problems can be corrected through technological solutions. There is no human made technology available to close the hole in the ozone layer, stabilize global temperature levels or prevent the ice caps from melting. Nor is it likely that such a technology will be invented in the future.

Institutions in society will also use different paradigms when dealing with environmental issues. The positivist view is both dominant and traditional. As such it often has power over arguments about the causes and effects of environmental change. Business, in particular, tends to subscribe to a positivist view and this is most clearly seen in the common arguments about the lack of scientific evidence upon which environmental damage is measured (e.g. over the existence of the greenhouse effect). Because the positivist approach implicitly ignores the precautionary principle, the traditional extrapolation of current trends, where relative environmental certainty is assumed and financial success criteria dominate over other more balanced measures, continues.

Governments use positivist arguments as well and therefore support the dominant paradigm. Government legislation tends to be based on a calculation of its effects and estimates of its future impacts, and government scientists argue for or against government initiatives with the use of scientific data and related statistics. Governments refuse to take action when there is no scientific evidence to support an argument, but are commonly embarrassed when the electorate as a whole decides that other perspectives do matter. The British government's mishandling of both the Shell Brent Spar and the British Beef crises in 1996 illustrates this well.

Meanwhile, less powerful institutions such as environmental lobby groups mostly adopt a more critical mode of analysis and argument. This stresses a wider range of perspectives although scientific evidence is still used effectively when useful. Arguments are commonly centred on rights and responsibilities which lead on to arguments about equity, equality and ethics. Such groups are becoming more powerful as distrust of politicians and business in general increases. Their arguments have a resonance with an increasingly sophisticated population who are now directly experiencing the effects of environmental damage. Most businesses continue to ignore these groups however and their arrogance holds on to the vestiges of power through a mixture of abuse, ridicule and a resort to the positivist paradigm.

Some commentators maintain that different paradigms are not mutually consistent, so that if one paradigm is adopted, another cannot be adopted (Burrell and Morgan 1979). Therefore to move paradigms would involve a major break with one's past work, which could be likened to a change of religion or a radical change of political attitude. However, it is too stringent an assumption that the four paradigms must be mutually exclusive as can be seen from a few companies that adopt a more interpretative view of modern business conduct and at the same time actively campaign for a change. An example is The Body Shop International with its animal protection, human rights and fair trade campaigns. However, examples of business adopting other paradigms than the traditional positivist one are few and far between.

When different institutions and individuals interpret the world differently it obviously causes conflict. Different ways of interpreting the world leads to different agendas for behaviour. This is evident in the conflict going on between Greenpeace and the chlorine industry. Greenpeace maintains that the chlorine industry is basically unsafe and largely unnecessary and should be abolished while chlorine manufacturers say that correct production and use of chlorine is environmentally non-harmful. This story is reflected elsewhere in industry and exists across countries and across cultures where tensions are perhaps the greatest. The positivist paradigm is an arrogant one and those who adopt it move ahead with little concern for wider ethical issues.

We can also use the four sector model outlined here as the basis for developing a more critical research agenda and we return to the issue in the final chapter of this book to discuss an agenda based on ethical theory and change, which might be seen as a mix of critical humanism and critical structuralism.

THE SOCIAL CONSTRUCTIVIST APPROACH

The framework used here in our analysis of how the corporate environmental agenda has been framed, is based on the interpretative paradigm and the critical humanist paradigm. It is, to some extent, based on a specific interpretive approach called social constructivism that has originated within the sociology of knowledge and psychology. There are a number of different applications of constructivism which differ in their initial characteristics. However, these share a number of fundamental likenesses (Burr 1995):

- Constructivism takes a critical stance relating to 'taken-for-granted' knowledge. It challenges the assumption that our observations are based upon objective, unbiased observations of the world 'as it really is' which is the hallmark of objectivist scientific approaches. This lies at the very heart of the interpretive paradigm described above. It rejects the premise that there are norms around which business has to be constructed.
- It holds that the way we understand the world and the categories, concepts and definitions we construct in order to do so, are historically and culturally specific. Accepted ways of interpreting the world depend on particular social and economic arrangements prevailing in that particular society at that particular time. Thus any analysis of business activity can never be value free.
- Our knowledge of the world is created and sustained by various interpretations. People construct knowledge and ways of looking at the world through daily interactions and in the course of social life. Knowledge is shared and communicated through language and symbols. The current 'truths' about business and the world in which it operates are therefore not something that exist independently of people: they are produced and accepted by humans.
- The constructivist approach holds that behaviour and interpretation cannot be separated. As we speak about different ways of interpreting the world around us we have to acknowledge that different constructions lead to different behaviours. Therefore arguments relating to there being 'no alternative' are spurious.

The interpretive and critical humanist paradigms are at the core of these characteristics. Such basic characteristics open the door for a more critical interpretation of society and the behaviour of people and institutions (including business) because they lay great stress on the cultural and temporal specificity of interpretations. This implies that the status quo is only one alternative out of many and that the fact that the status quo exists does not mean that it is the best alternative. Indeed, the status quo only exists because one particular set of values and beliefs become norms because they are held by those people, businesses and other institutions with power. And the more powerful business becomes, the more it is able to influence society as a whole.

A very important element of the interpretive paradigm and the critical attitude surrounds the concept of symbols and the human interpretation of symbols. By symbols we mean all aspects of human behaviour and action that is open to interpretation by humans (Mead 1934). They can be immaterial symbols such as those found in language, behaviour, facial expressions and music, or they could stem from artifacts such as cars, clothes, factories and houses. Interpreting symbols and basing behaviour on these interpretations is unique to the human species. Although one could argue that other animals do interpret symbols to a certain extent these form the basis of reactions rather than interpretations. And humans are the only species whose behaviour can be influenced by totally immaterial symbols such as religion and political ideologies.

According to Burrell and Morgan (1979) there are some basic assumptions about the relationship between symbols and human interpretation which are important here:

- Humans live in a symbolic environment as well as in a physical environment and can be 'stimulated' to act by symbols as well as by physical stimuli. For example, investors often base their investments in companies on financial data (symbols) without ever having laid eyes on the company in question. Equally, decisions of environmental managers can be based on the interpretation of figures from test equipment, the environmental policy laid out by the board of directors, the environmental objectives of the company, legal directives from local authorities, written complaints from local citizens, or the emergence of a new law. All of these are symbols according to our definition.
- Through symbols, humans have the capacity to stimulate others in ways other than those in which they themselves are stimulated. For example, by publishing an environmental report a company often hopes to influence the perceptions of its stakeholders in a favourable manner even though it may be a severely polluting company.
- Through communication and interpretation of symbols, humans can learn a huge number of meanings and values (and hence ways of behaving) from other humans. An example could be how knowledge and different ways of solving various environmental problems diffuses in an industry. The diffusion of various types of cleaner technology alternatives is a good example. One company develops the technology and through journals, conferences or word-of-mouth other companies follow suit. This is based on individuals or groups in these organizations exchanging or acquiring knowledge and learning new ways of behaving. However, although companies may benchmark and imitate each other in this way – there is no guarantee that the initial technological development was the best or most appropriate one. The same is true of other techniques and management styles which we discuss in more detail below.

Behaviour is therefore based on interpretation. This is a different view than the one adopted in traditional positivist approaches where the individual is seen as a rational, predictable and relatively simple black box existing between stimuli and response. The constructivist view maintains that there is always an on-going interpretation process where actions, events and objects are being given meaning, their relevance to the individual or group is being judged and action being taken on the basis of that judgement. The interpretation ultimately adopted is thus a construction of an individual or group of individuals. Indeed, much of management action is based on the interpretation and communication of symbols such as the interpretation of financial data, a judgement of the influence of external events on the company, speeches given at conferences, the publication of environmental reports, use of environmental indicators in decision making, designing television commercials and communicating the corporate strategy to employees.

An example of interpretations within the field of environmental management relates to the construction of knowledge about environmental problems. Hannigan (1995) has shown that it is primarily the scientific community, the media and politicians that contribute to the construction of environmental problems. Discovering environmental problems, communicating these to society and then deciding on courses of action is far from being a neutral, value free process of course. Scientific evidence, which in itself is very much a product of interpretation, is sometimes at the centre of any debate, but at other times it seems to be ignored or misunderstood. The media tends to concentrate on issues that have a dramatic appeal to them, and politicians are influenced by lobbyists, elections, internal party politics and other competing agendas. Furthermore, environmental problems are often ignored because the scientific community does not judge the scientific evidence presented as being valid. Thus the perceived seriousness of environmental problems does not have to be dependent on the actual or potential threat of the problem. How environmental problems are perceived can be more dependent on the social interactions that transform an environmental issue into an environmental problem.

In the context of corporate environmental management there are two levels inherent in the interpretation of symbols. The first and most obvious level relates to the interpretation of the problem at hand, how to respond to the problem and the possible outcomes of this response. This is the practical level. Solutions to environmental problems will have to be perceived to work. For example, efficiency has to increase, perceptions of stakeholders have to improve or products have to become free of a hazardous substance. The second level relates to the ideology and values that affect the interpretations of possible courses of action at the first level or in other words define what solutions are acceptable to the company and to the company's perception of society. This is examined in more detail below in the context of corporate interpretation frameworks.

In this context, scientific evidence does not carry the same weight as it once did. A recent example of this is the conflict around the intended sinking of Shell's Brent Spar oil platform into the North Sea. Although Shell had scientific evidence claiming that sinking the platform was the least environmentally harmful solution, it was the media which transmitted the alternative interpretation of other powerful pressure groups in society that eventually led to a different outcome. Further examples of the growing schism between science and public confidence include the recent bout of scares regarding 'mad cow' disease, plastic softeners in baby milk, the thinning of the ozone layer above public beaches and changes in the global climate. Spokesmen from the scientific community often assure the public that there is nothing to fear. The greenhouse effect is often said to mean little changes in global climate that will be beneficial rather than harmful. However, if scientists can not foresee with any accuracy the weather for the next few days, the public asks, how can they claim knowing anything certain about the long term effects of human behaviour on the climate of the world as a whole?

The basic problem is that scientists can only base their conclusions on evidence at hand. If some evidence comes along that 'proves' the opposite of what has become accepted wisdom because of more accurate measurements, different measurements or some unforeseen relationships or effects surfacing, then scientists change their claims. But this reliance on scientific evidence and facts as an approach to environmental problems, is clearly inadequate given the irreversibility of most of them and the potential seriousness of the effects on individuals and society. Admitting in ten years' time that minuscule doses of plastic softeners do seem to affect human reproduction after all, will not help people unable to have children due to the effects of these substances.

The emphasis put on scientific evidence clouds one of the most important approaches advocated by environmentalists, namely, the precautionary principle. By giving the benefit of doubt to people and the planet when there is a dispute or a large margin of error in scientific evidence, we at least err on the cautious side. If we are wrong in being cautious then little harm is done. Going with the scientific evidence which may turn out to be wrong is potentially much more dangerous. But despite some platitudes to the precautionary principle, this more cautious (some would argue responsible) approach is not on the agenda of corporate environmental management. The ICC Business Charter for Sustainable Development sees the precautionary principle being 'To modify the manufacture, marketing or use of products or services or the conduct of activities, consistent with scientific and technical understanding, to prevent serious irreversible environmental degradation' (see Welford 1996, p 110). Such a weak definition of the precautionary principle does not take us very far and once again it relies on scientific evidence at the centre of the decision making process.

Another important issue relates to how environmental problems are generally treated in the media. Traditional news presentation is often event fixated or blame seeking, which affects the way environmental problems are reported. Environmental problems are often pictured as recent outcomes of one specific event rather than the inevitable outcome of a series of political and societal decisions. This works very well for spectacularly visible events such as oil tankers running aground or banks of foam floating on rivers but for other types of problems such as the greenhouse effect, the thinning of the ozone layer or species eradication it does not work. For these global problems there is no one culprit that can be made to take the blame and therefore they are less news worthy and information provision is limited.

CORPORATE INTERPRETATION FRAMEWORKS

Given our previous discussion, we can view company environmental practices as being based on an interpretation of actions of other companies, institutions and individuals, and on events and conflicts occurring in the physical environment. Favoured interpretations can be said to form a framework through which the company sees the world. These frameworks can be located within the four different paradigms shown in Figure 3.1. However, given the commercial context in which business operates one can assume that most companies will base their frameworks on the positivist paradigm. Some companies, should it suit their strategy and values of the senior management, may apply a more interpretive paradigm but few, if any, companies approach their business with a critical attitude as advocated in critical humanism and critical structuralism. But how are specific frameworks of interpretation created and embedded in companies? The answer lies in a process of standardization and legitimation.

Standardization

The main process of embedding interpretation frameworks is standardization of corporate practices (see for example Berger and Luckmann 1966, who use the term institutionalization; and Cyert and March 1992, who use the term standard operating procedures). Basically, standardization of practices stems from the wish to minimize human effort and simplify decision making. Corporate actions, responses and interpretations become habitualised and 'given' in the organization. This could for example be routine ways of handling environmental complaints, the usual process preceding an environmental investment, the functions of an environmental management system or the extent of interactions between the environmental department and other departments. Even the standardization process becomes standardized as we have seen with the development of environmental management systems for certification according to BS 7750 or ISO 14000 standards. These require that every environmentally significant procedure, be it environmental auditing guidelines or how to change wastewater filters on certain machines, be written down and archived in the environmental management manual. This manual is the bible of the environmental management system and is supposed to provide the environmental officers and employees with the answers to most of the questions and problems that may arise. The process is therefore to standardize the interpretation of certain issues. This has come to form the bedrock of corporate environmental management.

Standardizing actions and responses implies some kind of control as well. A standardized pattern of conduct channels behaviour into one direction although alternative directions may exist. By doing things a certain way and adhering to a certain standardized interpretation, it often means that other, perhaps superior alternatives are ignored. For example if a company focuses on monetary returns on investment or other financial efficiency measures when making an environmental investment, it could overlook alternatives that do not conform to the prescriptions inherent in financial measurements.

This is often the case when companies try to reduce carbon dioxide (CO_2) emissions from their use of fossil fuels. Their attention is on directly reducing fossil fuel use by making their processes more efficient, planning transport routes more effectively or getting employees to save energy. All of these initiatives are related to increasing efficiency in the traditional way, comparing outputs with inputs. But there are other alternatives which more often than not are ignored. If we look at CO_2 emissions as a truly global problem then a company is amassing a CO_2 'debt' no matter what marginal progress in efficiency is achieved. The way to balance the books is thus not only to use fewer fossil fuels but to examine other alternatives to pay off this debt. An example could be for heavy CO_2 emitters to invest in forestry given that trees take CO_2 from the atmosphere during their lifetime. Thus, while pursuing energy saving alternatives, the company has a forest which absorbs some of its CO_2 contribution to the atmosphere. And seen in a global perspective this forest could even be on another continent. Another alternative might be to invest in alternative energy generation such as wind farms to cover some of the company's energy use. Thus the company might not use itself the energy generated by the windmills but by helping to generate cleaner energy it would be saving CO_2 emissions at another location.

When a specific informal standard is adopted and a company interpretation framework comes about, one could say that it gradually
'thickens' in apparent objectivity. People will behave as if the framework,
standard or code of conduct is an unchangeable fact and pass this on to
new members in the organization as 'the way we do things around here'.
This often means that dismissing the framework is not possible or
extremely difficult. This is often experienced by new enthusiastic
environmental managers hired into big old established companies.
There are established codes of conduct, systems tend to function in a
certain way, and behaviour is channelled towards certain specific goals.
To introduce radical new values and perspectives is more liable to break
the new manager than anything else. Thus as the adopted interpretations
of the world are standardized and passed on, individuals and groups of
individuals gradually lose the ability to see and evaluate alternative ways
of doing things. Only when crisis looms or existing standards prove
unable to solve the problem for which they were designed, will people
examine other alternatives.

The adoption of codes of conduct and standards within any organization necessarily raises a number of questions. The most obvious one
concerns the type of subculture which a standard brings with it. Does it
represent a piecemeal attempt to placate demands from pressure groups
and consumers or is it a more serious attempt at ethical behaviour for
example? We ought also to ask, how effective the codes are in promoting
what they stand for? Taken together these questions provide a measure
of the extent to which the standards are genuine and operational, rather
than cynical and self-deluding. Given that corporate environmental
management is increasingly standardized and framed around a number
of codes of conduct, it is worth pursuing these questions in a little more
depth.

Codes of conduct and particularly standards, which become accepted
across firms in an industry or even across industries, are very powerful
and we often see them written into contracts between organizations. We
might be inclined to think that a standard promoting some sort of
environmental improvement is a huge step forward and that companies
who follow others in adopting such standards should be congratulated.
But rather more analysis of the content and purpose of such a standard
is necessary before we can reach an answer to that question. Without
suggesting that environmental standards are indeed bad we must nevertheless consider whether, in fact, some standards push employees and
customers into a set of values which verge on indoctrination. Stakeholders in those sorts of situations come to possess what Marxists see as
false consciousness. In addition, the fact that a standard is widely
accepted does not guarantee that the values within it are not restricted
or inconsistent. Values contained in standards can also be restricted

when, for example (and typically), they exclude any consideration of the impact of a company's activities on indigenous populations in the developing world.

There is very little research on the generation, operation, monitoring and amendment of codes and standards. However, it is argued forcefully by Donaldson (1989) that because codes tend to be expressions of mixtures of technical, prudential and moral imperatives, and because they tend to vary in the extent to which they are or can be enforced, they cannot be regarded as the major vehicles for identifying and encouraging the practices which will raise the level of values in business and industry. Moreover, codes and standards are defined outside of the normal democratic framework which determines laws. They are constructed by agencies (often professional bodies or representatives of senior management in industry) with their own motivations, values and interests. On this subject Donaldson and Waller (1980) point to a statement of Bernard Shaw when he asserted that professions can be conspiracies against the laity, and their codes are widely held to be primarily aimed at the protection of the members of the profession, rather than the public. Much the same accusation might be levelled against industry standards. Moreover the matter of the development of codes and standards is bound up with the matter of enforcement. Codes which are not enforced or fail to deliver their expected outcomes for whatever reason, might be thought of as little more than cynical expressions of pious hopes.

Much of what has been discussed here can be illustrated by reference to the Responsible Care Programme, which in itself provides a formal standard for firms operating in the chemicals industry to adopt. The Responsible Care Programme might be seen as one of the earliest environmental management systems standards used across companies. It is a voluntary code where performance is measured in terms of continuous improvement. Responsible Care is unique to the chemical industry and originated in Canada in 1984. Launched in 1989 in the UK by the Chemical Manufacturers' Association (CMA) the cornerstone of the system is commitment. Chief Executives of member companies are invited to sign a set of guiding principles pledging their company to make health, safety and environmental performance an integral part of overall business policy. Adherence to the principles and objectives of Responsible Care is a condition of membership of the Chemical Industries Association. All employees and company contractors have to be made aware of these principles. The guiding principles also require companies to:

- conform to statutory regulations;
- operate to the best practices of the industry;
- assess the actual and potential health, safety and environmental impacts of their activities and products;

- work closely with the authorities and the community in achieving the required levels of performance;
- be open about activities and give relevant information to interested parties.

A company operating the Responsible Care Programme is required to have a clear company policy and the communication of this is seen as vital. The key principle being used in the Responsible Care Programme is self-assessment. However, the CMA does assess the effectiveness of the programme across all firms by collecting indicators of performance from the firms. However, in its three-year report of the Responsible Care Programme (ENDS 1993) the CMA was implicitly forced to admit that the Responsible Care Programme was not functioning in accordance with its aims. The main reason for this is that sites claiming to adhere to the Responsible Care standard were simply not adhering to its principles. Over the three year reporting period only 57 per cent of firms made returns for all three years and only 74 per cent made any returns at all. Even more importantly, one indicator of performance deals with waste and emissions where firms are supposed to report an environmental index by site designed to give a composite picture of gaseous, liquid and solid releases. Only one third of the total firms supposed to be operating Responsible Care reported this data in full, and of those who reported the index, over 30 per cent reported a worsening environmental impact.

Codes of conduct are therefore nothing if they are not adhered to, and voluntary approaches often slip down a list of priorities when other pressing issues arise. It is perhaps not surprising that the lack of response from the chemical industry over Responsible Care occurred during a particularly bad economic recession. However, at the core of a strategy for environmental improvement has to be commitment and no standard or code of conduct will survive without that commitment. Whilst some chemical companies are clearly committed to improving their environmental performance it seems that too many are not adhering to the spirit of Responsible Care. Indeed, whilst some make efforts to follow the guidelines of the programme many more treat Responsible Care as a smokescreen. Many of those managers in the chemical industry who appear confident of their procedures to improve environmental performance are certainly either suffering from the false consciousness which was suggested earlier or are making much more cynical attempts to hide their environmental impact in an attempt to hang on to market share and profitability.

This is not untypical of the general approach of corporate environmental management. There is a great deal of rhetoric surrounding eco-efficiency, stakeholder responsibility, environmental management systems, technology transfer and environmental auditing. However, whilst all of this is becoming increasingly standardized, pollution levels continue to increase. Nowhere in the rhetoric do we see any recognition of the fact that the environmental crisis results from a crisis in the way we operate our economies, societies and businesses. It is therefore a crisis of mindset which requires more than standards to clean up pollution, protect endangered wildlife and tell stakeholders how wonderful business is. More insidious, however, is the view that many leaders are fully aware that voluntary codes of conduct do little to bring about real change. They are there to placate and disarm an increasingly sceptical public. And, to date, as we get more and more geared up to expecting industry to adopt piecemeal environmental management systems standards with their self-determined objectives and targets, it seems that the approach is working just as it was intended to do.

Legitimation

The second major force in the creation and maintenance of interpretation frameworks surrounding corporate environmental management is legitimation. While standardization of interpretation frameworks concerns the way things are done and understood, legitimation involves the arguments surrounding why a certain course of action or a specific interpretation is acceptable. This is the process of explaining and justifying particular frameworks and making them plausible and available to managers and employees. In effect it is the process whereby certain approaches become accepted norms whilst others are disregarded. Here we distinguish between two basic levels of legitimation.

The first level concerns human language, and human experience objectified through language, along with prescriptions of behaviour transmitted through language. It is obvious that language has a big impact on the way we interpret the world and attach meaning to persons, events and objects. The language of the Inuits has more than a dozen different words for snow while English only has one. This is clearly because snow has a very important impact on the lives of those living in remote northern areas. One can also broaden the term language to include for example the language of mathematics, the language of accounting and the language of physics. There is therefore much in the application of language that legitimizes certain ways of seeing, certain ways of understanding and certain ways of communicating. And by this it excludes other ways of seeing, understanding and communicating. An Inuit conceptualizes snow differently from an English person and an accountant speaks differently about the workings of a business enterprise than a physicist.

For certain frameworks to become standardized in a company they must fit the language used in the company. The language of a company seeking to continually increase its profits will be very different to another company wanting to operate ethically in an egalitarian structure. A company wishing to implement an environmental management system must be able to communicate it and make it understandable to the members of the organization. And in doing that through language it implicitly constructs certain categories, perceptions and ways of understanding environmental issues. In other words, the languages used to communicate reality legitimize certain interpretations. A simplified example would be a company framing its environmental management within its marketing function and using marketing language and categories to communicate environmental programmes and initiatives to staff and employees. This would be very different from another company using engineering and technical language for its environmental management.

The language of much corporate environmental management is essentially the language of 'business as usual'. Stephan Schmidheiny and others from the World Business Council for Sustainable Development confirm this so well in their most recent book to push the eco-efficiency agenda: *Financing Change* (Schmidheiney et al 1996). The main thrust of the book is that business can be trusted and can be left alone to cure the environmental problems of the world. Any alternative interventionist approach is thrown out when it is argued:

> *We nowhere claim that tougher regulations improve a company's or country's competitiveness. In fact, given the ad hoc way in which regulations have proliferated, we have called for a pruning back until the ones that are left are necessary, transparent, evenly applied, and cost-effective. We have argued that more could be achieved with well-constructed economic instruments, including improvements in the competitiveness of eco-efficient companies. (p 68)*

The message is also one of self-congratulation:

> *Our main argument is that driven by ... many forces ... including a push from far sighted business leaders, the world is moving towards market frameworks which reward eco-efficiency more systematically ... Smart companies will help this happen. (p 69)*

Of course such false consciousness is amazing and alarming and completely at odds with what other respected commentators would argue. Michael Porter has made it clear that regulation can actually act as a stimulus to business to innovate and gain competitive advantage and that regulation can also be justified on the grounds of information provision, education and the need for the ubiquitous level playing field (see Porter and van der Linde 1995). And we have argued in the previous chapter that business leaders have been far from far-sighted in general. But the view seems to be that pushing this type of message often enough will mean that some of it will stick. It is an easy message fully consistent with eco-modernism which therefore happily finds receptive ears. The bottom line is once again exposed by Schmidheiney et al (1996):

> *Managers have to persuade stakeholders not only that they are moving efficiently in the right direction, but that they are exercising the same degree of financial prudence in pursuing eco-efficiency as they would exercise in pursuing market share (p 71)*

The second stage lifts legitimation from pragmatic reality to an ideological one. Ideology means, in the traditional definition, a body of ideas used to support a particular theory or bodies of knowledge. It binds different theories together and integrates, in our case, company interpretations into an all embracing frame of reference. An example could be the idea of economic growth and how it unites economic behaviour and economic theory on a path towards increased production and increased consumption.

Thus, here we have seen the attempts to make eco-efficiency the standard rallying cry for business and, more insidiously, to equate eco-efficiency with sustainable development. At the moment the concept is mostly rhetoric although one can be sure that technical fix solutions will follow. These arguments have been well rehearsed in the previous chapter and need not be repeated here. But the process of legitimation requires that eco-efficiency becomes firmly embedded in other norms surrounding business. Again Schmidheiny et al (1996) make their somewhat predictable contribution: 'High economic growth rates provide businesses with the opportunity to improve the eco-efficiency of their operations . . .' (p 42).

CORPORATE ENVIRONMENTAL MANAGEMENT REVEALED

We have now framed environmental management as a process of construction with interpretations becoming increasingly standardized and legitimized by certain codes of conduct, accepted norms, ideologies and bodies of knowledge. The question which arises relates to what sorts of corporate environmental management ideologies are in use today to legitimize the standardization of corporate environmental management.

One can identify two main ideas which dominate corporate environmental management thinking today. The first is the idea of the environmental management system which has become the most important vehicle to implement and interpret environmental management which is evident in the unabated popularity of standardized systems such as BS 7750, the EU eco-management and audit scheme (EMAS) and ISO 14000. The second is the concept of eco-efficiency which brings with it a clear set of values and techniques aimed at promulgating business as usual. Both ideas, which have a significant degree of overlap are creating another layer of management: indeed a new management trend.

Significant evidence exists that management trends which become popular exert a strong influence on the on-going techniques of corporate management. New concepts which are successfully implemented in certain organizations become accepted, become dominant and even when they are inappropriate become the norm (Mintzberg 1979). DiMaggio and Powell (1983) offer three explanations for this phenomenon. Firstly, organizations will submit to both formal and informal pressures from other organizations upon which they depend. Secondly, when faced with uncertainty organizations may model themselves on organizations that have seemed to be successful and adopt the sorts of techniques which they see being introduced. Thirdly, normative pressures which stem from a degree of professionalism amongst management can cause the adoption of 'fashionable' management techniques. Universities, training institutions, standard setters and professional associations are all vehicles for the development of these normative rules.

These are precisely the trends which we are seeing in contemporary approaches to environmental management which are often piecemeal and sporadic. This approach is not consistent with the concept of sustainable development because it does not go far enough in developing strategies which will reverse the trend towards environmental degradation. But the piecemeal approach is becoming the accepted ideology because it is being adopted by leading firms, espoused by academics and legitimized by standard setters and policy makers.

Moreover, this trend is further reinforced by so-called benchmarking analysis which is becoming increasingly common in industry. As a principle, benchmarking can be valuable but it can also reinforce inappropriate general techniques. Current environmental standards are not high and this in turn, gives the impression to imitators in industry that the environmental challenge facing industry is actually quite weak. The reverse is quite true and what is needed therefore is a change in the dominant ideology.

Such a change in ideology is, of course, difficult to achieve because environmental management standards have been set by industry itself.

They have been designed to be voluntary and designed so as not to conflict with the ideology associated with profit maximization in the short to medium term. Arguments such as the ones outlined above, suggesting that industry has not gone far enough, will therefore be treated with derision by industry and sidelined. The power which industry has in the current economic system is therefore a barrier to further development of the concepts of sustainable development. Thus the only way to bring about a change in this sub-optimal dominant ideology is to challenge the very basis of that power. Without a fundamental revolution in the way we organize our society, such a challenge can only come about through a legislative process.

The increasing importance of the concepts of the environmental management system and eco-efficiency imply that certain interpretations and behaviours are being legitimized. Referring to Figure 3.1 we argue that this legitimization and these concepts are very much based in the positivist quadrant. This implies that companies focus on constructing logical steps, distinguishing temporal phases, documenting procedures, concentrating on certain tangible environmental effects, aiming at continuous environmental management system improvement and striving for converting inputs to outputs with the minimum of waste, whilst maintaining traditional objectives of increasing profits, expanding sales, gaining market share and reducing costs. The terminology is based on the language of systems such as 'flows', 'processes', 'phases' and 'inputs' and the language of engineering such as 'efficiency', 'rationality', 'effectiveness' and 'optimization'. The dominant body of knowledge is based around the technological sciences implying that the solutions employed will be based on choosing technological solutions, implementing technological changes and selecting the right optimization methods or techniques. And the underlying ideology is still the aim of achieving as much growth as possible with the minimum of input. Although environmental impacts can be minimised on a relative basis (in other words, the company lessens its environmental impact compared to the size of its operations) the total impact continues to rise. Thus, although the company can show increases in efficiency, the availability of natural resources and the waste absorption capacities of the environment continue to decline. This is hardly consistent with sustainable development even though some commentators would have us believe otherwise.

Whether a company adopts a purely positivistic interpretation of the world or courageously strives to be more interpretive or critical, depends on the power relations between the groups espousing the different interpretations as well as the values of top management. The attitudes, values and actions of senior management will tend to form the culture in any organization. In particular, the chief executive will tend to be very important in influencing the behaviour of the next tier of executives, and down the line to the shop-floor employees. We know that senior management will tend to have a contagious influence and too often they will have a vested interest more associated with short-term performance than in acting in an environmentally responsible manner. We return to this issue in the next chapter.

Related to the top executive's influence over a company is the often mechanistic management systems and structures which traditional corporate environmental management approaches so often promote. These are in place because they are easy to control, but such structures will often stifle creativity. Moreover, any discussion relating to values will be second to structure and this will too often define the firm's immediate interests in terms of short-term performance. Customer and employee safety, integrity, and environmental protection will be secondary considerations.

CONCLUSIONS

This chapter has demonstrated that the most common way in which businesses analyse and explain events around them is very much centred around a restrictive positivist paradigm. There are alternative ways of viewing societal processes and environmental change, yet these have been sidelined because they tend to challenge the very foundations of business as usual. Businesses find it easier to push a simplistic and narrow view of the world which will not be inconsistent with their wider business objectives. Business embraces positivism for other reasons as well: it consists of a relatively simple set of ideas, it is operational and manageable; and it protects the status quo. Businesses resist other ways of looking at the world which we have discussed in this chapter because they tend to be more critical and challenge the traditional roles and structures of business. In effect, other approaches can sap the power of business, they are inherently less manageable and they challenge the business to change. Managers find such challenges very threatening.

Yet, the world is changing rapidly, people are becoming more sophisticated and business is increasingly distrusted. In the postmodern world business is now struggling to keep up with the changing perception around it. Scientific evidence alone is no longer sufficient to influence public perception. A reliance on technology is rapidly letting us down. Yet business clings on to its outdated and outmoded assumptions. It heralds concepts such as eco-efficiency as something new and good and radical. Nothing could be further from the truth. It has legitimized concepts such as environmental management systems and eco-efficiency quite successfully because it holds on to a great deal of societal power. But already those concepts are tired and have not produced any real change. Business is going to have to think again.

One reason for the great tensions which now exist between business, pressure groups and the general public is that businesses hold on to a narrow frame of reference whilst others are moving on. Whilst most of the corporate world clings on to positivism, others have become much more critical in their outlooks. The corporate world simply views this as misguided and in its typically arrogant way continues to plough the furrow of business as usual. Sooner or later the eco-modernist approach will be exposed as the 'greenwash' that it is. We have to hope that when that occurs it will not be too late to move against the golden trend.

References

Berger, L and Luckmann, T (1966) *The Social Construction of Reality*, New York, Doubleday

Burr, V (1995) *An Introduction to Social Constructivism*, London, Routledge

Burrell G and Morgan, G (1979) *Sociological Paradigms in Organizational Analysis*, London, Heinemann Books

Cyert, R M and March, J (1992) *A Behavioural Theory of the Firm*, Cambridge (MA), Blackwell

Donaldson, J (1989) *Key Issues in Business Ethics*, Academic Press Inc, San Diego

Donaldson, J and Waller, M (1980) 'Ethics and Organization', *Journal of Management Studies*, 17, 1

DiMaggio, P J and Powell, W (1983) 'The Iron Cage Revisited: Institutional Isomorphism and Collective Rational in Organizational Fields', *American Sociological Review*, 48, 147–60

Environmental Data Services (ENDS) (1993) 'Jury still out on Responsible Care'. *Industry Report no 55*, ENDS 222, July

Hannigan, J (1995) *Environmental Sociology: A Social Constructivist Approach*, London, Routledge

Mead, G H (1934) *Mind, Self and Society*, Chicago, University of Chicago Press

Mintzberg, H (1979) *The Structuring of Organizations*, Prentice Hall, New York

Porter, M and van der Linde, C (1995) 'Green and Competitive: Ending the Stalemate', *Harvard Business Review*, 73, 5

Schmidheiny, S, Zorraquin, F J L with the World Business Council for Sustainable Development (1996) *Financing Change: The Financial Community, Eco-efficiency and Sustainable Development*, MIT Press, Mass

Welford, R J (1996) *Corporate Environmental Management: Systems and Strategies*, Earthscan, London

4

Fading to Grey: the Use and Abuse of Corporate Executives' 'Representational Power'

Nick Mayhew

This chapter aims to raise questions about the role that corporate managers, particularly senior executives, are playing in defining and shaping the sustainable development agenda. It is intended as a polemical counter to the impression, given by much work in the business and environment field, that industrialists are passive actors, coming to terms with an externally-defined (and strangely uniform) 'environmentalism' with varying degrees of enthusiasm and success. This results in policy advice which rarely amounts to any more than exhorting business to 'do more' and encouraging 'business leadership'. The implication seems to be that once a critical mass of complementary 'corporate environmentalism' is reached – comprising initiatives such as the introduction of cleaner processes and technologies, the setting up of environmental management systems, the publication of environmental reports and so on – sustainable development will automatically ensue.

This chapter, by contrast, reveals the extent to which the corporate world is actively shaping environmentalism as it engages with it and is, in fact, hindering progress towards sustainable development as a result. Corporate actors are not disinterested parties; they have their own particular needs and goals – and they are powerful. This inevitably influences how they approach environmental matters, which in turn has considerable impact on the wider agenda and profound implications for the rest of society. The chapter therefore documents key ways in which corporate executives wield this self-interested 'representational power', actually fashioning the sustainable development agenda to suit their business priorities. The aim is to provoke greater scrutiny of the exact nature of important aspects of 'corporate environmentalism', and more circumspection regarding its contribution to sustainable development. The chapter also raises serious doubts about the value and legitimacy of business executives' assumption of a leadership role on the issue. The proposition is that executives need to be more self-conscious about the narrowness of the perspective underpinning their approach to environmental issues, and more aware of the flaws in this approach which thereby result. Thence, they have to become more open and amenable to the differing perspectives of others and, ultimately, to proactively reduce their 'representational power'.

Our starting point is a fundamental one – so fundamental, in fact, that it is often overlooked: the basic problem is that corporate executives currently represent, in a structural sense at least, a development paradigm which is completely antithetical to that of sustainable development. Korten (1995), for example, has described the basic contradiction of interests involved. For sustainable development to stand a chance, he writes:

> *we must . . . restructure economic relationships to focus on two priorities:*
>
> i) *balance human uses of the environment with the regenerative capacities of the ecosystem; and*
> ii) *allocate available natural capital in ways that ensure that all people have the opportunity to fulfil their physical needs adequately and to pursue their full social, cultural, intellectual and spiritual development.*

However:

> *Among the barriers we face to accomplishing this transformation is the powerful coalition of interests aligned behind an institutional agenda that is taking us in a quite different direction. These are the corporate interests that benefit when societies make the pursuit of economic growth the organizing principle of public policy.*

After Lipietz (1992), the term 'liberal-productivism' is used to describe this 'institutional agenda' militating against sustainable development. It serves as convenient shorthand for the presently hegemonic development paradigm comprising deregulated trade and investment patterns, the utmost faith in technology, an obsession with growth – of whatever

quality, a never-ending search for greater productivity and competitiveness, top-down managerial control and varying degrees of 'trickle-
down' wealth distribution. That this development model does,
undoubtedly, benefit corporate interests whilst acting simultaneously
against the interests of sustainable development is indicated by the
following sorts of statistics. For example, in 1991, total sales of the
world's ten largest corporations exceeded the aggregate gross national
product (GNP) of the world's 100 smallest countries (Hawken 1993);
about 70 per cent of world trade is currently controlled by a mere 500
transnational corporations (TNCs) (Lang and Hines 1993); and just 1
per cent of TNCs control half of the total stock of foreign direct
investment world-wide (United Nations 1993). In addition, between 1980
and 1993, the Fortune 500 industrial firms in the United States shed
nearly 4.4 million jobs, while the average chief executive officer's
compensation at the largest corporations increased by 6.1 times to $3.8
million (Korten 1995, p 218). Also, directors of British companies paid
themselves another 9 per cent more in earnings in 1995 than in the
previous year – equivalent to three times the rate of inflation and four
times the rate of growth in the economy (*The Independent* 1996). Meanwhile, one in three children in the UK are growing up in poverty (Hutton
1995); the richest 20 per cent of the global population receives 82.7 per
cent of world income (Korten 1995, p 107) and consumes some 80 per
cent of the world's resources (Schmidheiny 1994; Durning 1991); and
per capita water supply in developing countries has dropped by two-
thirds since 1970 (United Nations 1996).

Thus, despite the contradictions pervading the prevailing, liberal-
productivist development paradigm – threatening appalling 'systems
failure' – corporate executives tend towards promulgating a 'corporate
environmentalism' which furthers, rather than challenges, this paradigm. This chapter shows how this occurs, focusing on two, basic
dimensions of the process; it documents both how executives are
constructing and arguing their 'environmentalism', and the force with
which they are (re)presenting it. In the first case, we find that executives
are applying a highly ideological perspective to the issue, which is
presented as a form of rational objectivity even though it is derived from
entirely subjective interests. Thus, at the macro-level, corporate executives are managing to subordinate the goal of sustainable development
to the 'logic' of the free market and the 'rationality' of technological
progress, such that liberal-productivism is able to prevail. At the micro-
level, the operation of corporate bureaucracy (through which executive
power is reproduced) compounds these tendencies by requiring personnel to apply similar rationalities, complementing liberal-productivism.
Thus, scientific and market logics – so-called sound science, environmental management systems, cost-benefit analyses etc. – are applied to

the problem, although they are only able to provide very partial, if not regressive, solutions. This adds up to a top-down, technocratic approach to sustainable development which some have defined as 'eco-modernism' (see Chapter 2). In effect, sustainable development is defined such that corporate interests are not only protected, but generally enhanced.

(It is beyond the scope of this chapter to go into much further detail regarding exactly why this technocratic, 'eco-modernist' approach is so contrary to sustainable development. However, a principal failing is that it screens out – under the guise of a supposedly neutral rationalism – any consideration of the critical social and ethical aspects of the concept, like the need for greater socio-economic equity. Similarly, such technocracy militates against both bio- and cultural-diversity, leaving very little room for the valuation of nature (or increasingly, people) in ways other than by reference to their economic utility. Being inherently expansionist, the present paradigm also has great difficulty responding to the notion of 'limits'. A deathly economism, allied with a drab managerialism, is the result – whilst an increasingly intense productivism grows ever more global, creating ever greater inequality in its wake. For a more in-depth critique of liberal-productivism see, for example, Lipietz (1992); Korten (1995); Hawken (1993); Atkinson (1991); Jacobs (1991) and Gladwin (1994).)

As environmental pressure groups understand very well, it is one thing to apply a perspective and assert a position on a particular issue; it is quite another for this to have any wider impact. Thus, we also consider in some depth the second aspect of executives' 'representational power': the force with which they articulate their views. Management theorist, Robert Jackall (1988), writes of how corporate managers 'set both the frameworks and vocabularies for a great many public issues in our society' as a result of their 'pivotal institutional position'. Accordingly, this chapter provides numerous examples of how corporate executives are asserting their views on sustainable development issues via a wide range of institutional contexts, such that their influence is profound. Indeed, it goes on to suggest in a brief conclusion that this structural aspect of corporate environmentalism is of more concern than its actual content; rather than paying excessive attention to what executives are saying, more time should perhaps be spent contesting the fact that they have such a dominant voice in the first place.

The chapter is divided into two, contrasting sections. The first section, When Executive Cliques Rule the World, shows how corporate executives, via three key, world business organizations – the International Chamber of Commerce (ICC), the Business Council for Sustainable Development (BCSD) and the World Business Council for Sustainable Development (WBCSD) – have mobilized at a highly strategic level in response to the 'threat' of sustainable development. It not only sets out the arguments being utilized by executives to define the concept of sustainable development in a way consistent with 'business as usual', but demonstrates the substantial organizational effort devoted to ensuring that they are influential. (See Appendix for notes on a range of other organizations through which executives are wielding their 'representational power' with respect to sustainable development issues.) The second section, Danger! Executives at Work, shifts the focus to executives' more constrained *modus operandi* at the micro-level, where they have had to respond to sustainable development issues in a working context. Drawing on micro-sociological research, it reveals how the operation of that most pervasive institutional form, the hierarchical, corporate bureaucracy, is responsible for a 'processing' of sustainable development matters which, again, seems likely to preserve and promote corporate-led, liberal-productivism on a broad scale. Both sections are characterized by a very close reading of executives' language. This is because it is in executives' selection of words that the tensions in what they are attempting – i.e. the reconciliation of liberal-productivism with sustainable development – can be witnessed most clearly. However, it is the sharp juxtaposition of the rhetoric and smooth lobbying of the executive-led organizations portrayed in the first section, with the lumpy honesty captured in the second, that serves to deconstruct most effectively executives' current contribution to sustainable development. In particular, the material presented in the second section debunks the myth that executives operate according to some higher rationality; it clearly shows the political, and often highly expedient, nature of managerial decision-making.

In a book entitled, *Who Will Tell the People?* William Greider (1992) has already described how corporate personnel and their agendas are increasingly imposing on wider interests:

> *[The corporations'] . . . tremendous financial resources, the diversity of their interests, the squads of talented professionals – all these assets and some others are now relentlessly focused on the politics of governing . . . This new institutional reality is the centrepiece in the breakdown of contemporary democracy. Corporations exist to pursue their own profit-maximisation, not the collective aspirations of society. They are commanded by a hierarchy of managers, not by democratic deliberation.*

Documented below is clear evidence of the threat that this ascendant 'hierarchy of managers', committed to liberal-productivism, poses to a necessarily alternative, sustainable development paradigm.

WHEN EXECUTIVE CLIQUES RULE THE WORLD

This section reviews how corporate executives, through three world business organizations, have engaged with the issue of sustainable development at a strategic level. It shows how they have neutralized the 'threat' and gone on to mould the concept to accord with their business objectives (see also Chapter 2). The focus is on exactly how the corporate world has achieved this by way of argument – i.e. in a rhetorical sense – and through sheer institutional muscle. We begin with a comprehensive review of the activities of the International Chamber of Commerce, as this organization's environmentalism has provided a template for many other business organizations in turn. Our point of departure is the publication of the Brundtland Report (1987); thence we move on to how corporate executives asserted their case at and around the United Nations Conference on Environment and Development (UNCED) in 1992, before reviewing their principal activities up to the mid-1990s.

The International Chamber of Commerce (ICC)

Founded in 1919, the ICC boasts a membership of some 7500 companies and business associations in over 130 countries. Although it does not publish a complete membership list, it can be assumed that most of the largest TNCs in the world are members. The ICC (1992) describes itself as a non-governmental organization, 'serving world business by promoting trade and investment and the free market system'; one of its chief concerns is 'the promotion of self-regulation' (ICC UK undated). The ICC has top-level consultative status with the United Nations, including specialized UN agencies such as the United Nations Environment Programme (UNEP) and the United Nations Commission on Sustainable Development (UNCSD), where it 'defends the interests of private enterprise in developed and developing countries' (ICC 1992). Similarly, the ICC has regular and detailed discussions with organizations such as the World Trade Organization (WTO), the International Monetary Fund, the World Bank, the European Commission and the Organization for Economic Cooperation and Development (OECD), identifying its aim as the 'representation of business interests and influencing policy-making bodies' (ICC UK undated). Clearly, the ICC's *raison d'être* is the promotion of a corporate-led, liberal-productivist development paradigm. The question is: how can such an agenda possibly be reconciled with the goal of sustainable development?

The key to the ICC's position lies in its original framing of the problem – in its underlying assumptions. Thus, the ICC ignores the evidence suggesting that it is the consumption patterns and profligate life-styles of the world's wealthy that are largely responsible for unsustainable development patterns, and instead asserts that 'many environmental problems stem, not from growing affluence, but from growing poverty' (ICC 1992a). This then paves the way for an acritical call for economic growth: 'Without economic growth, societies cannot tackle poverty, improve the welfare of their peoples or protect the environment' (ICC 1993a). The ICC's case is unwittingly helped by the authoritative Brundtland Report (1987), which listed as one of the seven 'critical objectives' for sustainable development a revival of growth – of up to 3 per cent in the developed world and possibly more in the developing world. Although another of the listed objectives was to change the quality of this growth, as Eden (1994) has commented, the Report did 'open the door for the business perspective on sustainable development'. Thus, we find the ICC (1992b) praising the 'emphasis on the importance of economic growth providing that growth is sustainable'. Eden (1994, p 162) perceptively comments: 'Suggestively, this adds sustainability as a *secondary* aspect of economic growth, rather than justifying economic growth because of its nurturing of sustainable development as the Brundtland report seems to do'.

Having sucessfully defined the problem, the ICC manages to obliterate any distinction between sustainable development and liberal-productivism with ease: 'Sustainable development combines environmental protection with economic growth and development' (ICC 1993a).

Open international trade and movement of goods, services, management, capital, and technologies is indispensable to economic growth and is therefore a necessary element to enhance environmental protection . . . Environmental policies and regulations chosen, therefore, should be the least trade distorting and restrictive and not undermine the principles and workings of free market economies. (ICC undated a)

So, sustainable development and transnational, corporate capitalism would appear to be one and the same. An excellent example of how corporate executives have thus succeeded in transforming sustainable development into a business opportunity is provided by what the ICC says about the need for technology transfer. It starts by stressing 'the need for the development and dissemination of environmentally-sound technology and know-how . . .'; however, the ICC then points out, not only that it 'is industry which must provide and adopt this technology', but also that the 'development and implementation of environmentally-sound technology are costly investments which will only be undertaken by industry if there is an inherent commercial benefit' (ICC undated b). The case is complete when the ICC uses the capital-intensity of the solutions it is offering to argue for further corporate expansion; thus it talks of 'the need of major international companies to increase their global presence in order to amortize vast research and development spending' (ICC 1994a).

The ICC and the Earth Summit in Rio de Janeiro

The United Nations Conference on Environment and Development, held in Rio in June 1992, posed a substantial threat to corporate interests in a number of ways. Not least, sustainable development was in danger of becoming defined and widely understood as altogether contrary to the existing, corporate-friendly, liberal-productivist development paradigm. In particular, UNCED represented an opportunity for environmental interests, via the global media, to attribute a great deal of blame for global unsustainability to big business. Thus, the corporate sector needed to mobilize effectively. Responsibility for the ICC's reaction to UNCED was placed with its Environment Commission, which was chaired at the time by the Vice-Chairman of Norsk Hydro (a Norwegian TNC active in the oil, gas, chlorine and aluminium industries) and received substantial contributions from oil companies such as BP and Shell. In fact, the Commission set up a Working Party on Sustainable Development with a special UNCED brief, which was chaired by a Shell executive. It was this group that devised the ICC's 'Business Charter for Sustainable Development', a document containing 16 'Principles for Environmental Management', to which businesses were invited to commit by 'signing up'. This formed the centrepiece of ICC's UNCED strategy.

The ICC's primary objective was to set its own, less than demanding agenda, while simultaneously distracting others from attempts to devise TNC-constraining regulations. In the words of the ICC (1992c), it wished to 'establish the Charter as the international benchmark statement on business commitment to environmental protection'; and also 'to demonstrate to governments and society that business is taking its environmental responsibilities seriously, by helping to reduce the pressures on governments to over-legislate, thereby strengthening the voice of business in public policy debates' (ICC 1992a, p 87). The Charter, now translated into 23 languages, has proved a thoroughly effective instrument for this purpose. It is apparently comprehensive enough to make executives signing up to it look as though they are undertaking a major environmental commitment; yet it is sufficiently indefinite and undemanding to make wide-ranging executive support easy to come by. It is voluntary; there is no mechanism to ensure that signatories are abiding by the Principles, nor any form of measurement by which the extent of a company's commitment to a particular principle can be gauged: 'The ICC will not monitor compliance with the Charter . . . Public interest will, in reality, be the monitoring mechanism' (ICC 1991). Bizarrely, the ICC (1991) also states its belief that 'the public does not care how much we know. They want to know how much we care'! By October 1993, 1159 organizations had signed up to this Charter, including 144 of the world's 500 largest industrial TNCs.

Other elements of the ICC's UNCED strategy included the publication of a series of Business Briefs on a wide range of environment and development issues. These were 'designed to preserve economic growth and to protect the environment' (ICC 1992d). Just as the Business Charter attempted to reduce sustainable development to a series of management principles, so too did the Business Briefs argue that solutions lay in greater technocracy – again precluding attempts to tackle key social and ethical issues. The ICC's (1992a, p 35) statements on forests, for example, demonstrate how supposedly neutral 'rationalities' were (and are) asserted by corporate interests to serve a politically contentious purpose. It declares: 'well managed forests are a good example of sustainable development in practice', so immediately framing the issue to favour the application of corporate expertise. Such management then requires 'science-based methodologies for determining forest-related costs and benefits and the best policy to introduce these to the market' (ICC undated c). Thence, 'forest users should pay for the benefits they receive', while 'privately owned forest lands are better managed than publicly owned forest lands' (ICC 1992e). Thus, a set of normative principles is established, by which related matters then can be dealt with: for example, 'native peoples' . . . *legitimate* needs [will be] *considered*' (my emphasis) (ICC 1992e).

Having constructed a coherent position on the range of sustainable development issues confronting its membership, the ICC proceeded to ensure that this had maximum impact. Prior to UNCED, it lobbied key meetings and UN personnel relentlessly. For example, at one of the Preparatory Committees (Prepcoms) leading up to the event, its Business Briefs were presented in person to UNCED's Secretary General, Maurice Strong; members of the ICC also travelled to Stockholm specifically to persuade the Swedish government to withdraw their suggested Agenda 21 clause calling for TNCs to internalize environmental costs in their accounting and reporting procedures (confidential report 1992). In addition, the ICC lobbied negotiations on the Climate Change Convention, subsequently reporting how, 'to the satisfaction of business, the Convention approved at Rio refrained from setting mandatory targets for greenhouse gas emissions and followed other points proposed by the ICC throughout the negotiations' (ICC 1993b). When it came to UNCED itself, the ICC set up an 'Industry Press and Information Centre' to provide 'effective collaboration between industries in replying to criticism by environmental groups' (ICC 1992f). Moreover, the chairman of the ICC's Working Party on Sustainable Development was actually part of the UK government's delegation. Little wonder the ICC could look back on its UNCED work with much satisfaction: 'ICC lobbying ensured that business concerns and objectives were well known to government negotiators before the Earth Summit in Rio [and that] many of the final recommendations were in line with business views'.

Immediately following the Earth Summit, the ICC's Environment Commission maintained its regressive influence on sustainable development matters. Its report for 1993 (ICC 1994a, p6) opens by stating: 'Business is still able to influence the way agreements reached at the Earth Summit in June 1992 are translated into national legislation, and the Commission lost no time in producing recommendations . . .' Once again, the emphasis is firmly on ensuring that sustainable development-in-practice does not impose on key corporate interests. Among other initiatives, the Commission has managed the following: 'a detailed critique of the UNCED framework conventions on biodiversity and climate change'; a joint statement with the Commission on Intellectual and Industrial Property opposing 'phraseology that could encourage and sanction violation of private property rights'; and a statement to the International Negotiating Committee on climate change (August 1993) urging 'careful evaluation' of the impact of greenhouse gases and stressing the need for governments to avoid policies producing 'drastic short-term changes that might be economically damaging' (ICC 1994a, p7).

In January 1993, the ICC decided to add to these efforts by launching a new organization called WICE, the World Industry Council for the Environment, which attracted the membership of around 90 chief executives from companies including Shell, British Gas, NatWest, RTZ, BP, ICI, Waste Management International, AT&T, Mitsubishi and Norsk Hydro. Although this organization went on to merge with the BCSD in 1995 to form the World Business Council for Sustainable Development (see below), its efforts in the interim – 'to make a major, ongoing policy impact through a form of operation which is CEO-led . . . and agenda setting' – are worth noting (ICC 1992g). Of particular interest is the way WICE positioned itself so defensively – as 'the *advocate of business interests* on environmental questions' (my emphasis). Thus, it decided to 'analyse the likely effect of government policies and proposed environmental legislation on corporate interests and provide a forum for CEOs and senior executives to debate how these will impact on company-specific strategic interests'. It also set up a task-force to 'screen' the official documents (such as Agenda 21 and the Conventions) stemming from UNCED so as 'to identify . . . issues which can be used by green NGOs to put pressure on governments and/or industry' (ICC 1992g). WICE coupled this defensiveness with the overt promotion of *laissez-faire* technocracy, which it obviously understood to be complementary to its cause. Thus, one of its two, main stated objectives (ICC 1994) was 'to influence the direction of policy-making towards cost-effective and sound-science based policies', whilst promoting 'self-regulation in pursuit of sustainable development'. One Working Group (chaired by an ICI executive) was therefore set up to 'define . . . principles on [environmental] reporting, while avoiding stringent standards . . .' (ICC 1992g; 1993c).

To conclude, corporate executives are wielding vast 'representational power' with respect to environmental matters through the ICC. The range and scope of their activities would seem to have severe implications for any meaningful attempts, anywhere, to move towards sustainable development. By applying a technocratic frame of reference, they are managing to influence the sustainable development agenda, in such a way that denies the need for structural change, and often actually enhances their corporate interests. This points to a broader danger: that all interpretations of sustainable development will end up being framed by an eco-modernist perspective and legitimized according to whether or not they imply the generation of corporate profit.

We now take a more selective look at the corporate environmentalism of two other world business organizations, focusing particularly on how they differ from, or complement, that of the ICC. These are important to understand because, in promoting slightly different agendas and in possessing alternative identities, they provide a certain (largely superficial) variety of approach which makes the phenomenon of corporate environmentalism as a whole more difficult to size up and critique.

The Business Council for Sustainable Development (BCSD)

The BCSD was launched in February 1991 by millionaire businessman Stephan Schmidheiny, with the explicit aim of preparing a global business perspective on sustainable development for UNCED. This followed the Secretary General of UNCED, Maurice Strong, appointing Schmidheiny – a board director at both Nestlé and ABB – as his Principal Advisor for Business and Industry (Greenpeace International 1992). (They were old friends.) Strong is believed to have spurned the ICC because he thought the Rio Summit required a fresh business approach to environment and development issues; whether he actually wanted fresh ideas, or just a 'fresh face' to front corporate environmentalism-as-usual, remains unclear. However, it should be noted that while the BCSD was constructing its case, UNCED officials were simultaneously ensuring that the Summit agenda would not address the subject of TNCs and their responsibility for various forms of unsustainable development. Thus, through the BCSD, the corporate world was given a privileged role and voice in the UNCED process, without being subject to it.

The BCSD was set up as a Swiss private association and recruited 48 chief executives to contribute to its work 'in their personal capacities' (BCSD 1991b). These executives came from companies such as: Norsk Hydro, Shell, DuPont, Mitsubishi, John Laing, ABB and Dow Chemical. Their resulting contribution to UNCED was a book called *Changing Course: a Global Business Perspective on Development and Environment* (Schmidheiny 1992a) – which attracted considerable attention from the world's media and government officials. This extensive coverage stemmed from a comprehensive PR strategy, which involved Schmidheiny addressing many gatherings around the globe, including the UNCED Prepcoms, and other BCSD members giving 'a series of briefings on *Changing Course* to business and political leaders all over the world' (Schmidheiny 1992b). A copy of the book was delivered, often by hand, to the majority of the world's government leaders; President Bush, for instance, took receipt of the book over breakfast with Schmidheiny himself. The BCSD's coup was complete when Schmidheiny ended up being asked to address a plenary session at the actual Earth Summit.

Maurice Strong (BCSD 1991) summed up what the BCSD initiative was about when he said:

> The BCSD is helping the business community to set its own agenda on the issue of sustainable development [and] convincing governments and societies that the private sector can be their principal ally in future . . . The Council is also a key actor in describing what business and industry would like to see incorporated within Agenda 21 . . . [my emphasis]

Following UNCED, the BCSD decided to continue its work – complementing its lobbying activities with project work supposedly 'implementing' sustainable development (BCSD undated). It even gained some more members, including the newly-appointed chief executive of the Canadian power company, Ontario Hydro: Maurice Strong. However, in January 1995, the BCSD decided that little more was to be gained from its distinct positioning *vis-à-vis* the ICC and, as already noted, merged with WICE. However, four members of the BCSD had already been appointed to the High Level Advisory Board on Sustainable Development set up by the UN Secretary General to advise on post-UNCED development issues (BCSD 1994a). Also, another four members had been appointed to President Clinton's Council on Sustainable Development, and the Asian Development Bank had invited the BCSD to be policy advisor to its proposed new $100m Asia Sustainable

Development Fund (BCSD 1994a). Given this level of influence, the BCSD's environmentalism is worth assessing briefly, before moving on to look at the all-new WBCSD.

Whereas the ICC's positioning in the early 1990s was principally defensive, the BCSD's approach was more proactive and managerialist. The result was still a top-down, technocratic eco-modernism – but with rather more effort devoted to coopting and controlling other interests. Three examples of the BCSD's work follow, illustrating both its similarity to that of the ICC and its difference. The somewhat authoritarian dimension of the BCSD's work is important to recognize, as it represents a strategic strand that runs through a great deal of contemporary corporate environmentalism – both stemming from, and reinforcing, the problem of executives' excessive representational power.

The BCSD defines sustainable development to suit its own ends

One of the reasons the BCSD achieved such a high profile around UNCED was that it appeared to be open to the fact that sustainable development could well imply radical change. For example: 'The logic of sustainable development demands a revolutionary appraisal of the activities of the business and industrial community . . .' (BCSD 1991d) or 'A change towards sustainable forms of progress will require a change in civilisation, from one based on consumption towards one based on conservation . . . This implies some restrictions on growth' (BCSD 1991c). However, inconsistency is a prime strategy when one wishes to engage – or coopt – the interest(s) of a diverse target audience. Moving beyond the headlines to the substance of the BCSD's approach, these arguments end up being overwhelmed by another set of positions, which actually articulate to form a corporate environmentalist world-view that corresponds almost exactly to that of the ICC's. That is, the concept of sustainable development is defined in a way which facilitates economic orthodoxy and provides big business with the lead role: 'Sustainable development combines the objectives of growth with environmental protection for a better future' (BCSD undated a). 'It is development, growth and the creation of economic surpluses that are needed to deal with social issues like poverty and pollution' (Schmidheiny 1991). 'Open and accountable markets are the most effective way of generating wealth' (Faulkner 1992). 'The business and industrial private sector, which acts as the main generator of the world's wealth, must be at the fore-front of the environmental revolution' (BCSD 1991a). Thus, just like the ICC, the BCSD posits a top-down, technocratic development model which, by obscuring the difference between development and growth, ensures that sustainable development translates into an array of opportunities for 'business-as-usual'.

The BCSD pushes technological 'solutions', intent on expanding corporate control over the wider business environment

Like the ICC, the BCSD is keen to emphasize the role technology and its transfer can play in development. However, the BCSD does this by promoting, rather more so than the ICC, the disingenuous notion of 'technology cooperation', which actually provides a rationale for companies to further colonize their operating environment (especially in the developing world) for commercial ends. Thus, 'technology has failed because of the emphasis on the technical dimension and not enough on the business context. Technology cooperation is a new approach based on the long-term partnership between companies . . . [It is] about business development, capacity building and competitiveness in the new markets of developing countries' (Schmidheiny 1991a). The skill lies in exporting, not only technology, but services, management skills, organizational expertise, engineering know-how and so on. The circle is soon rounded: 'long-term partnership is hardly a new concept for the successful multinationals, for whom technology cooperation is synonymous with business development and their principal means of expansion' (BCSD 1992). This pragmatic approach was reinforced by the work of the BCSD's Technology Cooperation Advisory Group, comprising executives from companies such as ABB, Shell and Nissan. This perhaps explains the lack of circumspection regarding the problems associated with the development paradigm being promoted. The following passage appears in *Changing Course* (Schmidheiny 1992a, p 202):

> *Foreign direct investment from a multinational corporation is often the most effective way of exchanging the skills and technologies needed to further sustainable development in developing countries. In particular, foreign investors can contribute directly to the building of local management expertise and employee know-how through training programmes. This has* benefits not only for the company concerned, but also for the wider community . . . This has been the experience of Shell Petroleum Development Company of Nigeria. [*my emphasis*]

The combination of universal access for TNCs, provided by a liberal trading and investment policy environment, and the ideology of technology cooperation, actually allows the corporate world to institute sets of managed, hierarchical relations around the globe in its own image. The stratification of the 'global community' and the inequality within it is in danger of becoming subject, for the first time, to a sort of institutionalized homeostasis – courtesy of transnational management – in the name of sustainable development.

The BCSD appears to suggest an innovative, even radical, approach to micro-level management issues – but again, its executive membership is actually more interested in expanding its control

The BCSD (Faulkner 1992) proposes that

> *sustainable development means new relationships between corporations and their stakeholders, such as employees and citizens, built on the principles of transparency and accountability and requires new indicators of corporate performance well beyond the traditional bottom line.*

This could, of course, imply a quite radical upheaval of the corporate world: the BCSD (Schmidheiny 1992a, p 86) suggests that corporations of the future will have to 'add value' for all their stakeholders, not just customers and investors. It points out that this 'extends the idea of corporate responsibility in time and space . . .' However, crucial to the involvement and need-satisfaction of these stakeholders is the adequate provision of meaningful information about corporate activities. The trouble is that, although the BCSD berates companies for its poor disclosure record and the inadequacy of its sustainable development reporting, all it can propose as a way forward is 'accept[ing] as a baseline' the ICC's Business Charter principle of 'compliance and reporting' (Schmidheiny 1992a, p 95). On inspection, all this principle does, is to suggest that companies '*periodically* . . . provide *appropriate* information' (my emphasis) to stakeholders – thus leaving a great deal to executive discretion (ICC 1991a). Sustainable development therefore becomes a way for the corporate world to expand its remit and control without any devolution of power. Stakeholders are involved so that they can be hierarchically managed – pre-empting opportunities for them to challenge that hierarchy. The BCSD sees stakeholder involvement simply as a means to a competitive end; among the benefits identified by the BCSD (Schmidheiny 1992a, p 88) are 'public acceptance of corporate activity' and more 'self-regulation rather than legislation'.

The corporate world, through the mobilization of its executives, can take considerable satisfaction from the way it handled the concept of sustainable development during the early 1990s. The ideas inherent in the concept could have challenged the hegemony of the corporate-led, liberal-productivist paradigm profoundly – and yet, both before and during UNCED, and in the following years, it did not. Executive interests managed to broadly align the notion of sustainable development with its own interests and thus largely empty the concept of meaning. Chapter 30 of Agenda 21, for instance, is actually headed 'Strengthening the Role of Industry' and places much of its faith in 'responsible entrepreneurship' and a series of voluntary initiatives. Thus, the corporate world could proceed, under-regulated, largely as before. In 1993, the ICC (1994a, p 10; ICC UK 1993) reported how its work had led to 'the shelving of the UN's draft Code of Conduct on Transnational Corporations' and the 'downgrading' of the UN's Centre on Transnational Corporations. Meanwhile, ICC (1994a, p 2) lobbying – 'Never before has our world business organization campaigned with such insistence and for so long in support of an international agreement' – ensured the completion of the GATT Uruguay Round and the birth of the WTO, instituting liberal-productivism still further.

Undoubtedly, the corporate world has succeeded in neutralizing the threat of sustainable development in the short-term. However, many corporate heavyweights do realize that the plethora of social, environmental and ethical issues encompassed by this concept could yet represent a considerable threat to their business interests – and have committed to maintaining a strong presence on sustainable development matters. This is now being achieved mainly by the organization resulting from the merger of WICE and the BCSD in January 1995: the World Business Council for Sustainable Development.

The World Business Council for Sustainable Development (WBCSD)

The WBCSD comprises some 120 of the largest corporations in the world – represented by their chief executives. Most of these companies used to be members of either the BCSD, or WICE, or both. They include: British Gas, Thorn-EMI, PowerGen, Waste Management International, Shell, Nestlé, DuPont, Procter and Gamble, 3M, Dow Chemical, ABB, Volkswagen and BP. The WBCSD (WICE 1994) states that it is to 'give business leaders a powerful new voice on sustainable development issues'; however, its agenda stems directly from those of its parent organizations. It exhibits a mixture of the defensiveness of the ICC and WICE and the more insidious proactivity of the BCSD. Of course, although all these organizations attempt, or have attempted, to articulate a common 'corporate environmentalism', this still encompasses a diverse set of corporate understandings. Some members are truly defensive; others are more strategically-minded and Machiavellian; others, in 'becoming caught in the fly-paper of their own ideologies' (as one management theorist (Jackall 1988, p 160) has put it), do genuinely believe that their efforts represent the best way forward. This diversity, and the different agendas contained within it, are particularly evident in the WBCSD's activities and statements, a selection of which are scrutinized very briefly below.

- Most significantly, the WBCSD's Mission Statement (undated a) informs us that it is to 'provide business leadership as a catalyst for change towards sustainable development', and yet also 'promote the attainment of eco-efficiency'. This demonstrates its members' desire to be proactive on environmental matters on the one hand, whilst simultaneously reducing the sustainable development agenda to a series of top-down, technocratic measures on the other. Such eco-modernism is entirely congruent with the ICC's attempts, via its Business Charter, to confine sustainable development to a set of corporate environmental management tasks. It also continues the work of the BCSD, which originally coined the term eco-efficiency, defining it as 'adding maximum value with minimum resource use and minimum pollution'; the BCSD (1994a, p 10) also suggested that this 'should be the main corporate response to the goal of sustainable development'. Some WBCSD members may genuinely understand eco-efficiency to be The Answer. However, others evidently possess different views and motives; at a conference in late 1995, for instance, the WBCSD's Executive Director (Stigson 1995) defined 'eco-efficiency leadership' as 'creating more with less and coming out looking great!'
- Like its predecessors, the WBCSD paves the way for its asocial, technocratic approach by insisting on the primacy of economic growth, thus binding the concept of sustainable development to liberal-productivist ends. It describes its member companies as being 'united by shared commitment to the environment and to the principles of economic growth and sustainable development' (WBCSD 1996, p 2).
- Continuing the work of its precursor organizations, the WBCSD interferes in public policy-making to preserve macro-economic conditions allowing business-as-usual. It talks of the need for the 'right framework conditions' and describes how it 'strives to ensure that the policy-makers take proper account of business's perspective on sustainable development when they determine the framework conditions under which business operates.' It also 'argues that voluntary measures are to be preferred to legislation' (WBCSD 1996, pp 8, 10).
- Typically, the WBCSD produces reports with which to target policy-makers. For instance, a Working Group chaired by an RTZ executive, has issued a document entitled *Trade and Environment* (WBCSD undated); this concludes that:

Trade can help to optimize efficiency with which resources are used, provide higher levels of wealth to support environmental activities and facilitate the flow of technology . . . the protection of the environment and open trade can become more mutually supportive.

- The WBCSD is keen to turn sustainable development into a business opportunity. For example, a group of WBCSD member companies looked into the way liability for past environmental damage is handled in the Czech Republic – publishing a report (WBCSD 1996, p 18) that offered 'some trenchant and practical suggestions about what the Czech authorities and business should do to achieve the most sensible apportionment of responsibility for historical environmental damage, thereby helping to attract much-needed foreign investment capital'.

- Given its history, the WBCSD wields terrific influence. Apart from its 120 executive members, the WBCSD has regional and national Business Councils in the Czech Republic, Gulf of Mexico, Indonesia, Latin America, Malaysia, Nigeria, Poland and Thailand; it is working with a range of inter-governmental organizations, including the OECD, the WTO and World Bank. However, the extent to which this influence is contributing to sustainable development must be questioned when the WBCSD includes in its work 'driving forward a $10m educational initiative [to provide Russians with] the best of Western managerial practice and thinking' (WBCSD 1996, p 18).

DANGER! EXECUTIVES AT WORK

The previous section illustrated how corporate executives are mobilizing at a strategic level to ensure the domination of eco-modernist perspectives on sustainable development, which conform to the current, antithetical, liberal-productivist development paradigm. This then extends their remit and power, exacerbating the original problem. This section approaches this issue from another angle. It is one thing for executive interests to work to preserve favourable socio-economic structures in the face of sustainable development at the macro-level, but how do executives manage to prevent the sorts of social and environmental concerns bound up in the notion of sustainable development from challenging their interests at the micro-level, as they go about their business within their companies? It is, after all, at this micro-institutional level that competing viewpoints and realities are articulated and expressed and, via social and organizational processes, that real-life outcomes result. So what stops the environmental or broader ethical concerns of others – whom a globalized, liberal economy doesn't favour so – from challenging the development paradigm pursued by the corporate elite? The answer lies in the 'representational power' executives also possess at the micro-level, instituted by that most dominant of organizational forms – the hierarchical, corporate bureaucracy. As Hildyard (1991), editor of *The Ecologist*, writes:

The power enjoyed by corporate bureaucracies – and the concomitant disempowerment of local communities – is a central feature of the whole industrial state, indeed, the whole process we call 'development'. It is the key to understanding...the destruction of our environment and . . . the forces that now block change. For such bureaucracies now dominate our lives . . .

This domination occurs despite the more atomistic, 'freer' modes of economic activity supposedly at the heart of the liberal-productivist development model. Notwithstanding fashionable talk in business circles about decentralizing company operations and devolving power and responsibility, as the sociologists Lash and Urry (1994) make clear, 'the hierarchy' continues to flourish:

. . . the decline of the national state in the process of globalisation means that 'hierarchies', especially in transnational firms, have a more enhanced role to play in the new economic arrangements. In this sense, the more pronounced profile of hybrid forms of governance such as subcontracting, alliances or joint ventures does not imply a decline in the power of hierarchies. Instead this would seem to be emblematic of an enhanced role for hierarchies, but now as political actors, as political space is left to fill with the decline of the national state.

Lipietz (1992, p 34) also describes how 'liberal-productivism . . . amounts to a hierarchical individualism . . . where the collectivity acquires collective meaning only through the individualism of those who dominate it . . .'. Furthermore, such analyses are confirmed – in albeit anecdotal fashion – by research (Jackall 1988, p 36) recording the comments of corporate managers themselves: 'What we have now, despite rhetoric to the contrary, is a very centralised system . . . It's a kind of portfolio management. This accords perfectly with [the CEO's] temperament. He's a financial type of guy . . .' and 'Every big organization is set up for the benefit of those who control it; the boss gets what he wants.'

So, hierarchical, corporate bureaucracies play a central role in present-day socio-economic arrangements. They are also where and how executive power is re-negotiated and re-instituted at the micro-level on a day-to-day basis. By drawing on rare, micro-sociological research into the executive process and its interaction with environmental issues, the rest of this chapter attempts to convey, in a somewhat impressionistic manner, the ways in which this reproduction of executive power results in an adverse reaction to, and representation of, sustainable development issues 'on the ground'. It demonstrates exactly how the top-down, bureaucratic context in which executives operate results, either in a technocratic processing of environmental issues, or in their direct marginalization. It also shows how this working context enables executives to remain overly distanced from the social and environmental impact of their decision-making – precluding sufficient feedback and accountability. As at the macro-level, the executive *modus operandi* is shown, not only to preserve, but to sustain, liberal-productivism-as-usual.

In his study into the way corporate executives in the automotive, chemical, power and supermarket sectors are responding to environmental issues, Fineman (1994) describes how the bureaucracy of the corporate world has an impact on the way environmental issues are treated right from the beginning, as responsibility for dealing with them is allocated: 'So the environment, what it is and how it should be presented, undergoes its first major translation – into a PR issue, an engineering problem, a legal challenge, a marketing project, an accounting activity. It belongs everywhere and nowhere.' One of his main conclusions is therefore that: '"the environment" is frequently handled as just one of many business factors to add-in, drop, modify or haggle for in the politics of business.'

The essential trouble, of course, is that these 'politics of business' tend to revolve around an extremely narrow set of priorities. A manager in Fineman's (1996) study describes a typical scenario:

> *It's like this . . . I managed to get my Board to accept that we needed to spend £1 million to go green in the factory, and that will meet the way public opinion is shifting over the next five years. But then up pops my Marketing colleague and says that he could spend that £1 million now on an advertising campaign which would actually sell another 20,000 cars and keep 500 employed for another month. Guess who won the day?*

Clearly, financial considerations predominate. However, this is hardly a case of 'market rationality' prevailing in any straightforward sense. The politics of business cannot just be reduced to a matter of economics – because human perception and interpersonal relationships are also involved. In the above example, a 'greening' of the factory could easily end up producing the better material return. However, it is the Board executives' interpretations of the issues involved and their personal relationship with them that are determining. So although it might be assumed that the executive interest is simply aligned with, and representative of, the logic of profit maximization, the position is rather more nuanced. In the above case, the decision of those at the top of the hierarchy appears to have been shaped by fairly short-term economic goals, and apparently included some social considerations. These goals may well, in turn, have stemmed directly from the economics of the financial markets. However, it is possible that the Board's decision was actually swayed by a dominant executive's interpretation of the Board's legal obligations towards its shareholders. Or it could have related to the way a number of the directors' remuneration packages have been structured – or because of organizational politics demanding that the marketing manager be rewarded, or his environmental colleague 'shamed'. As management theorist, Robert Jackall (1988, p 66), has concluded: 'In the bureaucratic world, one's success...depends on...the capriciousness of one's superiors [as well as] the market'.

Whatever the motivations involved, Fineman (1994, p 2) is blunt about the actual outcome:

> *Corporate environmentalism as an ethically-green, cultural response, is largely a myth. It fits uneasily into the current realities of trading and corporate governance. 'Business and the environment' is often a gloss which disguises practices which are more like 'business or the environment'.*

This is the underlying reality. Despite the impression given by executives strategising in their cliques at the macro-level, given the deregulated, highly competitive business environment that these same executives are doing so much to promulgate, many fellow industrialists feel justified in subordinating social and environmental matters to more basic, 'bottom-line' concerns. Fineman (1994, p 8) stresses how the executives he interviewed 'were keen to remind [him] that they would never forget their ultimate god – the balance sheet'. Hence the blunt response of a supermarket director to Fineman's (1994, p 7) praise for his company's environmental report:

> *I guess you haven't seen our latest trading figures. It's been disastrous. All that environmental stuff is now out. We're into real survival mode.*

Another executive makes a similar point (Fineman 1996a):

> *It's fine being green when it doesn't cost you anything, or there's no pressure to perform. [Sneers] It's easy to hold those views and say it's really important because it's the long-term future of the world. But when someone says, 'Right, produce that on a 6% reduction in wages', it puts a slightly different view on it.*

Thus, the following comment seems to be indicative of a fairly common view (Fineman 1996a, p 9):

> *Of course, I [personally] have a lot of sympathy for the environment. I know we [as a company] sound pretty insensitive, but that's the way it is. We just haven't time to pay lip-service to issues which, at the end of the day, are tangential to what the core of the business is about.*

Because of the immediate stringency of 'the bottom line', the politics of business quickly becomes the task of simply trying to 'manage' sustainable development issues, so that they don't distract too much from the economic task in hand. This requires a certain canniness. In his acclaimed ethnography of the corporate process, Jackall (1988, p 60) describes how 'an adeptness at inconsistency, without moral uneasiness, is essential for executive success.' This is where executives' exertion of their 'representational power' starts to become obviously problematic. Jackall goes on to explain:

> *[This] means publicly demanding increased self-regulation of industry while privately acknowledging that the competitive welter of corporate life and of the market consistently obscures attention to social needs. It means lobbying intensively in the present to shape government regulations to one's immediate advantage and, ten years later, in the event of a catastrophe, arguing that the company acted strictly in accordance with the standards of the time ... It means, as well, making every effort to socialise the costs of industrial activity, arguing that one is furthering the common weal, while, of course, striving to privatise the benefits.*

Fineman's (1994, p 7) experience too was that executives would do all they could to 'argue and haggle' and 'exploit ambiguity'. He reports that

> *some companies had their own corporate specialists to turn to: lawyers who would comb national and international environmental legislation ... The companies with the power and resources to lobby government directly, do so; others join with their trade association to achieve the same end.*

Another manager interviewed by Jackall (1988, p 160) explains:

> *... this is the typical corporate response pattern – to hedge, dodge and try to avoid the issue in every possible way. You know [use] the old line: 'Nobody has conclusively proved that ...'*

Such insights certainly put the efforts of the executive-led organizations reviewed in the first section in perspective and show why such close attention needs to be paid to what they say. In stark contrast to these organizations' apparent commitment to sustainable development, and their faith in market-based measures to bring it about, Fineman (1994, p 7) decides from his viewpoint inside companies that 'the environment', not only transcends competitive interests, but is viewed as 'a common enemy'. Where environmental initiatives are in evidence, he (Fineman 1996a, p 9) attributes them to an executive 'pragmatism ... rooted in enlightened self-interest rather than a substantive sense of care or concern for others.' Fineman (1996a, p 7) supports this contention with assorted evidence, including the comments of a supermarket executive:

Listen [almost shouting] we're only interested in the money we're not going to spend! It's far better for {name} to be driven by money than by some vague feeling that it's good to be seen doing it. We're not in the business of telling our customers what they ought to feel.

Apart from illustrating corporate pragmatism, this is an example of how executives apply certain 'functional rationalities' to environmental (and other) issues. These rationalities derive from the 'ends-driven' nature of corporate bureaucracies – 'ends' related, not only to the ultimate goals of corporate growth and increased profitability, but also to the repro-duction of executive status and power. The particular rationality applied will depend on how the corporate bureaucracy engages initially with the issue concerned, as described above. Via this highly politicized process, wherein market and scientific rationalities hold most sway, a techno-cratic framing of the issue tends to result, which effectively screens out key dimensions of the environmental problematic. In her account of the environmentalism of superstore managers, Eden (1993, p 419) provides another example of a functional rationality, based on the logic of the market, being applied to green issues by executives:

It's not for us to dictate what our customers do and don't buy. It's not for us to say 'We're not gonna sell you aerosols, because we think they're bad'. We're retailers. We have to satisfy the demand of the population we service, and they tell us eventually through their purchases, what they do and don't want.

Thus, even those who accept that their businesses have a certain degree of social or moral responsibility, end up purveying a compromised and ultimately hopeless environmentalism. According to a supermarket manager (Eden 1993, p 417): 'We will do things which we think are morally and ethically correct, the sort of things which we think our customers expect us to do.' The problem is that the functional rationality invoked by corporate bureaucracies – in this case, that of the market – is limited. It can only explain and rationalize up to a point – beyond which, the logic of the executive position fails. Occasionally this is glimpsed (Eden 1993, p 419):

We are selling a [environmentally damaging] lifestyle . . . whether we like it or not, those are customer demands. Now there's an argument about whether we are guilty of creating those demands and whether we just fulfil those demands and that's a moral argument.

Of course, this isn't a 'moral argument' at all. That producers and retailers actually create and affect demand can be established as fact. In addition, the larger problem of the market generally reflecting the desires of the wealthy and being skewed in their favour – thus reproducing inequitable and unsustainable patterns of material well-being – can also be established through recourse to a more 'substantive' rationality. However, as Eden (1993, p 417) points out, it is in the corporate/executive interest to manage the environmentalist case by asserting the functional rationality of 'consumer sovereignty' instead.

> *[This] is used to relocate the source of power from business to the consumer, therefore conceptualising business as purely reactive and amoral, relegating the responsibility to a reactive one and thus downplaying the power of business.*

Another way in which executives seek to manage sustainable development concerns at the micro-level and thus defend their interests is to invoke the limited functional rationality of 'sound science'. Jackall describes how the expansion of industry and its powers has, historically, been inextricably linked with scientific advances, and how a great deal of the corporate world's legitimacy is therefore rooted in the scientific world-view. Scientific rationality is also a key, structuring principle of corporate bureaucracy itself: corporate organization and decision-making being founded in a belief in the value of a division of labour and responsibility, expertise, and distanced objective analysis – which supposedly ensures that the most rational decisions prevail. Thus, Fineman and Clarke (1996) record executives complaining about how campaign groups, by contrast, are 'too emotional' and don't know the 'true facts' – which is why their companies have to produce 'fact sheets' for the wider public, in order to 'keep the record straight'.

So executives call for greater 'proper understanding', more 'rational assessments' and complain that proposed environmental legislation isn't sufficiently underpinned by this curious notion of 'sound science'. However, as Jackall has stressed, the emphasis within the corporation on such rationalization is actually a product of the extreme uncertainty pervading corporate life – due to external factors such as the fickleness of consumers, and internal factors such as the indecipherability of much executive power play. In the face of an unpredictable and irrational world, executives need to be able to justify their thinking and decisions in politically expedient terms – whether or not they would be considered, on further reflection, to be rational in a substantive sense; hence Jackall's (1988, p 76) observation that 'vocabularies of rationality are always invoked to cloak decisions.' However, the self-aware fully understand that, in the end, what is or isn't regarded as 'rational', is socially constructed (see Chapter 3). One rationality can always be overturned by another if the social circumstances allow. As Jackall (1988, p 77) points out: 'many managers expect whatever ordered processes they do erect to be subverted or overturned by executive fiat, masquerading, of course, as an established bureaucratic procedure or considered judgement.' A manager he interviewed puts it more directly: 'The point is that in making decisions, people look up and look around. They rely on others, not because of inexperience, but because of the fear of failure.'

Thus, the rationality invoked by the corporate world is rarely representative of neutral, good sense; it is highly politicized. So, of course, 'sound science' is a chimera. The science mobilized by the corporate executive will never be disinterested; his or her 'representational power' will always be in evidence. This is revealed very clearly by the research of Purvis et al (1995) into the response to concerns about ozone-layer depletion of companies involved in the manufacture and use of products containing chlorofluorocarbons (CFCs). Their work demonstrates just how the representational power possessed by executives allows them to ignore or deflect pressures on them to pursue more sustainable strategies. The self-interest and lack of accountability signalled by the following comment from a manager in the pharmaceutical industry is typical:

> *It's at what stage do you say this is something I have to act on and that's a judgement between . . . how you understand and concur with the science and what the cost is going to be. Now I don't mean the cost in just money, I mean in terms of risk and disruption of everything else.*

Purvis et al (1995) conclude that

> *those who might be considered to have felt their activities to be most threatened sought to reduce that threat by emphasising the theoretical and uncertain basis of the science on which concern about ozone depletion rested. In some instances, this was complemented by an assertion of alternative realities . . .*

The writers then report how less powerful players, such as smaller companies, felt 'conned' by these alternative representations. For example, chemical producers had allegedly 'manipulated' the debate over ozone depletion because, according to one manager, they 'coined the phrase "CFC-free" and also coined the argument that [hydrochloro-fluorocarbons] HCFCs are not CFCs, therefore if you use HCFCs you can say you're CFC free. That's a very spurious argument in my view'.

However, it is Jackall (1988, p 127), in documenting the following comments by a manager in the chemical industry – also about CFCs and ozone depletion – who really illustrates the perils inherent in allowing aloof executives so much representational power:

> *It gets hard. Now, suppose that the ozone depletion theory were correct and you knew that these specific fifty people were going to get skin cancer because you produced CFCs. Well, there would be no question. You would just stop production. But suppose that you didn't know the fifty people and it wasn't clear that CFCs were at fault, or entirely at fault. What do you do then?*

As Jackall (1988, p 194) puts it: 'the very rationality of bureaucracy may stimulate remarkable patterns of irrationality . . .' Certainly, the very rationality of corporate organization – reproducing executives' representational power through its structure, culture (including language) and 'economy' – severely threatens progress towards sustainable development. The circle is vicious in that, as this representational power grows, so the functional rationalities of corporate bureaucracy come to pervade and structure society even more – enabling executives to further dominate. Allowing such narrow interests and inevitably inadequate understandings such a determining social role is, from first principles, unhealthy and unwise. However, it becomes dangerous when these understandings are as inadequate as, for instance, the DoE's 1995 survey, *Top management attitudes to energy and the environment* (ENDS 1995), suggests: only 26 per cent of the executives interviewed correctly identified carbon dioxide as the main greenhouse gas; another 24 per cent cited CFCs, 16 per cent blamed carbon monoxide and 5 per cent pointed to methane – while the 'don't knows' totalled 28 per cent.

Corporate bureaucracies have evolved to dominate the market-place and wider society; they have also developed as the result of social processes arising from business executives' desire for status and power – the achievement of which leaves them remote from broader concerns and even more liberated to pursue their own interests. This section has provided a further indication of the extent to which this executive interest is allied to that of a liberal socio-economic regime, wherein market disciplines and 'bottom-line' objectives predominate. It has also demonstrated how the hierarchical, corporate bureaucracy, serving this executive interest, engages with other interests via a highly politicized process – which is nevertheless presented in terms of the application of objective rationalities. These rationalities derive, both from the logic of the market, and from the actual structure (and thence social processes) underpinning the bureaucracy of the corporate world. Thus, 'functional rationalities' are applied to sustainable development issues, such that environmental interests are represented in expedient terms, and short-term, financial considerations are able to prevail. Hence, corporate executives' representational power at the micro-level, instituted and expressed through hierarchical bureaucracies, poses – just as at the macro-level – a major threat to sustainable development indeed.

CONCLUSION: TOWARDS A STRATEGIC RESPONSE

Yet the modern corporation presumes to act like a mediating institution – speaking on behalf of others and for the larger public good... With varying degrees of sophistication and intensity, hundreds of these large corporate political organizations are now astride the democratic landscape, organizing the ideas and agendas, financing electoral politics and overwhelming the competing voices of other, less well-endowed organiz- ations and citizens. They portray themselves as 'good citizens' doing their part for public affairs . . . The political space that once belonged to parties and other mediating institutions is usurped by narrow-minded economic interests. Citizens at large vaguely perceive that government is being steered by these forces and they naturally resent it.

William Greider (1992, p 332) in *Who Will Tell the People?*

This chapter has documented how, at both the macro- and micro-level, corporate executives wield excessive 'representational power' with respect to sustainable development issues. This power is rooted in the economic might of the corporation, but has organizational, social and cultural dimensions as well. The chapter has addressed the specific problem of how this power entails corporate executives interpreting and portraying (i.e. representing) sustainable development issues in a relatively unchallenged manner, such that liberal-productivism – in the corporate interest, against the wider social and environmental interest – is not only preserved, but often furthered. The result is an eco- modernism which promises an extremely grey, if not highly precarious, future. At the macro-level, executives are operating strategically through assorted business organizations, defining and redefining the notion of sustainable development through rhetoric, policy work, practical initiatives and brute lobbying strength. At the micro-level, executives' representational power is exerted through hierarchical corporate bureaucracies, resulting in various 'functional rationalities' and aloof executive opinions being applied to sustainable development issues, such that – in complimentary fashion – financial priorities are preserved and business-as-usual is able to prevail. Of course, it is the intensely compet- itive operating environment that demands such a narrow business focus

– which stems largely from executives' macro-level activities in the first place.

Jackall (1988, pp 126–7) writes of how the 'social insulation' of those near the top of corporate hierarchies and 'the sheer impersonality of the vast markets that corporations service . . . helps managers to achieve the distance and abstractness appropriate to and necessary for their roles.' Yet these same executives are setting 'both the frameworks and the vocabularies for a great many public issues in our society'. The problem lies in the incongruity of 'socially insulated' individuals setting the terms of existence for so much of the rest of society. Indeed, Fineman (1996a, p 16) has urged a critical examination of green 'leadership from the top'. It is his perception that, although such leadership 'may open up the green agenda', it could also 'railroad it'. He writes that

> *privileging a top executive perspective on 'ecology' or 'respect for others' contains an internal contradiction: it fails to engage with the values of non-executive personnel . . . [it] seeks to homogenise values and their expression, rather than build on diversity.*

It is a frequently missed point that, on the grounds of equity consider-ations alone, sustainable development is incompatible with social structures allowing elite groups excessive licence to put their case – whatever its apparent merits. Fundamentally, it is these structures, rather than what executives are doing or saying, that have to change as a priority. The suggestion here, therefore, is that sustainable development depends on a more widespread engagement with the notion of 'stake-holding' and beyond that, the practice of 'social auditing' (see Chapter 7). Opportunities do exist for the language of stakeholding to be seized upon in a strategic manner, both within and beyond the corporation, to further the goal of industrial democracy. This seems an obvious route towards executives becoming more aware of, and accountable to, the outcomes of their decision-making. A starting point is to ensure that the original definition of a stakeholder – as someone who affects, or is affected by, a company's operations – is preserved in the face of the more instrumental approach adopted by certain corporate interests (such as the BCSD, or even the RSA's 'Tomorrow's Company' Inquiry, for example).* Corporations are going to have to open up, whilst commit-ting considerable resources to engaging meaningfully with all those interests who consider themselves affected by their operations. As management theorist, Stanley Deetz (1992, p 43), suggests: 'Meaningful

---

* The Royal Society for the Encouragement of Arts, Manufacturers and Com-merce initiated an inquiry into 'Tomorrow's Company' in January 1993. The final report was published in June 1995.

democracy, which is positive in form and which invigorates citizens can take place through corporate restructuring . . . This becomes the leading political issue of the day.'

Such democracy at the micro-level would challenge the legitimacy of executives participating in elitist world business organizations such as the WBCSD, and thereby hinder their efforts to shore up liberal-productivism at the macro-level. However, greater participation in economic decision-making at the micro-level might usefully be complemented by more direct reductions in the representational power of executives at the macro-level, in international fora such as the WTO and the World Bank, for example. An acceptance of the need for the representation of other interests (such as environmental groups and grass-roots development organizations) has now been established in places like the UNCSD and, to an extent, UNCTAD. Practices within these institutions need to be continually monitored and reviewed to ensure the evolution of best possible working practice – and thence spread to other organizations. Still, the problem remains that much of the executive's agenda is accomplished informally, in an *ad hoc* way, once the likes of the WBCSD have formulated their policy positions. The priority, therefore, does have to be the reduction of executive 'reach' in the first place. That task has to begin at the micro-level: the original source of executives' excessive 'representational power'. It is no exaggeration to state that this power does currently represent the major obstacle to sustainable development. Brave steps from those within the corporate world, and rather more acuity from those without, are now urgently required.

Appendix

Additional organizations, operating between the levels of world business organization and individual corporation, through which corporate executives' wield 'representational power' with respect to sustainable development issues – with particular reference to the UK:

- Confederation of British Industries (CBI) – has a high-level Environmental Affairs Committee composed of around 20 business executives, whom it refuses to name. Also runs an Environment Business Forum which promotes voluntary environmental action designed to 'be helpful in pre-empting the threat of legislation.' (Davies, 1994)
- Advisory Committee on Business and the Environment (ACBE) – set up by the government in 1991 to 'promote dialogue with business on environmental issues' (DTI/DOE, 1996). Comprises about 25 business executives.

- Chemical Industries Association (CIA) – the chemical industry's trade association dedicated to 'influencing legislators and opinion formers'. Operates the industry's Responsible Care Programme: 'a voluntary initiative to gain public confidence in all aspects of health, safety and environmental performance'.
- Government Panel on Sustainable Development – comprises 5 'wise-persons' who advise the Prime Minister on sustainable development issues. These include Lord Alexander of Wheedon, Chairman of Nat West Bank and Non-Executive Director of mining company, RTZ-CRA.
- UK Round Table on Sustainable Development – a cross-sectoral body, convened by the government to 'help identify the agenda and priorities for sustainable development' (DOE, 1996). About 20 per cent of the 25–30 members are senior industrialists.
- Business in the Environment (BiE) – launched by Business in the Community in 1990, it 'helps raise business awareness of environmental issues; provides practical advice on developing and implementing environmental policies; and promotes examples of good environmental practice'. (BiE, undated)
- European Commission's Consultative Forum on the Environment – set up to serve a similar role at the European level as ACBE in the UK.
- European Round Table: a forum for around 40 blue-chip companies to devise policy positions and lobby on environmental issues at the European level.

Naturally, there is a host of other institutional forms through which corporate executives are directly influencing the sustainable development agenda, such as: the Government's Deregulation Task Force, the Board of the new Environment Agency, the governing body of the Prince of Wales' Business and the Environment Programme and even, the Economic and Social Research Council's (ESRC's) Global Environmental Change (GEC) Committee – responsible for the allocation of monies for academic research into sustainable development issues.

References

Atkinson, A (1991) *Principles of Political Ecology*, Bellhaven Press, London
BCSD (1991) *Interview with Maurice Strong*, Media Kit, BCSD, Geneva
BCSD (1991a) *Introduction*, Media Kit
BCSD (1991b) *Some Hard Questions*, Media Kit, BCSD, Geneva
BCSD (1991c) *What the BCSD Wants to Say and What the BCSD is Proposing*, Media Kit, BCSD, Geneva
BCSD (1991d) *What the BCSD Wants to Say*, Media Kit, BCSD, Geneva

BCSD (1992) *Towards Sustainable Development – an Indian Industry Perspective*, BCSD, Geneva

BCSD (1994a) Towards Changing Course, *1993 Annual Report*, BCSD, Geneva

BCSD (undated) *Business Council for Sustainabale Development*, BCSD, Geneva

BCSD (undated a) *Business Council for Sustainable Development*, BCSD, Geneva

BiE (undated) *Business in the Environment*, London

Brundtland (1987) *Our Common Future*, World Commission on Environment and Development, OUP, Oxford

Confidential report (1992) to Friends of the Earth (London) from observer at UNCED Prepcom IV

Davies, Howard (1994) Speech to the Environment Business Forum Convention, March 15

Deetz, S (1992) Disciplinary Power in the Modern Corporation, in M Alvesson and H Wilmott (eds) *Critical Management Studies*, Sage, London

DoE (1996) telephone conversation with Verity Sherwood, Sustainable Development Secretariat, June 13

DTI/DoE (1996) *Advisory Committee on Business and Environment Sixth Progress Report*, HMSO, London; April, p 2

Durning, A (1991) *Asking How Much is Enough? State of the World 1991*, Worldwatch Institute, Washington DC

Eden, S (1993) Constructing Environmental Responsibility: Perceptions from Retail Business, *Geoforum*, Vol 24 No 4

Eden, S (1994) Using sustainable development, *Global Environmental Change* 4 (2)

ENDS Report (1995) Business interest in energy saving levelling off, No 244, Environmental Data Services, London

Faulkner, J (1992) (Executive Director of BCSD) in *Foreward to Greenworld 2*, SustainAbility, London

Fineman, S (1994) Going Green – Corporate Angst, Action and Inaction, paper presented at the 12th International Labour Process Conference, Aston University

Fineman, S (1996) Constructing the Green Manager, manuscript to be published in the *British Journal of Management*

Fineman, S (1996a) Emotional Subtexts in Corporate Greening, manuscript to be published in *Organisation Studies*

Fineman, S and Clarke, K (1996) Green Stakeholders: Industry Interpretations and Response, manuscript to be published in the *Journal of Management Studies*

Gladwin (1994) *The social challenge of global sustainability*, paper given to the HRH Prince of Wales' Industry and Environment Executive Seminar, 12–16 September

Greenpeace International (1992) *The Greenpeace Book of Greenwash*, Greenpeace, Washington DC

Greider, W (1992) *Who Will Tell the People? The betrayal of American Democracy*, Simon and Schuster, New York

Hawken, P (1993) *The Ecology of Commerce*, Harper Collins, New York

Hildyard, N (1991) Editorial, *the Ecologist*, 21, 1, January/February

Hutton, W (1995) *The State We're In*, Jonathan Cape, London

ICC (1991) *The Business Charter for Sustainable Development: Model Questions and Answers*, ICC, Paris

ICC (1991a) *Business Charter for Sustainable Development: Principles for Environmental Management*, ICC, Paris

ICC (1992) *UNCED Press Briefing*, ICC, Paris, May

ICC (1992a) *From Ideas to Action*, ICC, Paris

ICC (1992b) *Environment Factsheet*, ICC, Paris, February

ICC (1992c) *Annual Report 1991*, ICC, Paris

ICC (1992d) *Business Presents its Case Before Earth Summit*, Press Release, ICC, Paris, 12 March

ICC (1992e) *Business Brief No. 6 Forests*, ICC, Paris

ICC (1992f) *Business World* Vol 2 No 6, ICC, Paris, June

ICC (1992g) *Environment and Sustainable Development: A voice and strategy for world business*, WICE, ICC, Paris

ICC (1993) *Annual Report 1992*, ICC, Paris

ICC (1993a) Statement by the World Industry Council for the Environment, ICC, Paris

ICC (1993b) *Annual Report 1992*, ICC, Paris

ICC (1993c) *WICE Workplan 1994*, ICC, Paris

ICC (1994) *WICE: World Industry Council for the Environment*, ICC, Paris

ICC (1994a) *Annual Report 1993*, ICC, Paris

ICC (undated a) Trade and Sustainable Development, *WICE Executive Brief*, ICC, Paris

ICC (undated b) Technology Cooperation, *WICE Executive Brief*, ICC, Paris

ICC (undated c) Sustainable Forest Management, *WICE Executive Brief*, ICC, Paris

ICC UK (1993) *Annual Report and Accounts 1992*, ICC, UK, London

ICC UK (undated) *Serving World Business*, ICC, UK, London

Jackall, R (1988) *Moral Mazes*, OUP, New York

Jacobs, M (1991) *The Green Economy*, Pluto Press, London

Korten, D (1995) *When Corporations Rule the World*, Earthscan

Lang, T and Hines, C (1993) *The New Protectionism*, Earthscan, London

Lash, S and Urry, J (1994) *Economies of Signs and Space*, Sage, London

Lipietz, A (1992) *Towards a New Economic Order*, Polity Press, London

Purvis et al (1995) *Fragmenting Uncertainties: British Business and Responses to Stratospheric Ozone Depletion*, Working Paper 95/12, School of Geography, University of Leeds.

Schmidheiny, S (1991) Address to ASEAN Regional Forum, 22 July

Schmidheiny, S (1991a) Address to 3rd Prepcom, Geneva, 30 August

Schmidheiny, S (1992a) Changing Course: *A Global Business Perspective on Development and Environment*, MIT Press, Cambridge, Massachusetts

Schmidheiny, S (1992b) Address to Smithsonian Conference, USA, 6 March

Schmidheiny, S (1994) Address to HRH Prince of Wales' Industry and Environment Executive Seminar, 12–16 September

Stigson, Bjorn (1995) (Executive Director WBCSD) at the UNED (UK) Annual Conference, London, 26 November

The Independent (1996) Editorial, Better value in the boardroom, 26 April

United Nations (1993) *World Investment Report*, United Nations, New York

United Nations (1996) *Human Development Report*, United Nations, New York

WBCSD (1996) *Annual Review 1995*, WBCSD, Geneva

WBCSD (undated) Trade and Environment: a business perspective, in WBCSD (1996) *Annual Review 1995* p 10

WBCSD (undated a) *World Business Council for Sustainable Development*, WBCSD, Geneva

WICE (1994) *Two Leading Organisations to Merge*, Press Release, 17 November

PART 2

Underlying Tensions

5

Ecological Eldorado: Eliminating Excess over Ecology

Tarja Ketola

Nearly all companies consistently exceed the limits of the ecosystem. They are rarely punished for this infringement immediately. If they cause an environmental shock (accident), they may be liable to pay for the clean-up and damages. However, most excesses over ecological limits are environmental stresses built up gradually, often unnoticed. In fact, in the short-term, many companies profit from abusing the environment. Polluting is a short cut to cutting costs.

In the longer term, however, the companies' poor environmental performance builds up to a huge liability to the ecosystem, the business environment and the companies themselves. The time lag between companies having been polluting on a large scale since the Second World War and its visible effects becoming apparent in the ecosystem is now closing in upon us. As a result, the carrying capacity of the ecosystem is rapidly diminishing. It cannot carry even the pollution loads it seemingly absorbed earlier, not to mention the additional adverse effects of ever-increasing production and consumption. The ecosystem is dying on us.

We are dependent on the ecosystem. It provides us with the vital life-support systems without which we would perish. The message of their destruction is finally coming through to us. We will look for the guilty parties and make them liable to compensate for the losses. The business environments of companies with their political, economic, socio-cultural and technological interest groups will in the future agree to integrate ecological factors into the profit and loss accounts and balance sheets of companies. Full costing is a fact of the future. But it will take a long time for the business environments to agree to it because they still benefit from companies exceeding the limits of the ecosystem. As yet their other – mainly economic – interests surpass their ecological interests. Still their ecological interests are beginning to have an economic flavour because many of the previously free or cheap resources – like clean air, light, water and food – are becoming commodities with a high price tag.

It will take years or even decades before our society and its business environments get their act together and force companies (and individuals) to change their mode of action. Some think that it will take too long. Others, optimists, believe that we can save our planet even if our life-style change takes decades. Meanwhile, the companies can continue to enjoy the profits from polluting – or they can get prepared for the future. It is their choice: exploit the ecosystem to their last breath or plan for the future survival and prosperity under new values. Some companies can operate in Ecological Eldorado, if it is achieved, others cannot.

Ecological Eldorado is a future world where there are great ecological riches and fabulous ecological opportunities. Human activities do not exceed the carrying capacity of the ecosystem. Instead, humans are one with nature. Different species live in an interdependent harmony. The Earth's life-support systems are carefully looked after. Biodiversity is conserved and enhanced.

The future of our planet is in our hands. If we do not choose the path which leads towards Ecological Eldorado, the adverse ecological impacts of our activities accelerate exponentially into a sharp downward spiral which will destroy the conditions providing for life on Earth. Planet Venus had similar original conditions to Planet Earth but, for some reason, it developed into a burning hot ball where life cannot survive. Our present activities may lead our planet to the same destiny.

We need to consider the way in which companies and their business environments can change their life-style to accommodate the values of Ecological Eldorado in which they will not exceed the limits of the ecosystem. There are two ways of ensuring that a company stays within the ecosystem boundaries – either through external interest groups enforcing the limits on companies, or through internal strategies to manage the business in a sustainable way. I will study both approaches, which could actually complement each other in the pursuit of Ecological Eldorado.

FRAMEWORK

A company is ultimately a subsystem of the ecosystem of this planet. Figure 5.1 illustrates this concrete systems approach to studying company operations.

Figure 5.1 A Company as a Subsystem of the Ecosystem

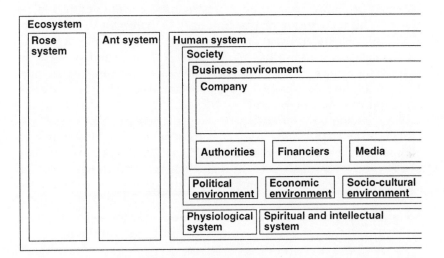

The ecosystem includes a human system and an abundance of non-human systems, e.g. an ant system and a rose system. These are global systems. The human system consists of physiological systems and spiritual and intellectual systems as well as of systems whereby people live in organized communities, i.e. societies. They are regional systems. Societies can be divided into subsystems in hundreds of different ways. For example, political analysts would study different kinds of political environments, sociologists would analyse social environments and anthropologists would research a variety of cultural environments. Alternatively we can consider the traditional business environments. These are local systems which are usually autonomous. A company operates within one or more business environments depending on the number and location of its operating units.

A company is dependent on the higher level systems: it needs its business environment for survival. The business environment, in turn, needs society, society needs the human system and the human system needs the ecosystem. Thus a company needs the ecosystem in order to survive. On the contrary, the ecosystem does not need the human system in order to survive as species are born and die out constantly. Humans are just one animal species. Hence the ecosystem does not need society, the business environment or a company either. Dependence is all one-sided.

However, the ecosystem can be destroyed by the human system, society, the business environment and even by a single company. The ecosystem can, of course, destroy any one of its subsystems. And each and every subsystem can destroy each other. In this sense there is interdependence between the elements of the ecosystem, which is only currently becoming recognized by the 'civilized' societies of the human system. This recognition may be leading to demands for the balance of terror in order to prevent the destruction of the ecosystem – and particularly humans within it. The approach of primitive societies towards the ecosystem has been much more positive: they have adapted to its limits and utilize its resources sustainably. For them, the ecosystem is an opportunity, not a threat.

Any company is therefore dependent on the ecosystem for its survival. On the other hand, the closest and most important subsystem of a company is its business environment. Figure 5.2 shows three building blocks used for an analysis of the relationships between the ecosystem, business environment and company operations.

Figure 5.2 The Building Blocks Used to Analyse the Relationships between the Ecosystem, Business Environment and Company Operations

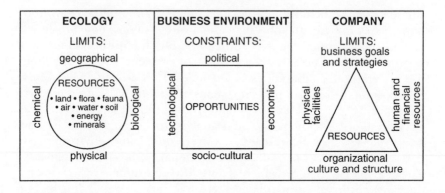

Ecological factors set limits to but also offer resources for company operations. There are geographical, biological, physical and chemical limits that restrict company operations. Exceeding these limits leads to environmental shocks or stresses. These can be distinguished according to the time they take to appear from the occurrence. Environmental shocks result from accidents and have an immediate effect. The effect of environmental stresses builds up gradually and is caused by normal company operations. Both shocks and stresses are human-induced hazards in the natural and man-made environment. They lead to pollution, other environmental degradation and ecological unsustainability. On the other hand, nature gives land, flora and fauna, air, water and soil as well as energy and minerals as resources to companies to use.

In the analysis of the business environment, political, economic, socio-cultural and technological factors (PEST-factors) are usually considered as constraints but they can just as well be regarded as opportunities. The same applies to the limits and resources of a company: organizational culture and structure, human and financial resources and physical facilities are two sides of the same coin which are directed by the business goals and strategies.

In Figure 5.3, I am utilizing the blocks of Figure 5.2 to illustrate four possible situations between the ecosystem, business environment and company operations. Roughly speaking, external interest groups impact on the business environment through PEST-factors and internal interest groups through business goals and strategies, organizational culture and structure and resources. In reality, however, external and internal groups are not separate but people can belong to both at the same time – like employees acting as their company's customers and shareholders as well as being members of its local people, general public and even environmental pressure groups.

In situation (a) of Figure 5.3, the circle, i.e. the ecosystem, is the ground on which business environment factors (the square) and com-

Figure 5.3 Four Relationships between the Ecosystem, the Business Environment and Company Operations (excess over ecological limits is shaded)

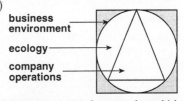

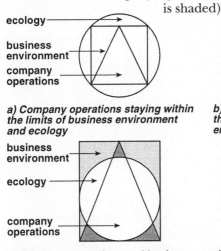

a) Company operations staying within the limits of business environment and ecology

b) Company operations staying within the limits of ecology while business environment exceeds them

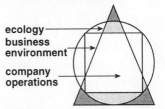

c) Company operations and business environment exceeding the limits of ecology

d) Company operations exceeding the limits of business environment and ecology

pany operations (the triangle) are laid. Both of them remain within the limits of the ecosystem. The square frames representing business environment limits (i.e. limits arising from PEST-factors) cut off the areas and activities which should remain outside potential industrial utilization. The triangle shows the materialized extent of company operations which thus remains within the limits of ecologically sustainable development. Situation (a) represents the environmental ideal: Ecological Eldorado. Such a situation does not (yet) exist here on Earth.

Company operations may stay within the ecological limits even if the general business environment exceeds these limits. In such a case, illustrated by situation (b) of Figure 5.3, company management has not simply adapted to the environmental pressures from the business environment but it has taken initiative to do more than required by external interest groups. The management recognizes that the long-term survival of the company depends on the survival of the ecosystem. Therefore, the main goal of the company is to live in harmony with nature. The company has advanced environmental values and visions based on its assessment of the ecological impacts of its activities. It constantly reassesses its impacts and develops its values and visions further for environmental policy reviews. Its environmental policies and strategies are fully integrated into other policies and strategies, in such a way that the environmental issues form the basis for other policies and strategies. The implementation of policies and strategies is carried out rigorously, so that the intended level of environmental performance is achieved to enable the company operations to stay within the limits of the ecosystem although its business environment exceeds them.

There are some companies which vigorously strive for situation (b). Some of the most well-known ones are The Body Shop and Ernst Winter & Sohn (GmbH & Co). The main reason why they cannot achieve situation (b) is that their products (cosmetics and diamond tools, respectively) are not really necessary for humankind. All human activities have an impact on the environment. Therefore, unnecessary activities should be avoided. Companies in basic food production like organic farming, or in clothes manufacturing like woollen mills have a better chance to achieve situation (b) if they base their operations on humane and ecologically sustainable practices with regard to all their processes and the whole life cycles of their products. Welford's (1996) advice for more sustainable manufacturing is a good guide: to produce less and higher quality with much lower environmental and social impacts at higher levels of employment.

Not only the area of business but also the size of the company matters. It is very difficult to control the many-sided and abundant ecological impacts of the operations of large companies. The operations of small companies are easier to redesign to achieve situation (b). Small companies can more easily operate within the ecological limits also because not so many contradictory pressures are exerted on them as on large companies by their business environment which, in situation (b), exceeds the limits of the ecosystem.

The difference between the concepts of 'society' and 'business environment' is noteworthy. Apart from being a subsystem of society in a geographical sense, a business environment also represents an elite group picked up from a society by a company. The weak and poor do not usually belong to a company's business environment. Therefore, a company's operations may well violate social and cultural values of some people and tribes, destroy their livelihood, and even exterminate them – with the blessing of the business environment: the powerful PEST interest groups. Some of these tribes live in complete harmony with nature. Their interests and the interest of nature coincide. This is why, the PEST interest groups often treat them as part of the natural environment (we all should be, actually, as the human system is a subsystem of the ecosystem). Their position is illustrated in situation (c).

In situation (c) company operations exceed the limits of the ecosystem but stay within the limits of the business environment. Consequently, the business environment has also crossed the boundaries of the ecosystem and thus given the company a permission to practise ecologically unsustainable operations. This situation is the current 'business as usual' mode that nearly all companies practise. From the environmental point of view, it is problematic because, in the short term, the ecological system cannot protest against excesses.

The willingness and ability of different PEST interest groups to look after the interests of the ecosystem varies. Governments, authorities, financiers and the strongest shareholders are in a powerful position but do not usually want to compromise their political and economic goals by ecological goals. Environmental groups usually try hardest to protect the ecosystem but they may have relatively little power in the short run because they are often considered less legitimate interest groups than many others. In addition, their narrow ecological goals may be in conflict with the overall interests of the ecosystem, and they have their own political and economic goals to meet. Other interest groups like local people, customers and employees also have to balance their conflicting interests. In other words, the PEST interest groups of the business environment may act unsustainably for their own short-term financial or other benefit. That is why, a company may be allowed to exceed the limits of the ecological system.

The strength of environmental pressure on a company from any interest group is a factor of the group's degree of concern for the ecosystem and its power to make a company conform. A single strong interest group with conviction can stop a company from breaking an 'ecological rule'. A joint effort by several interest groups can lead to a similar result. New legislation is not necessarily a final answer to exceeding ecological limits; the interpretation of a law or regulation and the degree of its enforcement depend on the general view within the business environment. Even with sophisticated environmental legislation, a company may be allowed to continue to infringe upon the boundaries of the ecosystem.

A good example of situation (c) are the oil companies. Their excesses over ecological limits are flagrant. But even among them, there are varied degrees of excess. Figure 5.4 illustrates the excess over the limits of the ecosystem of two British oil refineries, Shell Stanlow and Texaco Pembroke (for a detailed analysis, see Ketola 1995). The business environments of the two refineries are very similar. This shows as equally large squares in Figure 5.4. Texaco Pembroke lies in a more ecologically vulnerable area (partially within the boundaries of Pembrokeshire Coast National Park on the south bank of Milford Haven) than Shell Stanlow (in the town of Stanlow by Manchester Ship Canal which empties into the Mersey river). Therefore, Pembroke's ecological limits are more stringent than Stanlow's, which is illustrated by a smaller circle in Figure 5.4.

The general and environmental strategic management of the two refineries differ greatly from each other. In general, the strategic management of Texaco Pembroke allows and even enhances environmental change while in Shell Stanlow environmental change is discouraged. In particular, Shell's organizational culture, human and financial resources and Stanlow's physical facilities promote excess over ecological limits while Texaco's organizational culture, human and financial resources and Pembroke's physical facilities diminish its excess over ecological limits. That is why, the triangle of company operations shows a much greater excess over ecological limits for Stanlow than for Pembroke. Yet both cases are just variations of the 'business as usual' situation (c) where company operations exceed the limits of the ecosystem but not the limits of the business environment.

The only way to stop this kind of infringement by a company for good is to change the limits of business environment. If the PEST interest groups agree to reduce the business environment boundaries so that they stay within the limits of the ecological system, those company operations that still exceed the ecological limits will be easy to end because a company cannot exceed the limits of the business environment for long without being forced to comply or close down. For example, in 1987, the Finnish oil company, Neste, had to close down a chemicals factory it had just purchased in Sweden because it could not remove the local interest groups' distrust of that factory. Thus the boundaries of the factory's business environment reduced so that its operations became unacceptable.

Figure 5.4 Company Operations vs Business Environment vs Ecosystem (excess over ecological limits is shaded; the arrows indicate whether the area of company operations is increased or decreased by different factors)

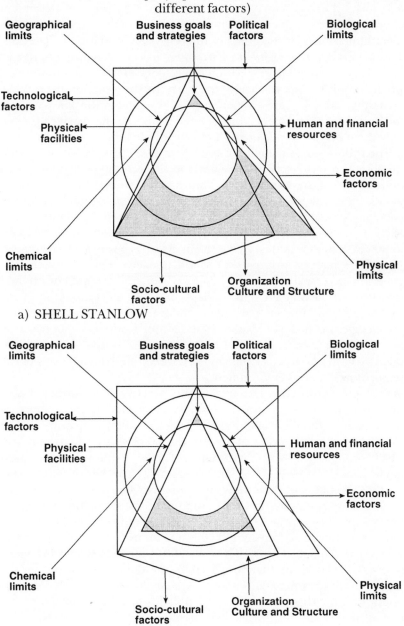

a) SHELL STANLOW

a) TEXACO PEMBROKE

However, most companies reconcile themselves to the new business environment boundaries. So, if a company's operations exceed the limits of both the business environment and ecology, the PEST interest groups will force the company to comply with the business environment boundaries. If a company still, after conforming to the business environment limits, exceeds the limits of the ecosystem, situation (c) prevails. This means that the business environment has not succeeded to reduce its activities enough to stay within the ecological limits as situation (a) would require. This is usually the case. In the very long term, the ecosystem can take care of itself. It takes revenge on the company and the business environment which exceed its limits, and may destroy not only them but whole societies – even the whole human system.

The willingness and ability of a company to keep its operations within the limits of business environment and the ecosystem depend on its policies which are based on its values and visions, and on how the policies are followed in practice. This, in turn, is dependent on the company's organizational culture and structure as well as on its human and financial resources. Normally, it becomes impossible for a company to survive if it constantly exceeds the limits of its business environment. The PEST interest groups simply will not let it behave against the generally accepted rules. The company's organizational culture and structure are flexible enough to adapt to these expectations. Similarly, the company will find enough human and financial resources to facilitate the changes needed. A company is, in fact, an abstract system made up of its interest groups, and not only a concrete system with physical boundaries. Therefore, a company's days are numbered if it exceeds the limits of its business environment.

Ecological Eldorado, presented in situation (a), clearly does not exist on Earth: the activities of most business environments and companies do not stay within the ecological limits. Consequently, the only relevant situations, from the point of view of the present, are situation (b), in which a company stays within the limits of ecology although the business environment exceeds them, and situation (c), in which a company exceeds the limits of the ecosystem but remains within the limits of its business environment. In both situations, the company managers' behaviour (their initiative and response to external pressures) determines whether the company will continue to stay within or continue to exceed the ecological limits. Thus one of the interest groups, managers, have a critical role. We therefore need to consider how managers see the business environment and the ecosystem in which their company operates, how they create and use policies to guide environmental management, and how other management areas help or hinder this guidance.

The issues that require investigation are: the vulnerability of the ecosystem, the strength of pressure from different PEST interest groups of the business environment, and the way in which a company's general strategic management facilitates or hinders strategic environmental management and its implementation. I will start by discussing the analysis of the vulnerability of the ecosystem.

ANALYSING THE ECOSYSTEM

A company can estimate the level of ecology by evaluating the vulnerability of local, regional and global ecology to its activities (see Figure 5.5). The arrows in Figure 5.5 show whether the effects increase or decrease the area of possible company operations. Very low or low vulnerability of ecology increases the limits of the ecosystem in which a company can operate sustainably, moderate vulnerability keeps the limits of the ecosystem about the same, and high or very high vulnerability of ecology reduces the limits of the ecosystem.

The vulnerability of the local and regional ecology depends on the type of surroundings in which the company operates and its environmental effects on it. Ecologically fragile areas like tropical rain forests, wetlands and coral reefs are very highly vulnerable to company

Figure 5.5 The Degree of Vulnerability of the Ecosystem

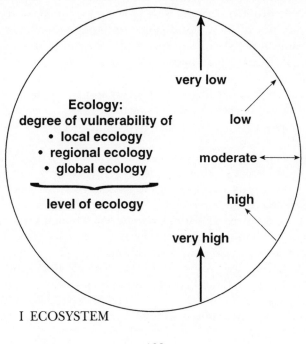

operations and other human activities. They are treasuries of flora and fauna as well as the provision of life-support systems and biodiversity. They are natural systems where human impact has been minimal and has not affected the ecosystem's structure (see Prescott-Allen 1991). These areas would be very difficult or impossible to compensate for, were they to be destroyed. That is why, companies need to be extremely cautious when they operate in the very highly vulnerable areas, and should think carefully whether it is absolutely necessary to operate there at all in order not to change their ecological structure. In these areas, the ecological limits to operations are very stringent.

Highly vulnerable areas are usually modified systems where human impact has been greater than that of other species but has not affected the structural components of the ecosystems (see Prescott-Allen 1991). These areas consist of coastlines, rivers, boreal forests, range land and national parks. They, too, give a significant contribution to the biodiversity and life-support of our planet. The ecological limits to operations in these areas are stringent so that the companies would not change the components of these ecosystems.

Moderately vulnerable areas are often cultivated systems, like farm-land, sown pasture, plantations and aquacultural ponds, where human impact has been greater than that of any other species and has cultivated the structural components of these ecosystems (see Prescott-Allen 1991). While highly vulnerable and vulnerable areas provide all species with food and other resources, moderately vulnerable areas have been developed to provide humans with food and other resources. Their vulnerability lies in their significance to us, humans. Since we have conducted business activities of many different kinds for thousands of years, our cultivated systems have adapted to the effects of most of them. Therefore, the ecological limits to company operations are more lenient in moderately vulnerable than in very highly and highly vulnerable areas. However, there is no room for increasing these limits because agriculture and animal husbandry, in particular, need large, relatively clean areas to produce edible food.

Areas with low vulnerability are usually built systems which have been developed by humans. They can be large urban areas or groups of buildings, roads, railways, airports and docks (see Prescott-Allen 1991). The main ecological limit to company operations in these areas is human health, safety and comfort. For this very reason – humans find their own species most adaptable – the limits of this ecosystem are constantly being extended to accommodate more operations.

Areas with very low vulnerability are already degraded systems: ecosystems whose habitability, productivity and diversity have been substantially reduced by human activities (see Prescott-Allen 1991). Many people think that it does not really matter any more what kind of or how intense operations companies conduct in areas with no animal life, no vegetation, extensive soil erosion and polluted water. It is considered that companies can thus increase their operations as much as they like in these areas without having to pay attention to ecological limits. Yet, the adverse environmental effects of the expansion of operations may spill over the boundaries of these areas of very low vulnerability and hence increase the degraded area at the expense of previously undegraded areas.

It is not only the type of surroundings in which a company operates that counts but also the quality and quantity of the environmental effects the operations cause to that local and regional ecosystem. The local adverse environmental effects of company operations range from different kinds of air, water and soil pollution to noise, congestion, and loss of scene and place. A company can identify these effects and measure them quite accurately. Regional environmental effects may be more difficult to assess and identify with the operations of individual companies. Sometimes these effects are straightforward: a company may be directly responsible for habitat loss, waste, chemical toxification and soil erosion. It is also possible to estimate each company's share of natural resource depletion, water quality and quantity, and even species extinction.

The most difficult issues to divide between different company (and other) operations are the global environmental effects. The greenhouse effect, ozone depletion, deforestation and desertification cannot be derived from the operations of individual companies. Nevertheless, as the chemical processes which cause these effects are unfolding, it is possible to point out which emissions, and hence which operations, belong to the major contributors to these effects. The vulnerability of global ecology to a company's operations can thus be derived from the types and quantities of emissions a company is responsible for.

The carrying capacity of the ecology seems to be decreasing. The ecosystems – whether natural, modified, cultivated or built – are reaching their saturation points and becoming degraded more quickly than before. The degradation of local ecosystems is unfortunate and affects many people, other animals and plants. However, humans, many other animals and some plants can move out of a degraded area if they did not perish there. The degradation of regional ecosystems is even more serious because it threatens the survival of higher numbers of people, other animals and plants. Fewer have a chance to escape and the relocation of the refugees (flora or fauna) is difficult because of the competition for living space in other regions which themselves may be degrading, thus offering less resources to live upon.

The worst threat to life on Earth comes from the degradation of the global ecosystem. It covers all natural, modified, cultivated and built systems. Global degradation may progress at different rates in different parts of the world, enabling massive migration from the more rapidly impoverished areas to the more slowly degrading areas. This accelerates the degradation of the latter areas. In the end, there will be nowhere to take refuge in – unless space travelling has taken off.

It is easy to laugh at these kinds of doomsday prophecies. But there are warning signs in many local and regional areas. Once they accumulate, the global ecosystem is in danger. However, it is still possible to turn the tide. The most crucial role in this game is played by the business environments of companies. They represent the most influential parts of our societies. They can, if they want to, exert enormous environmental pressure on companies and thereby change the course of our destiny.

ANALYSING THE BUSINESS ENVIRONMENT

A company has to obey the demands of its business environment if it wants to survive. That is why, its business environment is potentially the most powerful change agent in a company's environmental behaviour. However, the environmental pressures from different parts of the business environment have been varying a great deal, and have, in general, been too weak to make the necessary radical change to the environmental performance of companies.

A company can evaluate the strengths of environmental pressures from the political, economic, socio-cultural and technological factors of its business environment according to the principles explained below (see Figure 5.6). Very weak or weak strength of environmental pressure from the business environment increases the area of company operations that the business environment accepts, moderate pressure keeps it about the same, and strong or very strong pressure reduces the area of company operations acceptable to the business environment.

Political Factors

The easiest way to approach the political, economic, socio-cultural and technological factors of the business environment of a company is through its interest groups. Thus, the significance of political factors to a company's environmental positioning could be evaluated through the environmental pressures from the political interest groups, like legislators, local and regional authorities, business associations, trade unions, environmental pressure groups and the media. The strength of pressure from each interest group can be very weak, weak, moderate, strong or very strong.

Figure 5.6 The Strengths of Environmental Pressures from the PEST
Factors of the Business Environment

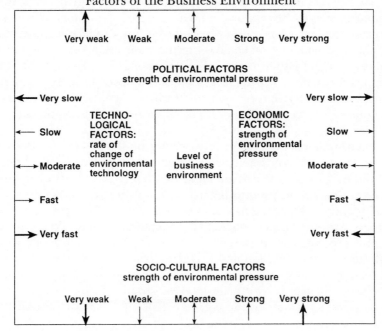

II BUSINESS ENVIRONMENT

For example, many banks may find the environmental pressures exerted
by legislators very weak, many computer companies may find them weak,
supermarkets may find them moderate, car manufacturers strong and
chemical companies very strong. The same companies may feel much
weaker environmental pressures from local and regional authorities
which look after the enforcement of the legislation.

Business associations, like the International Chamber of Commerce
(ICC), Confederation of British Industries (CBI) and the industry-
specific associations are representatives of companies and hence
legitimate interest groups. As far as environmental pressure is concerned,
they have a dual role: on the one hand, they encourage companies to
adopt environmentally friendlier principles and practices; on the other
hand, they lobby other political as well as economic interest groups so
that these would put less and weaker environmental pressure on the
companies.

While the industry associations have a powerful position, the workers'
associations, the trade unions, have little power over environmental
issues. The situation varies from one country to another. In Germany,
for example, the co-determination system gives employees and their

unions a chance to participate in environmental decision-making. Many European countries have a cooperative system which gives some opportunities for the unions to influence the environmental issues of their companies. Some European countries (e.g. Britain) and most other countries do not give much power to the trade unions. In all countries, environmental issues are ranked low among the priorities of trade unions. Particularly during recession, the basic employment problem is the first, and often the only, issue on the union agenda. Therefore, trade unions often exert only very weak environmental pressure on companies.

Environmental pressure groups' virility, on the other hand, does not suffer from recession. International groups like Greenpeace, the Friends of the Earth and World Wide Fund for Nature are constantly gaining power. Companies used to regard some of them as hooligans in the 1970s and early 1980s. Once some of the claims of the environmental groups proved true, and once they obtained positive results from their campaigns, engaged themselves in research, became more organized, and received recognition and financing from the public and organizations, the companies had to give in to some extent – but they still do not accept them as legitimate interest groups. Companies that find themselves as targets of these groups feel very strong environmental pressure.

Green parties have a different role from non-governmental environmental groups. In many countries, green parties have expanded their supporter basis and extended the scope of environmental issues over the years. They have shown that most political decisions made at the local, regional and national level have environmental consequences and affect people's everyday life. In many central and north European countries green parties have quite a lot of power although they are in the minority. They may play the pivotal role in local councils, in parliaments, or even in governments. If Greenpeace and others are considered radical outcasts, and treated with caution and contempt by companies, green parties are, because of their role as institutionalized environmental groups, legitimate political opponents which are difficult to ignore.

Companies have a similarly suspicious attitude towards the media as towards the environmental groups. Like the environmental pressure groups, the media willingly reveal the environmental shortcomings of companies to the public. Companies often complain that they cannot get their environmental achievements published but as soon as there is a negative environmental incident in any of their operations, the reporters make headlines out of them. One reason for this is that the companies' environmental accidents usually fulfil the most important criteria of what makes a good news story (see Peltu 1985): event-orientation, drama and conflict, negativity, human interest, photographability, topicality and local interest. However, the practice of keeping incidents secret, if possible, so that adverse publicity could be avoided, is gradually giving way to openness in many developed world companies. The companies have learnt from bitter experience that secrecy breeds rumours which are worse than the reality. By telling the truth immediately and explaining the actions being taken, public confidence in the company can be maintained. Yet openness is an object-ive, not necessary a reality, even in companies situated in developed countries. Environmental pressure groups and the media often cooperate. They have established roles: environmental groups take action, the media report it. The environmental pressure groups and the media together put more pressure on companies than any other interest groups. They are both still least willing to cooperate with companies.

All in all, the environmental pressures exerted by political interest groups have a common denominator: the degree of legitimacy felt by companies. Legislators and authorities are at one end of this spectrum, environmental groups and the media at the other end. Yet, the strengths of environmental pressures vary from industry to industry and – to some extent – from company to company within an industry.

Economic Factors

The significance of the economic factors of the business environment to a company's environmental positioning could be evaluated through the strengths of environmental pressures exerted by different economic interest groups, like governments, insurers, financiers, shareholders, customers, suppliers, distributors, contractors and competitors. The strength of pressure from each group can range from very weak to very strong.

Political and economic factors often go hand in hand. Therefore, it may be difficult to separate the environmental pressures exerted by legislators from those exerted by governments. But we can separate the pressures by considering that legislators exert environmental pressure on companies through legal instruments, like laws, while governments exert this pressure through market-based instruments, like taxes, tradable pollution rights and financial incentives.

From this point of view, for example, the British Government does not put much environmental pressure on companies compared to some other European governments which have introduced carbon and other eco-taxes. Tradable pollution rights, if used, may feel like a burden to companies which pollute heavily. But those companies which know how to negotiate good deals with authorities and then reduce their emissions so effectively that they stay well beyond the lenient consents, can earn huge sums of money by selling their pollution rights to the burdened companies or back to the government. These kinds of environmental business activities will offer great opportunities to large companies in the future. Taxes constitute negative environmental pressures on companies; tradable pollution rights can be either, depending on the company. Financial incentives offered by government to companies to improve their environmental performance belong to positive environmental pressures. The strengths of governmental environmental pressures are often not just company- but also industry-specific. Nevertheless, the governments, particularly the British Government, should take a longer-term view in its environmental policy and exert much more environmental pressure on companies in order to safeguard the future of British industry.

Insurers can exert strong environmental pressure on a company if they think that the probability of environmental shocks (accidents) caused by the company's operations is high and the damage caused by the materialized shocks is great. The evaluation of the likelihood and consequences of environmental shocks belongs to traditional insurance business. That is why, hazardous operations have always had high insurance premiums. Companies which think that the premiums are too high either quit those operations or find a less hazardous way of conducting them to bring the premiums down.

What is new in the insurance business are the environmental stresses (adverse environmental effects caused by emissions) companies are responsible for. Traditionally, it has not been possible to take an insurance policy against anything that is certain to happen. As the damage companies have done to the environment during the past 50 years begins to unfold, the question of who is responsible and liable to compensate for it will become a hot issue. Insurers are now checking their terms to guarantee non-liability. And what is more important, they are also becoming more cautious in agreeing on new policies. The small print will become longer when the insurers insure themselves against massive compensation claims caused by unforeseen environmental consequences.

Yet companies may become liable to clean land that has been contaminated by their operations maybe decades ago. And companies are bound by the 'polluter pays' principle in many countries. This covers not only soil pollution and waste disposal but also water pollution and, maybe in the future, air pollution damages. The scope of liability may expand from this local damage to regional and even global damage. Most companies cannot afford to pay for the damage caused by the environmental stresses exerted by their operations. This makes insurance policies in environmental stresses a lucrative but dangerous business for insurance companies. And it more than doubles their power to exert strong or very strong environmental pressure on companies.

Financiers are more vulnerable to the environmental liability of the damage their customers have caused than the insurers. They have fewer means to protect themselves against compensation claims because they have invested risk money in projects and can lose it if the environmental risk is materialized. In order to decide on the loans and secure them, financiers need to study the environmental consequences of the projects. Financiers have already begun to require an environmental impact assessment of the project (usually also required by local authorities) which gives a snapshot of the environmental risk posed by a company. Financiers and insurers are now developing environmental risk rating systems which would work in the same way as credit rating. Environmental risk rating would offer a more comprehensive picture of a company's susceptibility to environmental risks and could remarkably increase the environmental pressure financiers exert on companies.

Shareholders bring the basic capital to the business. In large companies an individual shareholder is not important. It is the stock markets that determine the financial success of large companies because big institutional investors buy and sell their shares according to fluctuations in those markets. Until a few years ago the investors did not base their decisions on, or even take account of environmental considerations. But things are changing. Piesse's (1992) study on the changes in the share price of some companies before and after environmental incidents in them shows this clearly. Dramatic negative environmental news usually has a dramatic negative effect on the share price and, what is noteworthy, a non-dramatic positive environmental piece of news can have a positive effect on the share price. It reveals the still rather invisible trend towards a more environmentally conscious stock market mechanism. Consequently, the stock market has a potential to exert strong environmental pressure on companies.

Shareholders are not just financiers; they are also the ultimate decision-makers of companies. Big investors can have a say on environmental issues during shareholder meetings, while small investors may only express their wishes and hope for support from the majority. However, the majority, that is, big institutional investors, are still usually preoccupied with economic considerations and small investors' environmental concerns are not heard. Nevertheless, the strength of environmental pressure from shareholder meetings varies considerably. In small companies it depends almost entirely on the environmental values of the individuals.

Customers can exert their environmental pressures on companies by deciding what to buy and where. Industrial and institutional customers as well as consumers need their products for their everyday activities. They usually make their decisions according to the price and quality of a product. The same people who, as representatives of environmental pressure groups, the media or the local community, protest against the environmental damage companies cause, change completely when they put on their customers' clothes. They do not buy energy made from sustainable resources or environmentally less damaging products if these are more expensive than the energy or other products they are used to buying. Industrial and institutional customers may, however, expect the company to follow similar environmental principles and practices as their own. If environmental management system (EMS) standards become as popular as quality system standards, these customers may demand that their suppliers adopt the same EMS standard as they have, in order to secure the environmental quality of their products.

It is rare for customers to boycott companies or products because they are dependent on them. Boycotting often means inconvenience and a need to think of alternatives. The few boycotts that have succeeded have required constant drumming by environmental groups and the media. They have mostly been one-off events. They have not changed anything fundamentally. Customers have a huge environmental pressure potential in their hands which they do not use. Therefore, most companies can still say that they do not feel much environmental pressure from their customers. However, customers' actions are fundamental in the pursuit of changing the course towards Ecological Eldorado. It is up to every one of us to become aware of our powers as customers and take our share of responsibility for the survival of our planet. Each and every one of us can make decisions as customers which together force companies to make their operations ecologically sustainable. Boycotts would be a very influential tool for collective customer action.

Suppliers, distributors and contractors usually exert hardly any environmental pressure on companies, either. They have their own means of living at risk. And, usually, they are 'in the same boat' with the companies, dealing with the same polluting products and processes. Therefore, they do not budge but keep still, instead, so that the more vocal interest groups would not pay attention to their own environmental shortcomings. Yet they could totally change companies' environmental behaviour.

Competitors also keep quiet because attention might turn to their activities if they complained about other companies' environmental behaviour. Only when one of them has already suffered from an environmental incident, the others may cautiously comment on it. However, competitors may use their environmental superiority to their competitive advantage. This may force a company to improve its environmental performance in one way or another. In addition, competitors cooperate through business associations and one competitor can lobby its association so that its environmental views become the association's views which the association can then try to 'sell' to its other members. Hence competitors have several ways of exerting environmental pressure on other companies. They usually prefer the quiet, devious methods.

The strength of this pressure varies considerably between and within industries. Competitors in some industries, like manufacturing, put little pressure on each other because environment is not yet realized to be an important issue there. Even car manufacturers seem to believe that the end-of-pipe catalytic converters solve most of the environmental problems of their products although a turnaround in thinking would be needed to eliminate the catastrophic impacts of our most disastrous invention: that one-ton death-gas spreading metal-plastic-rubber junk we carry around to save time. Competitors in the chemical industry think they can get away with the environmental issue by cooperating: setting internal wishy-washy standards, lobbying through their associations to prevent radical changes, and displaying a uniform front with well-rehearsed arguments against those who claim that they are just paying lip-service to the ecological problems they are causing. Threatening competitive moves – comparing favourably the ecological impacts of products or processes to those of the competitors, building a green image at the competitors' expense, alluring potential employees, shareholders and financiers by this green image and investing far more in environmental improvements and research than the competitors – are only used by few individual companies because of the lack of such superior environmental characteristics among companies and because of the fear of retaliation from the competitors. Yet, if they dared to utilize threatening moves, all companies in that industry would have to boost their environmental performance considerably to survive. What a powerful, unused tool!

All in all, the environmental pressures exerted by economic interest groups on companies have one thing in common: all these interest groups have much more pressure potential than they use. They have so far considered other issues – mostly their economic benefits – as more important than environmental issues when they have demanded something from the companies. This shows that economic and environmental goals still conflict with each other, although they could complement each other.

Socio-Cultural Factors

The significance of socio-cultural factors to a company's environmental positioning could be evaluated through the environmental pressures from local people, the public and non-governmental organizations (NGOs). It may be difficult to define what 'the public' means. In

Habermas's (1989) view, public opinion is a fiction. In reality, it is an opinion of certain influential interest groups. Depending on the type of society, it may reflect mostly the government's and authorities' views (totalitarian society) or environmental pressure groups' views (liberal society). Nevertheless, companies usually distinguish easily the pressure from the public from others. The strength of pressure from socio-cultural interest groups can again range from very weak to very strong.

Most companies represent Western market economy values. That is why, their socio-cultural damage in Europe, North America and Australia is more limited than in other parts of the world. In addition, Western societies give local people, the public and NGOs channels to express their views about the companies. Some Western countries even have a democratic system through which their citizens and local inhabitants can affect the decisions their national government and regional and local authorities make on the operations of companies. In any case, there is some public discussion about a planned project before it is implemented. However, often the public is dissatisfied with the environmental behaviour of the companies but expresses its grudge only in surveys. In fact, the media has an important – if involuntary – role as a bumper between the public and companies: it offers a forum where concerned citizens can unburden themselves.

In many countries, however, the media is not allowed to publish the grievances of the public. In these countries, the public is not heard. Instead of the public, local people and NGOs exerting environmental pressures on companies, the companies exert negative environmental pressures on them by not just damaging their environment but by destroying their livelihoods and means of survival.

Local people are more active than the general public because they can hear, see and smell the environmental effects of the operations of the companies in their local environment. Among non-governmental organizations, conservation societies and wildlife trusts have been established to take care of some aspect of the environment. They are active in their own area of expertise.

Other NGOs, like research centres and consultants also have a pragmatic approach. They take assignments from companies to solve or decrease a specified environmental problem. Their views may affect the company management, or may not. Their main goal is to get the job done and to be paid for it. Those research centres and consultants which are specialized in environmental issues, usually have similar or slightly more progressive environmental values and views than their clients. In the latter case, they often try to change their clients' values and views by showing them that it is (financially) worthwhile to do so.

Most universities are still practising their research according to the old principle of 'objectivity'. In reality, it is not possible to do objective research. The values are there, either hidden or openly expressed. Scientists seem to be the most conservative interest group of all. There seems to be no room for vocal environmentalists at universities. An academic with a visionary approach is labelled as a science fiction writer. As academic institutions are dependent on industry as financiers, the researchers adopt, either implicitly or explicitly, the values of the company they work for.

A philosopher, Niiniluoto, differentiates between technology scientists and management scientists (see Nykänen 1991). In his view, engineers are pragmatists: their research consists merely of finding means to reach the externally given goals. They are value-blind, unwilling to take a stand. Everything is reduced to what is most efficient. Their value-blindness has left technology unconnected to society. Management scientists, on the other hand, change their values like they change shirts. They follow the fashion, and, therefore, their advice cannot be taken seriously.

Students of these scientists are forced into the same mould. Their PhD theses are neat and tidy technical exercises with no vision or value basis. These little drills are then examined behind closed doors. This kind of research is far from, for example, Martin Luther's research theses which he nailed on Wittenberg's Castle Church door in 1517, and fiercely defended in a public debate. He – or his followers – could not prove his hypotheses true, nor could his opponents prove them false. Even reliable supporting or contradictory evidence has been hard to find. And yet Luther has had a profound impact on the development of the Western civilization. He had values. He had a vision. He was a true researcher. In our time, many students have realized that if they want to influence the future of our society they should leave university and work for an environmental group. These are the children of the 60s' and 70s' university radicals!

All in all, the environmental pressures exerted by socio-cultural interest groups on companies have one thing in common: they depend on the human and citizen rights practised by the country. In countries which give these rights, it is mostly the vocal middle class among local inhabitants and the public which puts some environmental pressure on companies. This pressure is seldom strong. However, the middle class within research organizations often keeps quiet to secure its earnings. In countries which do not give human and citizen rights, the public, local people and NGOs suffer from the ill-effects of the company operations in silence. If they try to protest, they may lose their freedom and lives.

Technological Factors

Technology is sold to companies by a group of suppliers but techno-logical factors refer to a wider interest. In the absence of direct interest groups, the rate of technological change could represent the techno-logical factors. In this way, technocracy is seen as a stakeholder group in the business environment. The rate of technological change can range from very slow to very fast.

In general, environmental shocks get more publicity than environ-mental stresses. Therefore, new mitigation measures for the shocks are developed more rapidly than for stresses. Publicity also affects the choice of mitigation method. Company management is often torn between taking, in their opinion, the environmentally sound, cost-effective option and the one perceived by the public to be the best. On the other hand, companies do not always know themselves which options are sound. Many operations that they believe to be environmentally benign can be demonstrated with life-cycle analyses to be disastrous.

In reality, the overall adverse impact of environmental stresses is far greater than that of the shocks. Roughly half of shocks and stresses can be prevented with such modern mitigation methods that are generally utilized by the developed world companies. Nearly all stresses and most of the shocks could be prevented if technologically possible, more expensive mitigating methods were used. Only very few companies want to utilize them because there is no guarantee that they will get their money back even in the long run.

Finally, there are some shocks and stresses that cannot be prevented. As for stresses, carelessness, negligence and ignorance constitute a human factor which turns even the most sophisticated environmental technologies into monsters belching out pollution. Errors are a primary reason for shocks, backed up with the above mentioned human factors. Education and training are cheap ways to prevent shocks and stresses caused by these reasons. Still, some are left, and, with the powers of nature, they are a serious potential problem, particularly in the 'shocks department'.

At their best, reactive methods can mitigate the damage done by an environmental shock, at their worst, they can exacerbate it. For both shocks and stresses, reactive mitigating methods are mostly inefficient, and thus a poor compensation for preventive methods.

The developed world can – if it wants to – overcome environmental shocks and stresses with money but the developing world cannot afford this because its money is spent on the everyday struggle for life. Furthermore, neither the latest know-how nor the modern environ-mental technology is available for the developing world companies. Therefore, it is not possible for those nations in the developing world, who have some environmental legislation, to enforce it effectively. Additionally, their authorities do not have expertise or monitoring equipment for enforcement.

Multinational companies have a potentially important role in know-how and technology transfer from the developed to the developing countries. They transfer technology, to some extent, within their own organizations. Therefore, their subsidiaries have a much better environmental record than indigenous companies. They could, however, expand this role considerably both internally and externally. Compliance with legislation seems to be the basic criterion for decisions they take. In many developing countries, there is little legislation and it is poorly enforced. This gives a large margin for technology decisions made for subsidiaries in these countries. This margin is taken advantage of because of the financial considerations ranking first if legislation does not put any pressure on decisions. This has lead to a grey area: developed world companies in the developing world know that whatever technologies they adopt, their environmental behaviour is inherently better than that of the domestic companies.

Porter and van der Linde (1995) claim that tough environmental standards trigger innovation in the area of environmental technology. Japan and Germany are good examples of rapidly developing technological solutions. However, even money, know-how, modern technology and enforced legislation do not prevent accidents or pollution altogether. Environmental shocks cannot be avoided because of the 'human factor'. Companies can only hope that the occurrence of shocks will follow the rule 'few and far between' – which it has not so far. Environmental stresses would be technologically almost avoidable if the operations were based on closed systems with recycling, but economic factors prevent these solutions from being implemented.

In conclusion, the rate of change of environmental technology depends, first of all, on the environmental problems perceived by the company management on the one hand, and by the external interest groups on the other. This leads to priorities which depend on the consequences to the company on the stock market. Those problems that are ranked high become institutionalized: either regulations are passed by the legislators or market-based mechanisms are created by the governments. Thus the pressure is the other way around: political and economic factors put pressure on companies which must then put pressure on technological interest groups to develop better technologies.

Environmental technology development focuses on providing methods for companies to comply with the legislation or deal with market-based instruments like taxes. This has led to the polarization of technology development. Environmental technologies to combat those shocks that threaten human life (fires, explosions, discharges of dangerous chemicals) take the first priority, and develop rather rapidly. Technologies to combat sulphur dioxide, nitrogen oxides and particulate emissions which have been proved damaging to the health of humans, other animals, plants and the ecosystem as a whole, have been on the agenda for decades and develop steadily. The heated debate about the greenhouse effect has begun technological innovation against carbon dioxide emissions. Most environmental problems, however, remain at the background. Technologies for them develop slowly because there are small markets for such innovations and little profit to make.

Altogether: PEST-Factors

The strengths of environmental pressure from the PEST interest groups of the business environment experienced by a company can be discovered through interviews. In a self-analysis, a company can bring together a group of managers and other personnel to discuss the environmental pressures, and thus achieve a rather accurate result through a debate. These results can be placed, e.g. on Ansoff's and McDonnell's (1990) levels of turbulence – repetitive, expanding, changing, discontinuous and surprising – to illustrate the type of the business environment in which a company operates.

Repetitive environmental pressure is familiar, recurring and slower than the company's response. It is usually local and, at the most, national, and gives priority to economic considerations. Expanding environmental pressure differs from repetitive pressure by being extrapolable rather than familiar and forecastable rather than recurring. It is expanding from national to regional concerns, and balances economic and technological considerations. Changing environmental pressure covers regional concerns, like those of Europe, and emphasizes technological considerations over economic ones. At this level, pressure is still extrapolable but predictable rather than forecastable and comparable to the company's response.

Discontinuous environmental pressure is adding some global concerns to regional ones and some socio-political considerations to technological ones. At this level, environmental pressure is discontinuous but still familiar and partially predictable. Surprising environmental pressure is discontinuous and novel, unpredictable with surprises, and faster than the company's response. It covers all kinds of concerns – national, regional and global – with emphasis on the global concerns, and pays special attention to socio-political considerations.

There is no direct connection between the strength of environmental pressure from a PEST interest groups and the level of business environment. Thus it cannot be said that if environmental pressure is very weak, the level of business environment is necessarily repetitive, or that if environmental pressure is very strong, the level of business environment is always surprising. However, there are some tentative correlations between the strength of pressure and the level of business environment – but the reality is much more complex than that. The meanings of the strengths of environmental pressures companies experience have more complicated interpretations. For these interpretations, the characteristics of different levels of business environments need to be considered. Therefore, the strength of environmental pressure needs to be compared to the complexity of that environmental pressure, its familiarity to the companies, the rapidity of change of that pressure and its visibility of future. In this way, some cautious conclusions can be drawn on the level of business environment in which a company operates. The level of these external pressures can then be compared with the company's level of the internal strategic management potential.

ANALYSING THE STRATEGIC MANAGEMENT POTENTIAL

Environmental Policy

We can draw two triangles of company operations, one for environmental policy (see Figure 5.7) and one for general strategic management (see Figure 5.8). The level of an environmental policy in Figure 5.7 shows the level of the strategic environmental management of a company. The arrows show whether the environmental policy increases or decreases the area of possible company operations. A very low level of environmental policy means that the policy allows a large area of operations, irrespective of whether they stay within the ecological limits or not. Such an environmental policy has probably been drafted only to comply with an environmental management system (EMS) standard or as a shallow public relations exercise. In this case, the existence of an environmental policy is important to the company but not its content as long as it does not make the company liable for anything.

A low level of environmental policy reacts on the environmental pressures from the business environment but still facilitates extensive operations. Such a policy often promises to comply with environmental legislation but does not go any further than that.

A moderate level of environmental policy illustrates some concern for environmental issues by the company itself. For this reason, the threshold to increase or decrease the area of company operations is rather high. The management considers carefully case by case whether new

Figure 5.7 The Level of the Environmental Policy of a Company

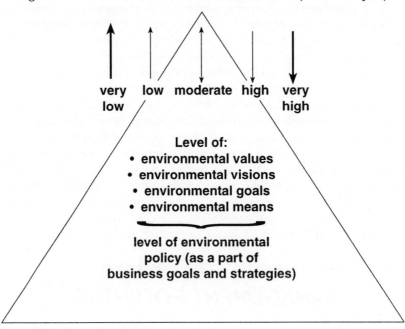

III ENVIRONMENTAL POLICY

projects can be started and what their impact on the environment would be. The managers also look into the environmental effects of the present operations but are reluctant to make great changes to them even when they have clear adverse effects on the environment. They want to exceed the requirements of environmental legislation so that there is a buffer zone between the requirements and the actual operations. This is often carefully expressed in the environmental policy statement.

A high level of environmental policy shows real concern for the environmental effects of the company. The management finds both environmental and economic goals important and tries to integrate them so that both could be achieved. The goals of the environmental policy usually include a commitment to go well beyond the mere compliance with environmental legislation. The company aims at being among the environmental leaders in its industry.

At a very high level, the company is very concerned about the environmental effects of its operations. The management prefer environmental goals to short-term economic goals. The company aims at being the environmental leader in its industry and states this clearly in its environmental policy. Its environmental performance is expected to be so far above the legal requirements that environmental legislation is not considered a reference point for future plans. Instead, the management searches for novel solutions to the company's remaining environmental problems.

The resulting environmental performance of a company depends on the level of the environmental policy, and on the extent to which and way in which the policy is implemented.

I have divided the topic of environmental policy into four parts (see Figure 5.7) although the first two – environmental values and visions – are not exactly parts of environmental policy statements. Instead they influence the development of these statements. Environmental goals and means, on the other hand, are written in the environmental policy statements. I will introduce each of these four parts below.

Firstly, the environmental values of a company will be under scrutiny. It is nowadays common for companies to support the idea of sustainable development. However, they have different views about the meaning of the concept. While most companies accept the definition of sustainable development expressed in the report *Our Common Future* (Brundtland 1987), it can be interpreted in many different ways (see Welford 1995). Each company approaches sustainable development from its own value basis. Therefore, the environmental values of a company can be reduced to a certain form of sustainable development.

Companies and people do not usually jump from one extreme to another in their environmental values but change their position gradually along the continuum of the forms of sustainable development. Therefore, instead of a polarized distinction between technocentric (or anthropocentric) and ecocentric sustainable development, a flowing classification with several alternatives is needed.

Colby (1990) distinguishes five categories along the line of anthropo-, eco- and biocentric sustainable development. His classification, which was originally meant for analyses on a national level but can also be used on a company level, seems useful for the purposes of this research – after one conceptual change. Colby's concept 'anthropocentric' is replaced here by 'technocentric'. Colby divides the technocentric paradigm into three categories: very strong, strong and modified. Thus he establishes a scale for sustainable development: very strong technocentric → strong technocentric → modified technocentric → ecocentric → biocentric. Very strong technocentrism (or frontier economics) believes that progress is achieved through infinite economic growth and prosperity. Strong technocentrism (or environmental protection) believes in trade-offs between ecology and economic growth. Modified technocentrism (or resource management) sees sustainability as a necessary constraint for green growth. Ecocentrism (or eco-development) believes in co-developing humans and nature. Biocentrism (deep ecology) believes in anti-growth constrained harmony with nature. It is possible to identify which kind of sustainable development a company (or its management) supports and locate it at a certain level of environmental values. A company which intends to survive in the long term, needs to have at least ecocentric – if not biocentric – values.

We can look at the environmental visions of companies in the same way as values. However, the difference is that visions are not as universal as values but are industry- and company-specific. Therefore, it depends on the individual company and its line of business what kinds of environmental visions it can have. Here I will show an example of environmental visions suitable for energy companies.

Energy experts have expressed many views of the future. Their views can be summarized into five different visions: oil age, oil and gas age, traditional mix, progressive mix and renewables age. In the first vision, the oil age continues with oil conquering even more market share. Natural gas increases its share, too. Coal, and, perhaps, nuclear power, are also important energy forms. In the second vision, oil and natural gas dominate with coal, and perhaps nuclear power, also being signifi-cant. This vision is called the oil and gas age. Although the most important energy forms in the third vision are still oil and gas with coal – and, maybe complemented by nuclear power – some renewables are also utilized. However, their share is small. In addition, some energy-efficiency measures will have been adopted. This is the traditional mix vision.

In the fourth vision, renewables are gradually replacing oil, gas, coal and, perhaps, nuclear power. Energy-efficiency measures are in effective use. This can be called the progressive mix vision. The fifth vision sees the renewables as the only energy form by 2030. Most of the energy required earlier can now be saved through very high energy efficiency. The name of this vision is, of course, the renewables age. The envir-onmental visions of an energy company can be located at these levels. An energy company wishing to extend its life-cycle well into the next century, needs to develop at least progressive mix – if not renewables age – visions. Similar classifications can be developed for any line of business.

The environmental goals of a company are based on their environ-mental values and visions. These goals are usually expressed in their environmental policy statements. The types of goals a company develops for itself vary. Ansoff's and McDonnell's (1990) levels of strategic aggressiveness – stable, reactive, anticipatory, entrepreneurial and creative – illustrate the different kinds of goals a company can have.

Stable goals are based on what has happened before in similar situations. The same things are expected to happen again exactly in the same way. For reactive goals, earlier experience is used as the basis of strategic decisions but something more is added to them. Anticipatory goals are based on extrapolation: elements of earlier experience can be utilized to forecast what will happen and proactive action can be taken to minimize the negative effects and maximize the positive effects. For entrepreneurial goals, earlier experience is not considered valid to give guidance for strategic decisions even through extrapolation. Instead, expected futures – like scenarios – are utilized as the basis for them. This means that the goals do not form a continuum but remain discontinuous. Creative goals are even more discontinuous. They have no external starting-point but arise from the managers' inner creativity. The environmental goals of a company can be divided into these five categories. Companies with a survival instinct have already realized that only entrepreneurial and creative environmental policy goals will allow them to prosper in the future.

The means (strategies) to reach the environmental goals can be categorized as well. Porter (1980) sees the means to achieve strategic goals as competitive moves. He makes a distinction between defensive, cooperative and threatening moves. Defensive moves try to prevent the battle, or at least to force the competitor to back down after a battle. Cooperative moves aim at avoiding the risk of warfare and making the industry as a whole better off. Threatening moves seek to improve the company's relative position but usually produce an immediate counter-threatening reaction from the competitors. As companies often use a mixture of competitive moves, this three-level classification can be stretched to five levels: defensive, defensive + cooperative, cooperative, cooperative + threatening and threatening moves. It is possible to divide the means with which a company attempts to achieve its environmental goals into these categories. Although cooperation is often desirable to combat environmental problems common to many companies, threatening moves are essential to implement the entrepreneurial and creative environmental policy goals of a company and also to push the competitors to improve their environmental performance.

Combining the results of the four parts of the environmental policy will show at which level the environmental policy of a company lies. This level can then be compared with the level of the general strategic management potential of the company to see if there is enough capability within the company to implement the environmental policy.

General Strategic Management

The level of general strategic management needs to match the level of environmental policy, so that it is possible to implement the policy in the company. The level of general strategic management, illustrated in Figure 5.8, consists of the level of integration and coordination between the environmental policy and the organizational culture and structure, business goals and strategies, human and financial resources as well as of the level of the company's environmental technology.

The arrows in Figure 5.8 show whether general strategic management increases or decreases the areas of possible company operations. Very low and low levels of integration and coordination between the environmental policy and general strategic management mean that general strategic management allows company operations to exceed ecological limits even if the environmental policy would not allow this. Moderate levels of integration show that environmental issues are taken into account to some extent in the strategic management of company operations. High and very high levels of integration illustrate similar or the same amount of concern for the environment in the general strategic management of company operations as the environmental policy expresses.

The business goals and strategies of a company can be compared to the environmental policy goals and means (strategies) to assess the level of coordination and integration between them. It would be advantageous

Figure 5.8 The Level of the General Strategic Management of a Company

IV GENERAL STRATEGIC MANAGEMENT

for a company if environmental goals and strategies and business goals and strategies were integrated, so that business goals and strategies would include the main environmental goals and strategies and environmental goals and strategies would include the main business goals and strategies. It would also be beneficial for a company if environmental and business goals and strategies were coordinated, so that environmental goals and strategies would advance business goals and strategies, and vice versa. For comparison, the business goals and strategies of a company need to be listed next to its environmental goals and strategies. The level of integration and coordination can range from very low to very high. Similar comparisons can be made about the environmental policy in relation to the organizational culture and structure, human and financial resources and the state of the physical facilities of a company.

All this boils down to the degree of environmental change the general strategic management of a company allows. Ansoff and McDonnell (1990) talk about the responsiveness of capability. One of their indicators showing this responsiveness is the type of a company's response to change: it may suppress change, adapt to change, seek familiar change, seek related change or seek novel change. In this chapter, I adopt these general levels of response to environmental change. Hence we can study how a company's response to environmental change shows itself in its business goals and strategies, organizational culture and structure, human and financial resources and physical facilities.

COMBINING THE ANALYSES: TOWARDS ECOLOGICAL ELDORADO

We can integrate the analyses of the ecosystem, business environment, environmental policy and general strategic management into Figure 5.9. It shows the levels of these different factors which represent the circle of the ecosystem, the square of the business environment and the triangle of company operations.

In part A of the model of Figure 5.9, the levels of the factors are evaluated, in part B, they are collected together for a comparison, and in part C, the matches and non-matches between the levels are discussed.

Once the levels of ecosystem, business environment, environmental policy and general strategic management have been evaluated in part A of Figure 5.9, the results can be collected together in a table in part B (for a more detailed analysis, see Ketola 1996). There are many combinations possible between these four factors, and even more within the environmental policy factor. However, the starting point is that, if a company wants its operations to stay within the ecological limits, its

Figure 5.9 The Ecological Positioning of a Company

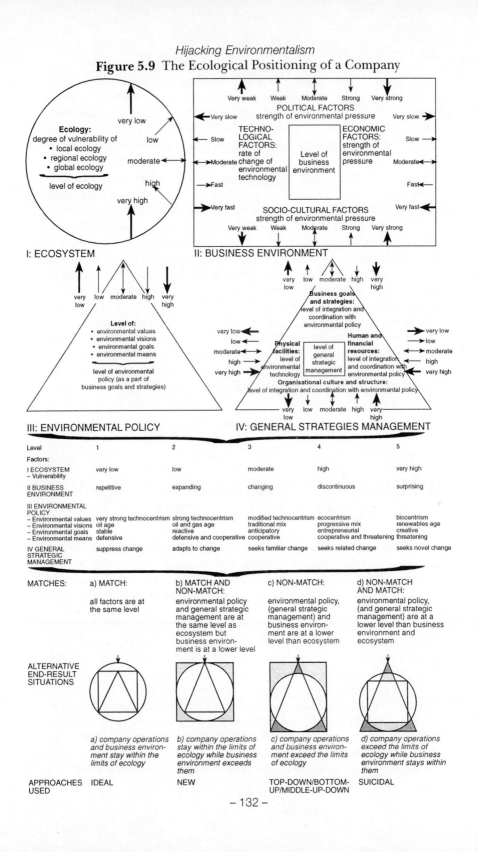

environmental policy and general strategic management need to be at the same or at a higher level than the level of the ecosystem. This is a necessary, but not a sufficient, prerequisite of staying within the ecological limits. The success of the implementation of the environmental policy determines the sufficiency. In an ideal situation (a), shown in part C of the model, all factors are at the same level (or, theoretically, the ecosystem may be at a lower level than the other factors). This is a match which means that the company operations and the business environment can stay within the limits of ecology.

If the company's environmental policy and general strategic management are at least at the same level as the ecosystem even if the level of the business environment is lower, company operations can again stay within the limits of ecology although the business environment exceeds them. In situations (a) and (b), it is important that within the company, general strategic management is at least at the same level as the environmental policy to allow the implementation of the policy.

In many cases, the levels of the business environment and environmental policy are lower than the level of the ecosystem. In this situation (c), company operations and the business environment exceed the ecological limits. It does not matter what the level of the company's general strategic management is, because there is no environmental policy advanced enough to stay within the ecological limits to be implemented. Naturally, in the long term, it helps if the level of general strategic management is the same as the level of ecology: the company only needs to develop its environmental policy, and not both the policy and the general capabilities. Situation (c) is a typical end-result of the traditional top-down, bottom-up and middle-up-down approaches to environmental change.

Theoretically, it is possible that the business environment is at the same level as the ecosystem but the environmental policy and (possibly) general strategic management of a company are at a lower level. However, this situation (d) could not last. It would be a suicidal situation for a company because the business environment would not allow any company to exceed its limits for long. A company would be forced to comply with the limits of the business environment, or to close down. These four different situations (a)–(d) are the main alternative end-results of the strategic environmental analysis carried out in the model of ecological positioning of Figure 5.9.

If a company analyses its position in the way the model suggests, it can choose its preferred future position and use the most suitable approach to achieve it. With the assistance of the model, a company can draft, maintain and utilize its environmental policy to attain the preferred position. The model is useful for a company's self-analysis at any time, and can be repeated regularly to recognize the changes. The model is particularly useful when a major environmental change needs to be carried out in a company. It is a planning tool for a change: it identifies the present position, gives direction to the change, evaluates progress during the change process and gives feedback on the success of the change. In large companies with corporate, divisional and operating unit levels, this tool needs to be used at each working level. The goals, progress and success of change at different working levels can be compared to each other to allow coordination, so that the best possible results from the change are achieved.

CONCLUSIONS

In this chapter, I have studied the strategic environmental management of companies through a systems approach. A company is a subsystem of its business environment which, in turn, is a subsystem of the ecosystem. Thus the operations of a company should remain within the limits of its business environment and the ecosystem. It would be suicidal for a company to exceed the limits set by its business environment. The fact that companies exceed the limits of the ecosystem means that these limits are exceeded also by their business environments.

There are two ways of making a company's operations stay within the limits of the ecosystem: either the external interest groups decide to decrease the limits of their business environment so that they stay within the ecological boundaries and then enforce these limits upon companies; or a company takes initiative to manage its operations in a sustainable way regardless of its business environment's excess over ecological limits.

As the cases of Shell and Texaco showed, the political, economic, socio-cultural and technological factors (PEST-factors) of the business environment exert such weak environmental pressures on companies as yet that they cannot be relied on to make a change fast enough. The companies' own initiative depends on their strategic management and its implementation which, for example, at Shell and Texaco would offer possibilities for a fast change if the values of these companies were upgraded and their organizational barriers were removed.

However, Shell, Texaco and other companies do not have much interest in making radical environmental changes. Such changes are considered to cost a great deal and bring hardly any additional income or competitive advantage to the companies involved. Yet the miserable state of the ecosystem we live in will necessarily lead to radical environmental changes in our society if we intend to survive. It will take some time before the consequences of the destruction of the life-support systems of this planet are understood by all of us. But once the message gets through there will be an outcry and all influential interest groups will take action against anyone who exceeds the ecological limits in order to save our ecosystem.

This is the reason why companies should now start weighing their short-term profits and growth coming from the exploitation of the ecosystem against their long-term survival and stability in the future world. If they begin to plan and implement environmental changes now and constantly upgrade their attempts, they will probably still have time to adjust to the coming change. Otherwise their days are numbered. They will either be forced to bankruptcy by their business environment which will demand the full costing of companies' ecological impacts in the new world of Ecological Eldorado – or they will perish with humans and other species when the ecosystem collapses. Just like us individuals, companies and their business environment interest groups are responsible for the survival of the humankind and other species on Earth. An Ecological Desperado would ruin the prospects for an Ecological Eldorado and kill us all.

References

Ansoff, H I and McDonnell, E (1990) *Implanting Strategic Management,* Second Edition, Prentice-Hall, London

Brundtland, G H (1987) *Our Common Future,* Report of the World Conference on the Environment and Development, Oxford UP, Oxford

Colby, M E (1990) Environmental Management and Development, The Evolution of Paradigms, *World Bank Discussion Papers,* no 80

Habermas, J (1989) *The Structural Transformation of the Public Sphere, An Inquiry into a Category of Bourgeois Society,* Polity Press, London

Ketola, T (1995) *A Map of Neverland: The Role of Policy in Strategic Environmental Management,* PhD thesis, Imperial College, London

Ketola, T (1996) Where is Our Common Future? – Directions: 'Second to the Right and Straight on till Morning', *Sustainable Development,* vol 4, no 2, August, pp 84–97

Nykänen, P (1991) Markkinausko yhdistää ja jakaa Eurooppaa, *Tekniikka & Talous,* 4.2.1991

Peltu, M (1985) The Role of Communications Media. In H Otway and M Peltu (eds) *Regulating Industrial Risks. Science, Hazards and Public Protection,* pp 128–48, Butterworths, London

Piesse, J (1992) Environmental Spending and Share Price Performance: The Petroleum Industry, *Business Strategy and the Environment,* vol 1, part 1, Spring, pp 45–54

Porter, M E (1980) *Competitive Strategy, Techniques for Analyzing Industries and Competitors,* Free Press, New York

Porter, M E and van der Linde, C (1995) Green and Competitive: Ending the Stalemate, *Harvard Business Review,* September–October, pp 120–34

Prescott-Allen, R (1991) Classification of Ecosystem Conditions, In IUCN, UNEP and WWF *Caring for the Earth, A Strategy for Sustainable Living*, p 34. Gland, Switzerland

Welford, R (1995) *Environmental Strategy and Sustainable Development, The Corporate Challenge for the 21st Century*, Routledge, London

Welford, R (1996) His comment on A Clegg's paper 'Sustainable Manufacture: Current Practice and Future Needs' at *The 1996 International Sustainable Development Research Conference*, 18–19 March, Manchester

6

The Big Brothers: Transnational Corporations, Trade Organizations and Multilateral Financial Institutions

Eloy Casagrande Junior and *Richard Welford*

The rhetoric of eco-modernism sees free international trade as important in spreading technological advances leading, in turn, to environmental improvement. There seems to be a common assumption that free trade is necessary and good, associated with a dominant discourse about competitive advantage, internationalization, globalization and growth of world markets. Of course, there is no such thing as completely free trade since tariffs, taxes and import controls do exist. Moreover, large firms have increasing amounts of oligopoly power allowing them to restrict trade when it suits their interests. Overall however, it is clear that the trend is and has been towards liberalization and deregulation in a world where the dominant transnational players are often companies rather than countries. This chapter seeks to explore those issues and questions whether such broad assumptions relating to the benefits of free trade are actually consistent with a move towards sustainable development.

Environmental problems are becoming increasingly international as pollution and ecosystem degradation cross national boundaries and when the cause of environmental effects of consumption or production are felt in other parts of the world than where a particular activity takes place. The process of international trade increases these cross border impacts and can itself have a negative (or indeed a positive) impact on the environment and related issues. We can categorize these effects in six main ways:

- Trade creates a dependency on the ecosystems of foreign countries as goods consumed in one place are either manufactured in another or where resources are derived from another.
- The consumption of goods imported from a country will also have an environmental impact in the country in which they are consumed (e.g. through the use of energy or the creation of a waste).
- Trade itself has a direct impact on the environment, mainly through impacts associated with transportation.
- Trade can transfer technology and employment from one location to another having a social and environmental impact on host and home country.
- Trade and economic globalization has greatly expanded the opportunities for the rich to pass on their environmental burdens to the poor by exporting both waste and polluting factories.
- Trade has a secondary impact on issues of equity as it results in impacts (positive or negative) on poverty, health, employment, human rights, democracy, labour laws and self-determination.

Within this general framework, we must, however, recognize that the global system is marked by a very great asymmetry. The most important economic, political and cultural-ideological goods that circulate around the globe tend to be owned and/or controlled by small groups in a relatively small number of countries (Sklair 1991). Whilst it is unquestionable that consumption is at the root of much environmental stress, we must remember that rich people consume far more than do poor people. We therefore begin with a situation which is inequitable and must consider whether the process of trade and the power of the transnational elites increases or decreases the problems associated with moving to a more sustainable future.

Within the eco-modernist rhetoric we find the claim that an open trading system is crucial in order to facilitate the transfer of technology which is environmentally beneficial. In part, the claim is that trade is necessary to make up for the economic, environmental and social deficits of those who have too little (the poor in the developing countries). According to Korten (1995) it often works the other way around, whereby the poor are further exploited and the environmental deficits of those who are already poor are increased whilst the rich benefit from transferring the polluting activities.

Underlying the process of trade and the power of the transnational corporation lies the root of the problem: consumption and its associated production. Insufficient information about the environmental impacts of these activities, a lack of property rights leading to an undervaluation of the natural environment and resources, a rich, uncaring population in the developed world, and a short-termist, profit-maximizing ethic amongst businesses result in an incomplete framework for our economic interactions. Connecting these problems to a free trade rhetoric makes the problem even more acute as the transfer of goods, services, environmental degradation and social problems becomes tied up with issues such as the power of the rich to determine the lives of the poor.

THE DOMINANCE OF THE TRANSNATIONAL CORPORATION

Our starting point is to consider whether the transnational corporations which are often regarded as forces for change with regard to environmental management are actually serious about delivering sustainability through eco-efficiency. In particular, it has been argued that the diffusion of technology through some transnational corporations (TNCs) can be a positive aspect for countries to enhance efficiency and growth (UNTCMD 1992), but it can also create socio-economic imbalances and inequalities. Moreover, the existence of large transnational organizations means that trade is not free at all but controlled by powerful undemocratic institutions. In particular, the existence of TNCs, strong oligopolies in certain world markets, creating unequal access to technology, and often creating competition between different countries trying to attract inward investment, contradicts the basic assumptions of *free* trade. One of the main concerns is that the developing countries enter global markets, which are neither free nor efficient, as unequal partners, with very limited negotiating power (UNDP 1992). It is therefore likely that the combined power of TNCs and international trade organizations can bring more damage than benefits to the health of this planet and its inhabitants. In the 27 principles agreed at the 1992 United Nations Conference on Environment and Development (UNCED or the Rio-Summit), in Brazil, as many as 10 principles could be related to major concerns regarding free trade and TNCs' policies with regard to their impacts on development and environmental protection.

TNCs benefit from having governments in their countries of domicile which see them as insiders within the national market, and their rivals as outsiders. Politicians are often seen to be willing to support and even countenance the activities of such TNCs. In reality however, TNCs are powerful cross border commercial organizations engaged in intense competition, designed to enhance their profitability and market share at the expense of their rivals. They are in control of more than 70 per cent of total international trade, helped by the European Union (EU), the Organization for Economic Co-operation and Development (OECD), the Group of Seven industrialized nations (G7) and trade organizations such as World Trade Organization (WTO), the North American Free Trade Agreement (NAFTA) and similar agreements in Asia and South America. In addition, there are international financial organizations such as the International Monetary Fund (IMF) and the World Bank which promote the globalization of the economy through their economic development programmes. They are the pillars of the so-called 'new economic order'. Interactions between industrial activities, economic growth and international trade is as old as trade itself and they have promoted the growth in material living standards throughout the world. Indications that these interactions are contributing to ecological degradation, social inequality and the deterioration of human health has become increasingly apparent.

According to the United Nations Conference on Trade and Development there are now about 37,000 TNCs, compared with 7000 in 1970 (UNCTAD 1993), and they retain more than 200,000 subsidiary companies world-wide. The world's largest 500 corporations accounted for around one-third of global production, and they control most of the world trade in tea, coffee, cocoa, cotton, forest products, tobacco, jute, copper, iron ore and bauxite (*The Ecologist* 1990). Only 20 transnational corporations control most of the world's agricultural trade. They are not interested in relieving hunger, only increasing their profits. They do this by ensuring that more and more goods are traded across countries.

From 1950, when the process of trade liberalization, through the early General Agreement on Tariffs and Trade (GATT), got under way, to about 1994, the volume of world merchandise trade increased at an annual rate of slightly more than 6 per cent and world output by close to 4 per cent. Thus, during those 45 years world merchandise trade multiplied 14 times and its output 5.5 times. However, the excess of trade growth over output growth varied: from an average of a half percentage point, in the period 1974–84 to nearly 3.5 percentage points in the most recent 10 years (WTO 1995).

Since the beginning of the 1980s, TNCs have benefited from the increase in global trade liberalization and capital flows. Their global domination is supported by economic models dictated by multilateral financial institutions and free trade associations. These are often consistent with free market monetarism practised by most developed countries and consistent with the types of austerity measures imposed on developing countries by the international financial institutions. These policies are all aimed at deregulating markets and increasing inter-national trade whilst implicitly ensuring a pool of cheap labour in order to keep production costs as low as possible.

Meanwhile, the very act of trade becomes a major contributor to environmental degradation. Without transportation, trade cannot take place, but transportation involving trade contributes significantly to energy-related pollution. As international trade has increased so the environmental degradation caused by transportation has increased several fold. For example, international truck transportation within the EU will increase substantially simply as a result of the development of the Single Market and deregulation within the transport sector. Truck transportation is expected to increase seven fold in North America during the next decade as a result of the North American Free Trade Agreement (NAFTA).

One of the major problems with transportation is that the means of transportation are largely derived from fossil fuels, resulting in air and water pollution. Air and sea transportation of people and goods is responsible for one-eighth of world oil consumption (Madeley 1992). One must add to this the even greater consumption of oil involved in road and rail transportation of imports and exports and the millions of miles driven in company cars to secure those important contracts in the first place. Thus international trade is responsible for the emissions of a large and increasing proportion of carbon dioxide, nitrogen oxides, sulphur dioxide and hydrocarbons into the atmosphere.

If the total costs of all environmental effects of fossil fuel use were reflected in the price of oil, it would be much higher and transportation would be much more expensive. Thus given the internalization of the true costs of international trade, production and consumption patterns would be very different. It would favour local production and consump-tion and where trade was still necessary there would be an incentive to find more environmentally efficient modes of transportation. Today, however, transportation costs are low and the environment is subsidising the consumption of internationally traded goods. When in Europe, we eat bananas from Central America and drink wine from Australia we pay only a fraction of the true cost involved in that consumption.

Meanwhile, international trade continues to grow. In 1992, the total sales of transnational corporations reached US$ 5.5 trillions, more than Japan's gross national product (GNP) and almost that of the United States (UNCTAD, 1993). In 1995, the top ten TNCs' sales were about US$910 billion, over five times greater than the GNPs of sub-Saharan Africa (excluding South Africa). The profits of the top twenty five TNCs amounted to around US$83 billion (*Business Week* 1996). According to the WTO, where GATT is now accommodated, it is government policies which can speed up, slow down or even reverse progress on commercial global integration. However, governments are often under pressures from TNCs and trade organizations to lift trade barriers. Corporate money to help political candidates get elected, the creation of employment, and much needed corporation tax contributions, make TNCs powerful players in the global economy. This has led directly to a whole range of social and environmental crises as money and economics comes to dominate social and ecological considerations.

By way of an example, one of the first harmful consequences of free trade was felt both in the countryside and urban areas of developing countries. The Brazilian slums (known as favelas), would not exist if a technological revolution had not been applied to agriculture in Brazil and removed millions of people from the land. The result was a great concentration of property ownership at national and regional levels. Forty four per cent of the farmland is held by 1 per cent of an elite of landlords. The lack of an agrarian reform creates violence between big landlords and poor farmers. It is the landlords' elite who have access to government subsidies and credits to produce export-oriented products. Meanwhile, poor farmers are invading non cultivated private land to plant their crops in order to feed their families. Policies such as this not only lead to social inequality and economic instability but also can damage the domestic market and consumer choice. In 1995, Brazil's coffee production was cut in half due to the effects of frost and drought. The consequence is that Brazil, for the first time in more than three hundred years, now imports Mexican and Guatemalan coffee to meet domestic demand, because its own crop is entirely contracted for export.

In poorer areas of the world, integration into the global economy may provide more foreign exchange to service accumulated debt, but it often has grave implications for local populations and the environment. The most fertile land is given over to export crops, while desertification and famine attack subsistence farmers. Soil erosion increases with the over exploitation of the land, deforestation rises and, river and underground water are contaminated by intense use of pesticides and chemical waste discharge.

BORN IN THE USA

TNCs from the USA, Western Europe and Japan are in control of the global market. However, the USA corporations were the first to conquer markets abroad. The history of the TNCs is directly associated with the history of Foreign Direct Investment (FDI). The flow of USA funds into Europe and Japan after the Second World War was the driving force enabling USA corporations to penetrate foreign markets. This process was assisted by the establishment of globalized Fordist production methods and technologies. Today, USA TNCs (producing any kind of product) buy labour in the low-wage markets and sell their (low-cost) products in the remaining high-wage, high-income, high-price markets. They have now incorporated new practices learned from global competition and some Japanese management practices and called it post-Fordism. However, USA TNCs still follow an old strategy. They continue to stress economies of scale, they continue to seek the lowest price for quality suppliers wherever in the world they happen to be, and they continue to locate final assembly plants close to customers and parts manufacturing in outlying, lower-cost sites (McGrath and Hoole 1992).

Examples of the socio-environmental consequences of these policies on developing countries can be found as near as Mexico, or as far away as Asia. Many environmentalists are concerned that agreements made under the NAFTA, for example, weaken environmental legislation or make environmental laws unenforceable, especially, in Mexican territory. At the beginning of the 1990s, according to a document endorsed by eighteen USA environmental organizations, over two-thirds of the export-only factories (Maquiladoras) had failed to return their hazardous waste from Mexico to the USA for proper treatment as is legally required. On the social consequences, we have seen the new global market result in the loss of workers' power and resulting lower wages. The USA TNCs, as well their European counterparts, have slowly destroyed the power of labour unions, often with the help of Conservative administrations. Temporary work, reduced benefits, cutbacks in training and job insecurity are products of the industrialized countries. Meanwhile, in their own domestic markets there is a consequent social crisis growing through increasing levels of long term unemployment. Increasing numbers of (particularly young) people are disenfranchised by society, forced to live on social benefits and often become homeless. In many big cities there is a violent revolution waiting to happen.

One may assume that the transfer of employment from the developed to the developing countries may nevertheless have some benefits for the latter. But low wage markets make little contribution to the eradication of poverty in developing and the least developed countries. Nike, the American sportswear maker, refers to itself as a 'network firm'. It keeps all its product development and marketing in Beaverton, Oregon, its home town, but subcontracts production to independent firms in 40 different locations employing some 75,000 workers, mostly in Indonesia. A pair of Nike training shoes sells for up to $150 in the USA or £100 in the UK. In 1996 they are produced for around $6 (£4) by girls and young women paid as little as fifteen cents per hour. The workers are housed in company barracks, there are no unions, overtime is often mandatory, and if there is a strike, the military is called in to break it up (Korten

1995). In 1992, the basketball star, Michael Jordan, was reported to have received $20 million for promoting Nike shoes. This exceeded the entire annual payroll of all the Indonesian factories which made them (Barnet and Cavanagh 1994).

In Bangladesh, large American retailers such as Wal-Mart, K-Mart and Sears, are having their shirts made by culturally passive Islamic women toiling 60 hours a week and making US$ 30 per month. The labour cost per shirt is roughly four cents. They assert the need to lower costs in order to remain competitive, but their main competitors are all there in Bangladesh as well, enjoying the same windfall of cheap labour (Collingsworth et al 1994) but maintaining the price of shirts in their domestic markets. Elsewhere in the world, clothes with expensive designer labels are produced using cheap labour, packaged back in the country of sale, in boxes often costing more than the garment itself, and sold at very exclusive prices to those whose satisfaction is somehow derived from a demonstration of not-so-naked affluence.

Avon, the international cosmetics company, has 70,000 saleswomen taking Avon messages to every rural doorstep in the Brazilian Amazon Basin. Avon is 'promising' beauty to people who do not know how to read or write and where the average household income is $3 per day. By taking advantage of the naivety of the uneducated population of the region, Avon advertises its products as a 'rejuvenation miracle'. People stop buying food and clothes to buy 'Renew', Avon's skin-renewal product costing $40 a jar. These examples illustrate an economic system that shifts rewards away from those who produce real value, to those whose primary function is to create marketing illusions to convince consumers to buy products they do not need at inflated prices.

Huge profits can therefore be derived by shifting production to low wage economies. And if wages in one host country rise, the firm simply shifts production elsewhere (*The Economist* 1995a). Rather than lowering prices, all the evidence suggests that when one company moves its manufacturing to find cheap labour, profit margins simply rise. Thus any distribution effect does not occur between domestic markets and developing economies, but between domestic markets and the (already rich) owners of capital and their appointed senior managers (who consume vast amounts of profit internally through enormous salaries, expense accounts and perks). Rather than the ubiquitous win-win situation talked of by international strategists (and now by the corporate environmentalists) this is definitely a lose-lose situation.

Moreover, this transfer of production activity to the developing countries has rarely taken with it high health, safety and environmental policies. In Chile, for example, the use of toxic pesticides by the export-oriented fruit industry is accused of causing birth defects among field farm workers. The Chilean fruit industry is one of the biggest importers of pesticides from the USA and is controlled by only six large corporations, including American companies such as Dole, Standard Trading, and Unifruit. Many of these pesticides, banned in the USA and Europe, include Lindane, Paraquat, and Parathion. A study carried out by Dr Victoria Mella of the Instituto de Ecologica Politica in the fruit growing Central Valley, in 1988–90, found that three times as many babies were born without brains and with exposed spines and water retention in the brain, compared to periods before the fruit industry began heavy use of pesticides. Methyl bromide, for example, used in the fumigation of grapes to be exported, is believed to be the cause of death of workers and even children in nearby schools poisoned by the gas (NAFTA & Inter-American Monitor 1995b). Nearly 5 per cent of the fruit consumed in North America in the winter season comes from the work of around 600,000 Chilean farm workers in the fields and 100,000 working in packing plants. The fruit industry is using 60 per cent of the US$ 38 million worth of pesticides imported by Chile annually. The use of methyl bromide is now spreading rapidly to other developing countries. There are safer alternatives available but these cost more money. China is now using methyl bromide to fumigate its vegetables and cut flowers for export. In addition, methyl bromide is an ozone depleting substance which may already be responsible for around 15 per cent of ozone depletion (*New Scientist* 1995).

Lower safety at work standards for exported-oriented fruit production can also be found in Mexico and is completely acceptable under NAFTA rules. Pesticide-contaminated fruit from Mexico can be kept out of the USA market if it fails to meet the same standards for pesticide residuals as USA fruits. But Mexican fruit cannot be kept out on the grounds that Mexican farm workers are suffering from pesticides poisoning more than USA farm workers. Life and health are clearly less valuable outside of the USA than they are inside.

WHAT PRICE AN 'ECONOMIC MIRACLE'?

According to Daly (1993) the free trade TNCs seek to maximize profits and production without any real regard to the considerations that represent hidden social and environmental costs. In fact, they care little even when they are not so hidden. They argue that when growth has made people wealthy enough, they will have the funds to clean up the damage done by growth. Conversely, environmentalists and now some economists, suspect that growth is increasing environmental costs faster than the benefits from production, thereby making us poorer, not richer (Daly 1993).

Most economists have been arguing about the benefits of exported-oriented economies, particularly, after the 'economic miracle' experienced by the East Asian countries; Hong Kong, South Korea, Taiwan and Singapore, in the 1970s and 1980s. From 1981–90, the average growth rate of the gross domestic product (GDP) of East Asian countries was 8.8 per cent (Kirkpatrick 1994). Yet when we consider the success of the NICs (newly industrializing countries), the Tigers or the Dragons, we must realize that their international and domestic achievements have not relied on free market policies alone. They have incorporated active government intervention in industrial policy programmes, following and expanding on the example of Japan. The Japanese style production model has had great influence on the development model of the NICs. It has stressed a flexible specialization based production model which grew first inside Japan, helped by large government intervention to enhance supply and demand. Internationally, Japanese TNCs had originally relied upon networks of giant trading companies to penetrate world markets. But later, the flexible specialization based manufacturing process expanded abroad not only to be close to local markets, but also because of the high value of the yen which increased domestic production and labour costs relative to those elsewhere. The establishment of Japanese TNCs abroad had also been helped by the interest of new host-nations in wishing to halt or reverse the decline of older industrial regions. Japanese corporations specializing in automobiles, electronics, rubber, and machine tools were soon transplanted to the United States, Western Europe, South America and South East Asian countries (Cusumano 1985 and Morris 1991).

A combination of promotion for technological cooperation from Japan's Ministry of International Trade and Industry (MITI), the growth of Japanese joint-ventures with local producers, and loans from the Japan Export/Import Bank to indigenous east Asian components manufacturers, assemblers and dealers, have also helped corporations in the NICs to consolidate their strong position in the international market (Cumings 1984). As in Japan, the success of NICs were part of national industrial strategies; the difference is that they took less than ten years to create a significant export capability.

The fact that the NICs have achieved high rates of economic growth (in terms of conventional measures of GNP) without following any programme developed by the World Bank and the IMF, has impressed many economists. But it is important to observe that all these 'economic miracles' have been measured by orthodox economic methods. Since all the economic activities associated with monetary values are added up indiscriminately in conventional GNP measures, it is perfectly possible that an increase in luxury production and consumption, in social costs and health care, in military expenditure and in environmental rehabilitation and pollution protection, are counted as positive contributions in GNP. More realistic approaches are showing that the NICs' 'economic miracle' was based on a mobilization of resources rather than on any real increases in efficiency. Evidence that the high rates of economic growth of the East Asian countries are not sustainable in the long term has been provided in Krugman's (1994) study, *The Myth of Asia's Miracle*. Krugman argues that the East Asian growth is almost wholly attributable to increased inputs, notably, of labour and capital. Examples of high and unsustainable rates of economic growth, have been observed in the former Soviet Union and in Brazil in the past. The rapid economic growth of the Soviet Union in the early 1960s is not dissimilar to the more recent 'economic miracle' of East Asian countries. Krugman (1994) argues that in both cases, the rapid growth in output could be fully explained by a rapid growth in inputs: expansion of employment, increases in education levels, and, above all, massive investment in physical capital with serious environmental consequences. Similarly, for ten years, from the mid-1960s until the beginning of its debt crisis, the Brazilian economy grew at 11 per cent a year (a period also called an 'economic miracle'). The resulting financial, social and environmental chaos is now self-evident. Today, Brazil's average economic growth is less than 4 per cent a year.

Brazil is a good example of another myth. The myth that increases in economic growth will provide a greater 'pie' to share. Even with a gross domestic product (GDP) of over US$ 600 billion, the Brazilian 'pie' was never shared. The process of growth has not been oriented to raise the income and productivity of the poor and to promote a sustainable use of the natural resources and the environment. Since the mid-1960s, the country has been through several economic programmes implemented by the former military regime and more democratic governments in the past ten years. However, Brazil still has an excessively wide income distribution and a level of poverty amongst a significant part of the population, comparable with some of the poorest areas of the world. A 1993 study conducted by the National Domestic Sampling Survey (PNDA), revealed that while the poorest 10 per cent of the population received 0.7 per cent of the national income, the richest 10 per cent took 50 per cent of the country's total income. The survey also reveals high levels of unemployment, poor working conditions and a high incidence of the use of child labour.

Meanwhile, the Brazilian economy has been opened up to foreign competition and average tariffs have fallen from 42 per cent in 1990 to 14 per cent (*Financial Times* 1995). This increasingly open market only benefits that part of the middle class who rush to import cars and consumer durables. In contrast, the domestic industrial sector is suffering from the impact of a rapid increase in imported products into the domestic market. In a study conducted among medium and large industries (which account for 65 per cent of employment), by Brazil's National Industrial Confederation, less than half the companies surveyed were found to be prepared for such international competition. In November of 1995, 14 per cent of the Brazilian work force was unemployed in the greater Sao Paulo area, around 1.14 million workers, the highest rate in ten years. But by December, according to the Commercial Association of Sao Paulo (ACSP), another record was established when 1,329 companies were declared bankrupt with consequent increases in unemployment. The situation remained the same in the beginning of 1996, January saw 802 bankruptcy declarations and in the first fifteen days of February, a further 856 companies became bankrupt. Currently there is an average of 78 requests per day (A Folha de Sao Paulo 1996). Recent trade agreements establishing the 'Mercosul', a grouping of Brazil, Argentina, Uruguay and Paraguay have done little to help small indigenous industries. However, large transnational organizations have managed to increase their trading activities and have been largely the beneficiaries of increasing export activity. Between 1991 and 1995 such activity in Argentina increased exports to Brazil from $1.4 billion to $5.3 billion.

Meanwhile, despite the fact that in the Tiger economies the income distribution is more equal than is to be found in Brazil and other Latin American countries, there is still evidence that economic growth has led to huge social and environmental costs, a lack of democracy and continuing violation of human rights in the East Asian countries. Intense pollution, in turn, damaging human health, has been caused by companies externalizing their environmental costs in an attempt to constantly drive down production costs in the fierce international marketplace. Meanwhile, as the demand for cheap labour increases, high rates of urban population growth lead to declining physical and social infrastructures. These are the real consequences of the 'economic miracle'. In Taiwan, for example, there are three factories per square kilometre. More than 50 per cent of river water is badly polluted and only 1 per cent of human waste receives primary treatment. In the countryside, some 20 per cent of farmland is polluted by industrial waste water and 30 per cent of the rice grown is contaminated by heavy metals (Bello 1992). In South Korea, agreements on free trade which allow the import of cheap USA food is destroying a once prosperous farming sector and driving 500,000 people off the land every year (Swift 1995). In Thailand, a striving 'Tiger' candidate, the annual deforestation rate between 1965 and 1989 was 2.6 per cent, one of the highest in Asia (World Bank 1992).

The NIC models of economic growth have an even darker side however. For many years now there have been hundreds of accusations made by organizations such as Human Rights Asia-Watch and other NGOs relating to humans rights abuses, torture, exploitation, political repression, the use of child labour and the dangerous and often prison-like work conditions in factories. In many Asian and Western corporations established in the region, workers have to work excessively long hours for subsistence wages. In South Korea, an average of five workers are killed on the job every day and an additional 390 are injured: one of the highest occupational-accident rates in the world (Hart-Landersberg 1993). In Myanmar (Burma), child labour is being used to build roads, railways and hotels in an attempt to attract Western tourists to the area. Such labour, termed 'voluntary' by the military dictatorship, is unpaid and to refuse to do it can lead to imprisonment for up to seven years (Pilger 1996). In many countries, agreements with repressive police forces are common in the suppression of any formation of labour union. But there is little concern for the outcry from the pressure groups. Indeed, Chinese officials have made their position quite clear: if you want to benefit from China's cheap labour market you have to tacitly consent to the human rights abuses; if you don't like it then stay out; there will be others to take your place.

As in the case of the Japanese corporations, the East Asian TNCs are now looking towards less developed countries to establish and expand their production facilities. The increase of production costs in their own territories is driving manufacturing not only to China, Thailand, Malaysia, Indonesia and Vietnam, the new business neighbours, but also to Central America, following the USA example. The targets are countries such as Honduras where they can pay three USA dollars a day for young women (between the age of 14 and 20) to work long hours with no real employment rights and certainly no rights to form unions (Cox 1993). Those who see growth and globalization as the redeemer for poverty and underdevelopment would do well to consider these and the mass of other evidence pointing in the same direction.

We have reached a situation where the global economic system is rewarding corporations and their executives with generous profits, salaries and benefits packages for contracting out their production to sweatshops, often paying subsistence wages. Managers keep their jobs and increase their salaries by replacing high wage labour with low wage labour. When Glaxo Wellcome was discharging 7,500 staff in the UK, for example, it was accused by unions of paying out £16.2 million in annual salaries and pensions to its 28 directors (*The Guardian* 1996). Their actions create a frightened domestic population who are no longer sure that they will have a job tomorrow. Such uncertainty makes the whole economy shaky as workers are unwilling to take on financial commitments which they may never be able to service. In the long run they are creating their own demise.

Elsewhere, the activities of large companies and their 'fat cat' executives result in the destruction of primal forests, the displacement of tens of thousands of employees and increasing levels of unemployment by the introduction of labour-saving technologies, the dumping of toxic wastes, the imprisonment and often the murder of political activists, the curtailing of human rights, the destruction of species, and so the list goes on. For this, our high flying executives are generously rewarded, often idolized, and their strategies (bad bits left out) analysed by ambitious students of business wishing to emulate their heroes, convinced that some day they too will form part of the super-rich elite.

Meanwhile the true costs of such actions are never experienced by those who make the decisions. The costs are, of course, borne by the system's weaker members: these include the displaced workers who are unemployed; those who do work but are paid so little that they cannot feed themselves or their families so that their health deteriorates; the workers whose very life is simply work, housed by their employers and essentially modern day slaves; the forest dwellers deprived of their homes, culture and livelihoods; the poor who live next to toxic dumps; those born with pollution-related disabilities; the children in workhouses; those imprisoned for their attempts to bring about democracy; and those (increasing numbers of people) who simply see very little meaning to life any more. The consequence of delinking the benefits from the costs is that whilst the majority suffer, the minority are actually rewarded for their decisions. In other words, the decision-makers receive positive feedback, rewarding them for the devastation which they are causing. This truly is a self-destructing system. Adding insult to injury, the rich then point to the miserable environmental conditions in which the poor sometimes have to live as proof that the poor are less environmentally responsible than themselves.

THE ROLE OF THE INTERNATIONAL FINANCIAL INSTITUTIONS

Lending over US$ 23 billion a year to more than 100 countries, the World Bank is, today, undoubtedly one of the most powerful institutions in the world. Working close with the IMF, it virtually controls the economies of the 70 developing countries now subject to Bank or IMF dictated Structural Adjustment Programmes (SAPs) (Hildyard 1994). Meanwhile the external debt of developing countries has multiplied over thirteen fold in the last two decades: from US$100 billion in 1979 to

US$1350 billion in 1990 (Poppovick and Pinheiro 1993). The IMF accounts for 22 per cent of the $30.5 billion owed by the poorest countries to multilateral creditors. It now receives more in debt repayments from African countries than it provides in finance (Killick 1995). SAPs have been imposed by both institutions on seriously indebted developing countries as a condition for loan rescheduling. These programmes require countries to reduce public expenditure, cut wages, open up markets, privatize state enterprises and maximize export-oriented production. These policies are based on traditional Conservative economics of the Reagan and Thatcher era which assumed that unregulated, free market forces would always result in optimum outcomes. Today, a walk through any American or British city in order to witness the pollution, poverty, homelessness and crime which has been created during this era gives human form to the statistics on the distribution of wealth, income and employment.

The World Bank's repayment flows are now greater than the volume of new lending to the developing countries. Servicing external debt is removing significant national resources from poor countries, and the SAPs are penalizing debtor countries, suffocating economic growth and significantly impacting on human development as a result. This is partly because half of the money lent to the world's poorest countries has actually gone to companies in the world's richest countries as payment for goods, services and consultancy! Now, the World Bank and the IMF are actively pushing the 'Tiger' model as a solution for the economic problems of developing and less developed countries. However, there is strong evidence to doubt that such an Asian model will bring long term prosperity to countries with different cultures, traditions and expectations. Not only because of Krugman's analysis of the Tiger's unconvincing long term 'economic miracle', but also because it is clear that in this global economic system it is difficult to maintain a stable and high growth path. After all, the powerful transnational corporations actually have an incentive to support and create planned underdevelopment of the poorest countries of the world in order to maintain a pool of cheap labour.

The world is a very uncertain place and the future is difficult to predict. We live an a new era of global information, yet even with all the statistics available, no one could have accurately predicted or even anticipated the collapse of world stock markets in 1987, the disintegration of the Soviet Union or the 1994 Mexican currency crisis. Yet the powerful financial institutions base their models on rationality and certainty that their monetarist inspired models are correct. Global models based on neo-classical assumptions about the economy and which try to translate a 'success' model directly from one culture to a different one are not going to bring about the Pareto improvements assumed. Such economic models applied globally are as much an illusion as is the control of Adam Smith's invisible hand on the market. Any kind of development model simply has to take into consideration the local and regional structure of every society, which has so far has been ignored in the programmes implemented by the international financial institutions. In addition, the social and environmental degradation which we have seen in so many of the 'success' countries is a warning to those who see the panacea as achieving rapid economic growth at any price.

One of the visible consequences of the policies described above is that worldwide, the rich are getting richer, the poor are getting poorer, and the people in the middle are becoming less and less secure about their futures. It is estimated that between 1960 and 1989 there was an eightfold increase in the absolute difference in incomes between the richest fifth and poorest fifth of the world population (UNDP 1992). The polarization is most noticeable in the poorer regions of Asia, Africa and Latin America and, in the ex-socialist European countries converted to the new capitalism. An explanation of this increasing gap between rich and poor is traceable to globalization. Those segments of the population in both rich and poor countries that are linked most directly to the global economy have fared well, but they are very small in relative terms. Those with a more local economic orientation, whether they are among the upper class or the lower classes, have fared badly.

TOWARDS SUSTAINABLE DEVELOPMENT?

The promotion of the concept of sustainable development has already generated many definitions and plenty of controversy. There is little doubt that, as many environmentalists argue, it has been overused, misused and abused by policy makers, politicians and business corporations. For many businesses, for example, sustainable development has become a slogan associated with a strong economic efficiency theme rather than an understanding of the wider issues and any real commitment towards more radical change. There seems little attempt by business or others to really understand the reality of the world's unsustainability. Despite the fact that some agreements have been signed and promises have been made in line with the principles of Agenda 21, environmentalists and some scientists are still worrying about the inadequate progress made towards finding solutions to even the most immediate environmental problems. Global warming, ozone depletion, destruction of biodiversity and the increasingly global poverty are still waiting for effective measures.

From the discussions above, what is clear is that the international harmonization of tough environmental standards will not be possible. There will always be an incentive for countries to ignore strong standards in order to attract the transnational corporations to more 'competitive' locations. Moreover, it is clear that transnational corporations themselves would not tolerate the sorts of controls which would have to be introduced if we were serious about environmental protection. They are currently rewarded for causing environmental destruction and apart from a few apologist environmental strategies in their developed world operations and the use of rhetoric associated with eco-modernism and technology transfer, they have no incentive to change. Thus to control the production and distribution activities of the transnational corporations is impossible. However, the TNC cannot exist without its end markets where it sells its low cost products for high prices. Control of these is possible if Western governments were committed to sustainable development. Individual states should have the right to introduce product norms and standards which regulate the local environmental effects of consumption and which ban products which have been produced in such a way which has an intolerable impact on the environment, human health or basic human rights. Until governments do that however, we may have to rely on mobilizing those people who do have a conscience and organizing more sophisticated consumer boycotts.

In order to correct unsustainability at an international development level, it is also important to acknowledge the interrelationships between the participation of civil society in development programmes, the control of environmental degradation and the reduction of social inequality. It is fundamental to rethink development in its socio-environmental dimension and to generate programmes at a local level where people's basic needs are best satisfied. We need to recognize that the lack or absence of democracy, freedom of speech and trade union activity contribute directly to environmental damage in many countries. It is also essential that ethics be incorporated into the programmes of the international financial institutions, trade organizations' agreements and the policies of the transnational corporations.

In 1992, the USA, Germany, Japan and the UK, declared that it was impossible to reach a consensus over a code of conduct for TNCs. Attempts to achieve this have been made by the United Nations (UN) since 1976. By 1995, a new code was developed by Consumers International (an organization of 200 consumer unions from more than 80 countries) and distributed to TNCs, following the failure of the UN initiative. However, the Charter has already met resistance from powerful companies such as Shell, which claim to have their own codes of conduct. But by the end of the same year, many environmentalists and the general public had expressed serious doubts over such codes and specifically about the 'Shell Business Principles' which were supposed to regulate the activities of its operations. Shell's attempt to dump the Brent Spar oil platform in the North Atlantic exposed its corporate arrogance. It failed to detect or act upon the public concern in Europe when alerted by the campaigns of environmental organizations such as Greenpeace. Shell also demonstrated totally passive behaviour when nine Nigerian protesters who campaigned against Shell's harmful operations in their country were threatened with being hanged and subsequently executed by a repressive military regime. Shell has also shown little concern over the social upheaval and environmental degradation resulting from its thirty years of operation around the River Niger Delta.

There must be a great deal of doubt surrounding whether it is possible to ensure a healthy environment for all people, as a basic human right, in this 'new economic (dis)order'. A fundamental prerequisite for individuals exercising human, economic and political rights is to be healthy. Worldwide, there are at least 1 billion people, mostly the poor, who do not have access to drinking water, at least 1.7 billion who do not have access to sanitation and around 2 billion people without an electricity supply. The consequences of poverty affect rich societies as much as the poor societies when people are forced to emigrate from African countries to European countries, for example. This creates increasing social problems in these countries and it is now apparent that a number of Western European countries are tightening their immigration legislation and making it tougher for asylum seekers to find refuge.

It ought now to be clear that poverty is one of the direct results of globalization and that the environment, social structures and weaker segments of the world's population cannot be left to the manipulation of the market and stronger political powers (represented by the developed world and the transnational corporations) without causing untold chaos and suffering. Without physical survival, individuals in poor countries can clearly do nothing whatever to protect themselves or the environment. But the free market has effectively reduced that physical health and disabled social participation by hindering the scope of action and interaction. It is imperative to guarantee that all segments of society have their basic needs satisfied in order to have more active participation in actions towards a healthier world. Sustainable development is not about just an improvement in quality of life (too commonly measured in terms of cars or televisions per household) however, it must above all address the promotion of social justice.

International and national authorities must now be pressed to establish effective mechanisms for real democracy and a change of priorities towards ensuring the implementation of collective norms and actions devoted to human survival, an equitable distribution of benefits and environmental quality protection. Decision-making processes are concentrated in the hands of a few rich countries and companies (or in the elites of poor countries) that defend strong private interests and need to be compelled to accept the participation of all the sectors of society. Ethics must be introduced into the international trade dimension but we must recognize that these will only be taken seriously when people who are affected directly by international development strategies are not marginalized but part of the decision-making process.

References

Barnet, R J and Cavanagh, J (1994) *Global Dreams: Imperial Corporations and the New World Order*, Simon and Schuster, New York

Bello, W (1992) *Dragons in Distress*, Penguin Books, London

Business Week (1996) 'Here come those slow-growth blues', vol 148, March 4, international edition, New York

Collingsworth, T, Goold, J F and Harvey, P F (1994) Time for a Global New Deal, *Foreign Affairs*, 73 (1), January–February, The Council on Foreign Relations, New York

Cox, S (1993) The rag trade goes South, *New Internationalist*, 246, August

Cumings, B (1984) The origin and development of the Northeast Asian Political economy: Industrial sectors, product cycles, and political consequences, *International Organization*, 38

Cusumano, M (1985) *The Japanese automobile industry*, Harvard University Press, Cambridge, Mass.

Daly, H E (1993) The Perils of Free Trade, *Scientific American*, 269, November

Financial Times (1995) Brazil Survey, May 17, London

Folha de Sao Paulo (1996) Brazilian newspaper, February 16, Sao Paulo

Hart-Landersberg, M (1993) *The Rush to Development*, Monthly Review Press, New York

Hildyard, N (1994) The Big Brother Bank, *Geographical*, The Royal Geographic Society, London, June

Killick, T (1995) *IMF Programmes in Developing Countries*, Overseas Development Programme and Routledge, London

Kirkpatrick, C (1994) Regionalisation, Regionalism and East Asian Economic Cooperation, *The World Economy*, 17, (2), March, Blackwell

Korten, D C (1995) *When Corporations Rule the World*, Earthscan, London

Krugman, P (1994) The Myth of Asia's Miracle, *Foreign Affairs*, 73 (6), November–December, The Council on Foreign Relations, New York

Madeley, J (1992) *Trade and the Poor*, Intermediate Technology Publications, London.

McGrath, M E and Hoole, R W (1992) Manufacturing's new economies of scale, *Harvard Business Review*, Boston

Morris, J (1991) *Japan and the Global Economy*, Routledge, London

NAFTA & Inter-American Trade Monitor (1995) The Institute for Agriculture and Trade Policy, 2, (30), December 1, 1995, Minneapolis, after Sagaris, L (1995) The Killing Fields, *Chicago Tribune*, November 5, Chicago

New Scientist (1995) 'Ozone deal could backfire', vol 148, December 16

Poppovick, M and Pinheiro, S (1993) How to consolidate democracy? A human rights approach, *International Social Science Journal*, (143), March, UNESCO-Blackwell Publishers, Oxford.

Pilger, J (1996) The Burmese Gulag, *The Guardian*, 5th May

Sklair, L (1991) *Sociology of the Global System*, Harvester Wheatsheaf, London

Swift, R (1995) Unmasking the miracle, *New Internationalist*, (263), January. London

The Ecologist (1990) The Uruguay round: gunboat diplomacy by another name, Editorial (20), London

The Economist (1995) A Survey of Multinationals, June 24th–30th, London

The Guardian (1996) Fury Over Glaxo 'Fat Cats', March 23, London

UNDP (1992) United Nations Development Programme, *Human Development Report 1992*, Oxford University Press, New York

UNCTAD (1993) United Nations Conference in Trade and Development, *Report on Trade and Development*, Geneva

UNTCMD (1992) United Nations Transnational Corporations and Management Division, *World Investment Report 1992: TNCs as Engines to Growth*, New York

World Bank (1992) *World Development Report*, Washington DC

WTO (1995) World Trade Organization, *International Trade – Trends and Statistics*, New York

7

Organizing for Sustainable Development: Structure, Culture and Social Auditing

David Jones and *Richard Welford*

In earlier chapters of this book it was argued that the internal structures common in business alienate individual workers and remove their powers of self-determination. Modernism has dictated hierarchical management systems rather than more cooperative forms of organization, and more contemporary management techniques (e.g. total quality management and business process re-engineering) have done little to improve this. Yet an important part of sustainability is to ensure long term equity and equality, globally, locally (and in the workplace), to make individuals more responsible for their activities (including their jobs) and to build on the cooperation of people. For businesses, local environmental action means including everyone in the workforce in a search for opportunities for environmental improvement. Moreover, environmental issues are best handled with the participation of all concerned citizens. Each individual should have information and the opportunity to participate in decision-making processes. This requires us to look at the organization and culture of a business in more depth.

This chapter argues that if businesses are to move towards sustainability then they need to shift from traditional unitarist structures to more pluralistic cultural development strategies. The unitarist structure involves a pre-planned, top-down, management driven system with aims of assimilation and integration of the workforce, elimination of conflicting interests and perspectives and creation of shared meanings and values (Bate 1994). This represents the most popular corporate strategy of the post-war period in the West. In contrast, the pluralist option involves a bottom-up, sideways-on, top-down emergent strategy with aims of accommodation, interdependence, collaboration and peaceful co-existence between participating interest groups (Bate 1994). This represents the regular favourite of the cooperative movement, bioregionalists and many deep green ecologists. It is, more importantly, more consistent with the achievement of sustainable development than rigid hierarchical management.

THE IMPORTANCE OF CULTURE AND ORGANIZATION

The application of the concept of culture to organizations became widespread through the 1980s, but was pioneered by some innovative thinkers earlier (for example, Crozier 1964; Turner 1971; Pettigrew 1979). Subsequent researchers distinguished two broad senses of organizational culture, the more popular view of culture as a variable to be managed in organizations, and the view that culture is a metaphor or fundamental means of conceptualizing organizations (Smircich 1983). According to this latter view, culture is not something an organization has, but something an organization is and management cannot control culture because management is a part of that culture (Nicholson 1984). This debate, which culminates in querying the existence of organizational culture at all, has attracted much academic interest but has not deterred widespread acceptance of the concept. Despite the plausible contention that culture is not something that organizations have, there is a popular understanding that organizational culture exists and that it is important (Schein 1983).

Frequently understood as a 'multi-layered' phenomenon, organizational culture includes deep-seated and enduring values, at the most fundamental or inner level, with artifacts and symbols, procedures and arrangements, shared doings and sayings, characterizing the outer and more superficial layers of organizational culture. There are some doubts that an organization can influence the substantive content of its own culture, because the underlying values of any organizational culture are deeply rooted in broader national, racial and religious cultures (Schein 1983). More amenable to change are the outer layers of culture, the rituals, the symbols, heroes, attitudes, objectives and structures.

The importance of focusing on organizational culture for a business wishing to move towards sustainability seems to be self-evident. It must be recognized that ultimately, any long term success depends on the attitudes, skills, knowledge and experiences of the people involved in the development and implementation of the policies towards sustainability

(Beaumont, et al 1993; Welford 1995). To date, work has primarily focused upon a call for a cultural change to mainstream business. This would affect all levels of an organizational culture, from underlying assumptions and beliefs to espoused values and artifacts. However, few authors have attempted to study organizations who are already committed to and are moving towards sustainability, defined in its most holistic sense i.e. actively combining their financial responsibility with their long term environmental and social responsibility. These companies are led by values and ethics. Instead of culture change, these organizations are developing the outer layers of their culture towards sustainability.

THE DOMINANCE OF UNITARIST STRUCTURES AND CULTURES

The unitarist structure in business has been very much a product of modernism with its emphasis on order, control, hierarchy and continuation of 'business as usual'. A unitarist cultural development strategy is invariably expressed in the call for a strong management culture: one where, in general, there is acceptance of structure and authority throughout the organization which, in turn, is powerful in determining individual behaviour. In other words, an 'effective' organization has a unitary system bound together by a common task and common values. Just whose values they are is open to some debate, but since they are enshrined and promulgated by management they are certainly the vestiges of modernism. Thus it is not surprising to find that the argument of the unitarist approach is that by engendering high levels of commitment to the organization among employees, good performance follows. This is therefore an argument very much about efficiency, defined in traditional output and money terms. Companies that employ the unitarist strategy of cultural development believe that their companies will be healthier, more innovative and generally more effective when the cultures of its parts have been fully integrated into a single, consistent uniform whole. In other words when the overall corporate culture is 'strong' and diversity is eliminated. Therefore, order and efficiency are achieved by merging diversity into a single, common orientation towards the organization's dominant ideology. The general aim is therefore away from diversity and heterogeneity among staff and employees towards greater uniformity and standardization. Within such a strategy, plurality is eliminated and the environment is commonly undervalued.

Thus little has changed from the management ideologies of the 1960s and 1970s when industrial sociologists, industrial relations theorists and political scientists talked about the need for a unitary frame of reference. Indeed, research shows that a majority of businesses conceptualize the most 'desirable' culture in this way (Meek 1988; Young 1989) although it is often described as an 'integrative' culture. A unitary system has one source of authority and one focus of loyalty, which is why it suggests the team analogy. What pattern of behaviour do we expect from the members of a successful and healthily functioning team? We expect them to strive gently towards a common objective, each pulling his or her weight to the best of his or her ability. Each person accepts their place and function gladly, following the leadership of the one so appointed. There are no opposition groups or factions, and therefore no rival leaders within the team. Nor are there any outside it: the team stands alone, its members owing allegiance to their own leaders but to no others. New management techniques imported into Europe from Japan and North America have done little to replace the traditional top-down hierarchical approaches. They may have flattened middle management structures and introduced teamworking but their emphasis is still on tight control via systems management. Moreover, new approaches involving much more 'flexible' work practices further enshrine the power of senior management, who are more able to hire and fire workers. Meanwhile workers are left with an increase in shift-working, uncertain temporary contracts, part-time employment and even the prospect of turning up to work only to be turned away again (without pay) because no orders have arrived. Never, since workers queued at pitheads hoping that colliery owners would look kindly on them, have we seen valuable human capital reduced to indispensable factors of production.

The unitarist strategy in organizations is very much part of modernism. It is characterized by strong hierarchical leadership, the diffusion and popularization of a particular corporate culture and world view. As Child (1984) argues, a unitarist strategy is consciously designed for developing pragmatic acceptance into a much more enthusiastic support for management's purposes (or creating a false consciousness). It is about putting in place structures which get workers involved in management's aspirations, dictating rigid behaviour patterns and working within a tightly defined system. These were the roots of mass production line technologies and organization. But any examination of the structures and systems implicit in total quality management, for example, will reveal that not much has changed. The ultimate aim of this sort of approach is to get employees to act in accordance with systems and structures and adhere to the corporate culture because they 'feel' something for their company and come to respect, even idolize and worship, what it stands for. Therefore, Bate (1994) argues that the range of positive feelings and expectations that strong culture strategies seek to engender towards the company and its leaders is wide, not only taking in loyalty, commitment, dedication, devotion, enthusiasm but even love and passion.

As an example of the high expectations of a unitarist strategy, Bate (1994) points out that one of the main feelings, strong culture companies are seeking to engender towards the company and its products, is getting people to feel that they have to or want to put work before their families. A quote from Deal and Kennedy's book, *Corporate Culture* (1982) illustrates this point: 'I'm sorry I'm so late getting home, but the customer had a problem and we never leave a customer with a problem'. Another example is what the Honda worker cited in *In Search of Excellence* might well have said, 'I'm sorry I'm so late getting home this evening. I have been straightening the wiper blades on all the Hondas I have seen on the way home because I just can't stand to see a flaw in a Honda' (Peters and Waterman 1982, p 37). These examples show that working in a strong culture is not viewed as a 9 to 5 affair. It has to be a way of life, a consuming passion, a mission.

Thus if there is any environmental strategy in the organization, it will be one which is 'dictated' and promulgated by interested managers. As was demonstrated in Chapter 2, this strategy is more likely to adhere to industry norms and standards and be based around concepts of eco-efficiency. The natural commitment towards the environment, which can be found in any organization, along with workers' experiences, aspirations, ideas and emotions will be sidelined in favour of a marginalist, top-down approach, consistent not with principles of sustainable development, but with traditional corporate aims and objectives. The environment will not be centre-stage and is therefore unlikely to be fully embraced by all workers.

THE EFFECTIVENESS OF THE UNITARIST STRATEGY

The apparent beauty of the tightly knit top-down system is that so long as workers understand the system and know their place within it, they can be relied on to set their own standards and discipline themselves, while being aware of the 'deal': freedom is conditional upon the ability to 'deliver'. In theory employees, like the patients in a hospital, tend to do what they are told because they value (and depend on) the care and attention they are receiving and do not wish to run the risk of being cast out into a hostile, uncertain and lonely world. They want to be good patients (Bate 1994). The lure of a strong culture is that it can feel stable and secure, it can be warm, comfortable, supportive and protecting. But it can also be brainwashing.

However, employees not only derive a sense of meaning and belonging from complying with a strong culture, they often simultaneously experience a sense of anxiety, shame and guilt when they judge themselves to fail. As Deal and Kennedy (1982, p 56) point out, employees in strong culture companies are not permitted to fail in any way. Therefore, for employees who do not conform to the corporate values, the psychological price is great and employment prospects poor. After all, as our ubiquitous quality management system standards now tell us: non-conformity requires corrective action.

The proponents of unitarist structures and systems actually suffer from false consciousness. They believe that their systems work and that workers are on their side. But workers often do not succumb to the thought controls and do not allow themselves to be absorbed into the greater whole. They have a number of social and psychological defences which prevent this from happening. Instead of the deep internalization of corporate values encouraged by the 'corporate culture gurus', a more likely orientation is one of conditional identification or even calculative compliance. In other words, employees are commonly willing to adhere to the values of the corporation only insofar and so long as they calculate that material or symbolic advantage is being derived from it. In so far as this involves the performance of certain roles, the worker retains a subjective detachment from the organization, often putting on an act of compliance and then 'sniggering' behind the backs of management. Managers might be convinced – workers rarely are.

Furthermore, workers may partially submit to managers' cultural assaults but they also resist them by developing their own subcultures and counter-cultures. These challenge or poke fun at the managerial shibboleths, expressing cynicism and detachment at managerial attempts to whip up commitment and enthusiasm. Those who call themselves the 'gurus' forget the fact that within every organization there is a large uncolonised terrain, a terrain which is not and cannot be managed, in which people, both individually and in groups, can engage in all kinds of unsupervised, spontaneous activity. No matter how much power resides in the ruling group, there will always be a part of the organization where control attempts can be subverted and robbed of their effectiveness by informal, grass roots processes. Thus it ought to be clear that no organization can be exclusively managed in a coercive manner from the top down. Even when the odds are stacked against it, the informal system will be able to repel most kinds of ideological invasion if it desires. If top management decides everything and afterwards informs the employees, this clearly creates discontent and conflicts. The implementation of a decision then becomes slow and difficult due to internal resistance.

Control through unitarist structures, systems and strategies is not the simple and straightforward affair that cultural engineers would like it to be. In an uncertain world employees may yearn for meaning, but it does not follow that they will simply 'buy' that meaning (Gabriel 1991). A reliance on a unitarist strategy using a management defined vision is so often ineffective. Those who promote systems such as total quality management will always tell you about their successes – they will rarely admit to the very common failures. Corporate strategy literature substantiates this finding, expressing serious doubts about the ease with which management vision can be communicated to employees. For example, Coulson-Thomas (1992) draws on three sets of survey data to argue that 'a wide gulf has emerged between "rhetoric and reality" of attempts to "communicate" visions and "missions": instead of inspiration and motivation there is disillusionment and distrust' (p 81). Proponents of unitarism are keen to stress that this is because of 'mistakes' in communicating visions and missions. But their arguments remain very strong on prescription, and very limited on evidence of real and lasting success.

One important lesson that needs to be learnt about unitarist strategies for cultural order is that senior management are often blind to the increasing pluralism of organizations (particularly growing organizations). They do not see (or prefer not to see) the hundreds of small interest groups, with incompletely overlapping memberships, widely differing power bases and a multitude of techniques for exercising influence on decisions salient to them (Polsby 1966). Nor do they acknowledge that in such a pluralistic system, management's assumed superiority is no longer sufficient to permit the luxury of imposed solutions or directives (Fox 1973). In consequence, they are often ill-prepared for the resistance that they encounter on the way, and for the bargaining process that will be necessary if they are to create some kind of order.

PLURALIST CULTURAL DEVELOPMENT STRATEGY

Other cultural development research has shown that for practical reasons associated with employee acceptance, even the most committed 'strong culture' companies, need to attend to pluralism (Bate, 1994). Therefore, whilst representing for many people, a vision of what an organization ought to be like, the unitary frame of reference does not adequately reflect what it is really like or could ever be like. Unitarism towards sustainable development is a utopian ideal but pluralism is the inescapable reality. Central to Agenda 21 are calls for workers (and their trade unions) to be more involved in the industrial change which will be necessary to achieve sustainable development. Businesses are called on to foster dialogue with workers, forming a partnership capable of shaping and implementing environment and development strategies at local, national and international level. This can only be achieved with increased participation of the workforce within a more pluralist framework.

For pluralists, the challenge in maintaining order or ensuring sensible and controlled development is not to ignore, suppress, gloss over or eliminate differences between people (actions that were likely at best to enjoy only a limited and temporary success), but to develop greater sensitivity towards multicultural differences, accepting and welcoming, and continually looking for ways of expressing, accommodating and reconciling them. In short, companies need to realize that they need to manage the inherent 'pluralism' within and external to their organization. Thus if management is to be successful, rather than cosmetic or deceptive, it will have to comprehend comparative values and belief systems. The starting point here is for managers to understand themselves, first, and then go on to recognize the value of diversity.

This view substantiates research on environmental management and business level sustainability. Gray (1994) points out that the very critical nature of the environmental and social problems that one is seeking to address plus the sheer complexity of the issues and the increasing level of ignorance of humanity's interaction with the biosphere do not lend themselves to the assumption of 'rational', allocative decision-making by selected groups of the privileged. He argues for decision-making to be democratic, in the widest sense of the term, because it is society as a whole which must make the choices and trade-offs that are essential in the path to sustainable development. Welford (1995) argues for new forms of industrial organization as part of the equity dimension of sustainability. This would involve seeking to increase employees' decision-making powers, to increase democracy in the workplace and to share profits with the workforce, alongside improving environmental performance. This revolves around respecting the values of everybody associated with a firm or organization and the need for more open procedures and less hierarchical bureaucracy in decision making to be developed within firms. Similarly, employee participation is first and foremost a question of recognizing the individual and collective interests of the employees, of the quality of working life and the nature of the relationship between management and employees: the social constitution of the firm. Furthermore, a research exercise by Welford and Jones (1996) has pointed out the importance of empowerment strategies in moving towards sustainability, arguing that it is by empowerment that we can begin to challenge and change traditional balances of power. The logical next step must be to implement participation measures: participation in decision-making as well as financial (profit-sharing) participation and other non-financial rewards. Essentially we are searching for evidence of an equitable distribution of benefits. Ultimately the sustainable organization will be able to demonstrate that it is moving towards systems which provide for increased levels of industrial democracy.

With a more pluralist strategy, differences and conflicts of interest between individuals and groups are the order of the day and no amount of wishful thinking is ever going to change that basic fact. Nor could any single group ever hope to be able to impose its will unilaterally on the others or to be able to count on undivided loyalty, because power in the modern organization is too diffuse, and rarely coincides with formal authority structures. We have to accept the existence of different sources of leadership and attachment. The challenge for management in a pluralist organization is not to unify, integrate or liquidate sectional groups and their special interests in the name of some overriding corporate existence, but to control and balance the activities of constituent groups so as to provide for the maximum degree of freedom of association and action for sectional and group purposes consistent with the general interest of the organization. The aim is to provide leadership, not direction. But leadership is only possible where there exists a 'followership'. Thus, more cooperative, interactive and participative management is always likely to prove more successful in moving the organization forward.

An important point to note is that there is some evidence that organizations can not only tolerate many subcultures, but also benefit from the discourse about values which they inevitably spawn (Sinclair 1993). Indeed organizations which embrace pluralism tend to be learning organizations, rather than structures driven by dictat. Therefore, rather than pursuing the strong corporate culture, the task for managers becomes one of understanding and unleashing the commitment of subcultures towards goals which are consistent with, or ideally advance, those of the organization (Martin and Siehl 1983). Pluralists argue that the unitarist strategy is the antithesis of individual ethics, that such a culture demands a 'surrender of individual integrity' to the organization (Silk and Vogel 1976). They argue that by relinquishing power to subcultures, communally-mediated control is effectively increased, by sponsoring autonomy, commitment can be nourished, by encouraging connections between organizational subcultures and wider community groups, the organization's reserves are enhanced.

For a pluralist, the essential steps in the process of management are firstly, self scrutiny, weighing up individual obligations and responsibilities, secondly, weighing up professional and organizational responsibilities, taking personal responsibility for a decision and critically analysing the underlying assumptions of each course of action to better understand value choices, before finally applying decision standards and deciding. A key ingredient of this kind of more ethical management is the process of self awareness and self scrutiny that precedes it. Thus this puts weight on the process of thought that precedes action, to qualify behaviour before proceeding with action. Because such thought requires a level of reflexivity and ongoing self-inspection, it is not enough to adhere single-mindedly to simple standards of behaviour prescribed by others. For example, being ethical may require doing the opposite of what is comfortable, acceptable or expected by the culture. Managers must be wary of simply doing things which represent the continuation of accepted norms and practices. Such an approach does not impose a corporate culture, instead, it aims to stimulate more ethically aware behaviour of members of subcultures by collaboratively surfacing an awareness of subcultural differences, competing and common values and their effects on outcomes.

The pluralist strategy does not rely on management as the architects of the moral code, but works by encouraging individuals to understand and challenge the ethics and values they bring to the organization. This view has been confirmed by Post and Altman (1991) in their study of companies moving towards sustainable development. They base their methodology upon research done by Bartunek and Moch (1987), who argue that a change agent must not prescribe a particular value system, but instead be responsible for helping employees to self-reflect and develop the capacity to change one's point of view, and therefore to explore one's own situation through a different light. Similarly, research on the implementation of environmental management techniques (Callenbach et al 1993) suggests that people of different colour, women, labour, and other groups affected differently by company actions can be the eco-manager's best allies in bringing unique insights and solutions to problems. Ecological transformation is limited and likely to prove fragile without diverse participation, perspectives, and bases of support.

Environmentalists, and even some scientists, are increasingly arguing that diversity is more than a phenomenon of nature, but rather a value, a quality that should be striven for, protected and defended. If diversity is good, then loss of diversity is bad. Furthermore, research on team behaviour in organizations (Janis and Mann 1977) supports the conclusion that diversity of backgrounds, perspectives and values is an asset that protects the group from the hazards of 'groupthink'. This is especially significant within highly volatile financial and social environments where it is essential that the members of the strategic decision-making team have highly differentiated perspectives (Bourgeois 1984). Furthermore, people do not understand or interpret environmental concepts with one voice. They hold contrasting beliefs and values systems which are often in conflict with the dominant interpretations of the firm. These differences can not only create barriers to change but also openings for change.

As Callenbach et al (1993) argue, in every company, as in society as a whole, conflicts and contradictions will invariably appear that cannot be simply resolved in favour of one side or the other. Thus they say we need stability and change, order and freedom, tradition and innovation, planning and *laissez-faire*. They argue that a systemically orientated manager (an integral part of eco-management) knows that the contradictions within the company are signs of its variety and vitality, and thus contribute to the system's viability. Without conflicts there can be no development. A systemic manager will therefore try to take into account both sides of a contradiction, knowing that both will be important depending on the context.

Another significant benefit from adopting the more pluralist approach is that it is capable of embracing even wider dimensions of business. Whilst the unitarist model is one of internal control and direction, pluralism is more about participation and joint determination. This can be extended beyond the traditional boundaries of business to an assessment of the needs, desires, values and aspirations of external stakeholders. For a business to act in a more sustainable manner links with suppliers, customers, lenders and other interested parties are vital. Pluralism therefore embraces a wider assessment of the company's objectives and behaviour and as we shall see below, facilitates a much more sophisticated mode of assessing a company's contribution to environmental protection and sustainable development through techniques such as social auditing.

TOWARDS A WORKABLE MODEL OF PLURALISM

The danger of drifting towards the extreme end of a spectrum of pluralism is that nurturing processes of self-inspection and critique among individuals and subcultures of the organization may induce a morally self-aware group, which satisfies ethicists in its processes, but may not necessarily produce virtuous sustainable behaviours or outcomes. If everything has a different meaning for each organizational member and if everybody has different ideas on what should be done, creativity may flourish for a while, but the whole edifice is likely to collapse from lack of consistency, co-ordination and direction (Murphy 1989). The major shortcoming with this extreme is that of implementation. Difference, if valued purely for its own sake, might be a recipe for organizational anarchy. Accepting the legitimacy of differences in organizational culture cannot and should not lead to the kind of cultural relativism which presumes there is some justification for any and all cultural differences (Metcalfe and Richards 1987). There are very significant obstacles to the realization of this management for diversity approach, paralleled in attempts to manage workforces comprised of more racially-diverse groups and more women. The management of diversity by recognizing and valuing difference and strategically sponsoring the cultivation of complementary contributions is a new and unfamiliar managerial paradigm, which confronts many obstacles (Adler 1985). People in organizations and especially managers are uncomfortable with ambiguity and tend to view such a process as abdicating managerial prerogatives and responsibilities and relinquishing power.

However, realizing the potential of a more pluralistic response, it has been argued that a company needs to implement processes which provide a greater respect for diversity and democracy to its workplace. But by realizing the drawbacks of a solely pluralistic strategy, it is clear that the company needs to retain the useful elements of a more unitarist strategy. A positive way forward is to combine the strong leadership and commitment (to move towards values associated with sustainable development) found in unitarism with a strategy aimed at respecting any alternative values. Moreover, by adopting this more participative style, the pluralist strategy would, in fact, extend values associated with environmental protection and sustainable development. There must therefore be a commitment to providing mechanisms that will resolve, or at the very least contain, the disharmonies that exist between divergent systems of meaning within the culture whilst developing a strong consensus, over-arching framework (or system) and commitment to the improvement of environmental performance within the organization.

Therefore, this strategy eliminates the failing unitarist strategy of holding the anarchistic tendencies of corporate pluralism in check, but also recognizes that there must be an overall green objective. The education of not only the workforce, but management as well is an essential element in achieving a common consensus promoting environmentalism. The challenge for environmental management is to find a balance between bureaucracy and dynamics.

ASSESSING THE PERFORMANCE OF PLURALISM: THE SOCIAL AUDITING PROCESS

As was argued above, there needs to be a wider involvement of all company stakeholders in a move towards sustainable development. The pluralist approach facilitates this and allows for an assessment of progress through techniques such as social auditing. Thus social auditing takes account of not only the internal pluralism within an organization but external pluralism as well. It also supports a greater degree of organizational transparency as advocated by Welford and Jones (1996). Social auditing is therefore a process to induce and promote new forms of democracy and accountability in the workplace and beyond.

The rationale behind using a social auditing approach for a business wishing to move towards sustainability, is to acknowledge the rights of information to a wide constituency i.e. to attend to societal pluralism. Firms using the social auditing process would be conceived of as lying at the centre of a network of social relationships which are articulated in a manner akin to a stakeholder model. Stakeholders are commonly understood to be those groups or individuals who can affect or are affected by the organization's social performance and objectives (Freeman 1984). Put another way, social auditing recognizes the concepts of stewardship and accountability and this in turn acknowledges that the whole of society has rights to information about actions taken on its behalf (e.g. by businesses). Thus the social auditing process allows the business to engage with its stakeholders (representing, in part, societal interests), listen to and respond to their views and, where necessary, explain and justify its actions. But it is not only a one-way flow. Businesses are also able to influence their stakeholders so that the ultimate outcome is derived from consensus.

Respect for pluralism is developed as organizations become more transparent. That is, information is used to reduce the distance between the organization and the external (and internal) participants so that stakeholders can 'see into' the organization, assess what it is doing with the resources that determine future options and react (or not react) accordingly. As Gray (1994) argues, the impact of this information on this constituency and their associated response can be assumed to encourage the new practices necessary for sustainable development. If accountability and transparency is embraced, then the corporation will find itself more closely in tune with its wider constituents and the company will develop its culture from a recognition of different stakeholder expectations and needs. But this is by no means an easy process. There will be trade-offs that have to be made if sustainability is to be pursued.

The social auditing process means that employees' (internal stakeholders') values and expectations are accounted for alongside other external stakeholders' values and expectations. The social audit provides a medium in which the employee's values and expectations can be measured against other employees from different departments, levels or backgrounds as well as against various other stakeholders. The resulting deeper appreciation of the diverse stakeholder pressures upon a company breeds a greater respect and trust between stakeholders. A relationship characterized by trust and mutual respect is a fruitful basis for employee participation. An open dialogue between management and employees on raised problems are necessary to deal with conflicts and resistance.

The social audit gives the employee a chance to compare and contrast core company values with not only their own values but other employees' and other external stakeholders' values and expectations. The important point to stress is the importance to a social audit of an over-arching and explicit values framework written in terms of corporate values, visions, aims and objectives. This is important because it provides the basic parameters for the ongoing dialogue between the various stakeholders and management. An explicit values framework avoids the anarchic flaws of this type of 'accounting receptivity'. In other words it avoids a business degenerating into an unmanageable scramble of values, multiple aims and multiple measures of performance. In this way a firm can provide a sustainable direction to its activities. The importance of an explicit values framework for a business wishing to move towards sustainable development was one of the recommendations from the prior research of Welford and Jones (1996). Therefore, in order to measure the organization's social performance, not only is stakeholder performance against core values measured, but also company performance against stakeholder values. Figure 7.1 represents a stakeholder consultation model. It shows the two-way flow of learning and accountability necessary to fully realize the virtues of a pluralistic strategy. The company reports to and learns from the stakeholder and the stakeholder is invited to assess the organization's performance and aspirations. The company is also able to influence the stakeholder, particularly where its own aspirations may be higher than some of its stakeholders.

The social audit is operationalized through the three assessment loops depicted in Figure 7.1. At the centre of the assessment process are the core values of the organization, made explicit in the organization's values framework which is published and made widely available. The extent to which the organization is perceived to be adhering to these core values is determined through consultation with a range of stakeholders and (often key) informants (expert opinion, publicly recognized figures etc). Where company performance is perceived to be poor it will be either because that action really is poor or because the organization has not communicated its performance accurately or effectively. In either case, action to improve performance (or its communication) will have to be taken. Such action may require some alteration of the organization's values framework. This process is represented by loop 1.

At the same time the organization compares its own core values with

Figure 7.1 The Social Auditing Process

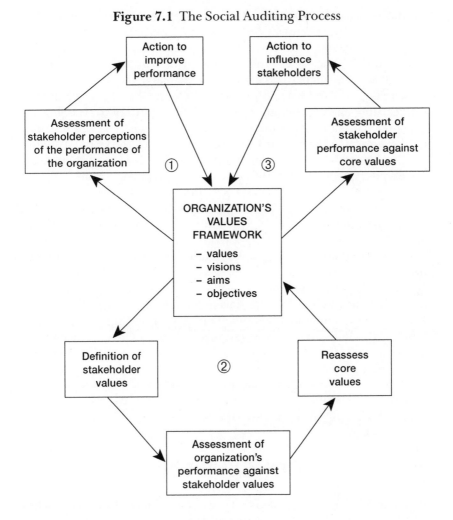

those of its stakeholders (loop 2). The process is firstly to define its stakeholders' values (again through consultation) and then to compare the organization's performance against these stakeholder values. Where necessary (because gaps or deficiencies are identified) core values can be reassessed and the values framework rewritten to reflect this.

The third loop involves action to influence stakeholders through the assessment of stakeholder performance against core values. Here, we may find the situation where the organization considers its values to be superior to those of its stakeholders. Through education and campaigning initiatives the organization takes action to influence stakeholders. According to Welford (1995) this might be seen as central to a company's green marketing strategy.

Thus stakeholders influence the organization through their perceptions of company performance based on its own values (loop 1) and through an assessment of performance based on stakeholders' own values (loop 2). The organization, in turn, tries to influence stakeholders through an assessment of stakeholder performance against its own core values (loop 3). Welford and Jones (1996) argue that this implicit two-way learning and accountability is especially important to recognize in the context of moving towards sustainable development. Their research results argue that the existence of consultation frameworks and dialogue must be at the heart of sustainability measures. This must include all stakeholders, widely defined. Moreover, through such a process, the organization can actually become a facilitator of change. Transparent, open institutional structures are required in the firm so that any stakeholder has the ability to challenge and question the organization over any issue. Thus, we are looking for two-way processes here with interaction and dialogue shifting the organization on to a more sustainable path.

The social auditing process occurs on a regular basis (perhaps annually) and disclosed to the stakeholders in a systematic, periodic, verified and documented manner. This regular auditing procedure is important as it allows for an evolutionary process of taking stakeholder interests more directly into account and having to report on activities according to their interests. It is a learning process where the organization seeks to improve its environmental, social and ethical activities over time. It should be a process of dialogue and discussion with all parties benefiting from the procedures.

CONCLUSIONS

In this chapter we have argued that the popular hierarchical approaches to organizational arrangements and structure in the workplace are impractical. They are very much the vestiges of modernism with its narrowly defined approach to environmental improvement. Top-down management control is often inefficient, brings with it a particular view about the industrial process and wider economic system and is based on the assumption that management knows best. It is alienating and not consistent with the spirit of Agenda 21 which calls for more cooperation and participation with workers and their trade unions. Employees with differing values and commitment, see through and often rebel against directed top management control. This can often lead to the formation of subversive subcultures and the so-called 'unmanaged organization'. The type of feelings embodied in this situation are fear of failure, powerlessness, mistrust and disillusion.

There is a clear need for a systematic framework to involve employees in top-level dialogue and decision-making. There is also a need for strong leadership but this is only possible with a solid 'followership'. In the move towards sustainable development at the level of business activity we have made the case for a participatory strategy. But employees must see the point of participating. It must be more than mere lip-service. Strong views from the workforce (and indeed, other stakeholders) must be acted upon and positive outcomes from participatory arrangements may need to be rewarded. Over time, within the participatory framework, certain staff will become instrumental and they will become a powerful resource for education and awareness raising. Whilst their views are only as valid as anyone else's, one should not forget that they will often be able to synthesize and communicate the feelings and views of people around them.

Therefore, the case has been made for a more pluralist, democratic strategy, which more fully respects diverse goals, values and aspirations. But it is not only internal structures which matter. As a powerful social actor the business has a responsibility to respond to and, where appropriate, influence its external stakeholders as well as its internal ones. This needs to be managed and measured within a broad social auditing approach where performance of the company is measured against core values of the company as well as the values of a range of stakeholders. The social auditing process allows the organization to be transparent and accountable. It engages a wide range of stakeholders in a two-way dialogue about the activities and performance of the stakeholders closest to the company: the workers, and therefore treats them as a valuable resource rather than a neo-classical factor of production. It is argued that such an approach rejects the traditional approach of modernism and is more consistent with the general move towards real environmental improvement and social responsibility. Moreover, by empowering the worker and other stakeholders within a more pluralist setting, we are likely to achieve the changes in industrial organization and activity needed to bring about sustainable development.

References

Adler, N (1985) Introduction, in *Women in Management Worldwide* (eds Adler, N and Izraeli, D), M E Sharpe, New York

Bartunek, J M and Moch, M K (1987) First-order, second-order and third-order change and organizational development interventions: a cognitive approach, *Journal of Applied Behavioural Science*, 23, 483–500

Bate, P (1994) *Strategies for cultural change*, Butterworth-Heinemann, Oxford

Beaumont, J R, Pedersen, L M and Whitaker, B D (1993) *Managing the Environment*, Butterworth-Heinemann, Oxford

Bourgeois, L (1984) Strategic management and determinism, *Academy of Management Review*, 9, 4

Callenbach, E, Capra, F, Goldman, L, Lutz, R and Marburg, S (1993) *Eco-Management: The Elmwood guide to ecological auditing and sustainable business*, Berrett-Koehler Publishers, San Francisco

Child, J (1984) *Organization: a guide to problems and practice*, 2nd ed, Harper and Row, London

Coulson-Thomas, C (1992) Strategic vision or strategic con?: Rhetoric or reality, *Long Range Planning*, 25(1), 81–9

Crozier, M (1964) *The Bureaucratic Phenomenon*, Tavistock, London

Deal, T E and Kennedy A A (1982) *Corporate cultures. The rites and rituals of corporate life*, Addison-Wesley, Reading, Mass

Fox, A (1973) Industrial relations: a social critique of pluralist ideology, in *Man and Organization* (ed J Child), Allen and Unwin, London

Freeman, E (1984) *Strategic management: A stakeholder approach*, Pitman Publishing, Boston, Mass

Gabriel, Y (1991) An organizational stories and myths: why it is easier to slay a dragon than to kill a myth, *International Sociology*, 6(4), 427–42

Gray, R H (1994) Corporate reporting for sustainable development: accounting for sustainability in 2000 AD, *Environmental Values*, 3(1), 17–45

Janis, L and Mann, L (1977) *Decision-Making: A psychological analysis of conflict, choice and commitment*, The Free Press, New York

Martin and Siehl (1983) Organizational culture and counter culture: an uneasy symbiosis, *Organizational Dynamics*, 12(2), 52–64

Meek, L V (1988) Organizational culture: origins and weaknesses, *Organization Studies*, 9(4), 453–73

Metcalfe, L and Richards, S (1987) Evolving management cultures, in *Managing public organizations: Lessons from contemporary European experience* (eds J Kooiman and K Eliassen), Sage, London

Murphy, P (1989) Creating ethical corporate structures, *Sloan Management Review*, 30, 2, 81–7

Nicholson, N (1984) Organizational culture, ideology and management, in *Leaders and Managers* (eds) J Hunt, D Hosking, C Schriesheim and R Stewart, Pergamon Press, London

Peters, T J and Waterman, R H (1982) *In Search of Excellence*, Harper and Row, New York

Pettigrew, A M (1979) On studying organizational culture, *Administrative Science Quarterly*, 24

Polsby, N W (1966) *Community power and political theory*, Yale University Press, New Haven, Conn.

Post, J E and Altman, B (1991) *Corporate environmentalism: The challenge of organizational learning*, National Academy of Management Meeting, Miami, Fl

Schein, E (1983) The role of the founder in creating organizational culture, *Organizational dynamics*, Summer

Silk, L and Vogel, D (1976) *Ethics and Profits: The crisis of confidence in America*, Simon and Schuster, New York

Sinclair, A (1993) Approaches to organizational culture and ethics, *Journal of Business Ethics*, 12, 63–73

Smircich, L (1983) Concepts of culture and organizational analysis, *Administrative Science Quarterly*, 28

Turner, B (1971) *Exploring the industrial subculture*, Macmillan, London

Welford, R (1995) *Environmental Strategy and Sustainable Development*, Routledge, London

Welford, R and Jones, D R (1996) 'Beyond environmentalism and towards the sustainable organization' in *Corporate Environmental Management: Systems and Strategies*, R J Welford (ed) Earthscan, London

Young, E (1989) On the naming of the rose: interests and multiple meanings as elements of organizational culture, *Organization Studies*, 10, 2, 187–206

PART 3

Searching for Solutions

8

Models of Sustainable Development for Business

Richard Welford

There exists a strange and fruitless search for a single definition of sustainable development amongst people who do not fully understand that we are really talking here of a process rather than a tangible outcome. This search is most apparent amongst positivist researchers who grope for a hard core of definitions and data which they can manipulate to produce simple solutions and singular answers to very complex concepts. Such simplifications cannot exist in the postmodern world and they simply hide a scientific research bias which is not appropriate to a highly political issue such as sustainable development. The search for a single definition of this concept is futile even though it may maintain the employment of a few academics.

As an ultimate broad vision and as a description of how we might get to that vision, the concept of sustainability may nevertheless be immensely valuable. However strategies are needed to translate conceptual ideas into practical reality. This requires a more radical assessment of environmental strategy than we have seen to date. The challenge that faces the economic system is how to continue to fulfil its vital role within modern society whilst ensuring sustainability. The emphasis to date has been on piecemeal moves towards environmental improvement and this move has often been in the wrong direction. It also lacks the sense of urgency and commitment which is required. There is now a need to carefully assess how economic activities can be sustainable and this implies acceptance of the view that not all growth and development will be good. We must accept that sustainability is not something that will be achieved overnight, but in the longer term, entire economies and individual businesses need to look towards a new type of development and growth. This, in turn, requires them to look at their own ethics, their objectives and their own forms of organization, corporate culture and communication. Moreover, it requires us to give some direction to business by mapping out the path towards sustainability.

One major obstacle preventing sustainability from being achieved is the overall level of consumption experienced in the Western world. Consumers who are relatively wealthy seem reluctant to significantly reduce their own levels of consumption. While increasingly governments are adopting economic instruments such as taxes, subsidies and product labelling schemes to reduce and channel consumption towards more environmentally friendly alternatives, there is also a need for education amongst consumers. In addition, though, industry has a role to play in educating their customers and suppliers and all businesses must be encouraged to further increase their own internal environmental efficiency by reassessing the very ways in which they do business and measuring and assessing their social and environmental performance.

The fact which lies behind the concept of sustainable development is that there is a trade-off between continuous economic growth and the sustainability of the environment. Over time, through greater and greater exploitation, growth causes pollution and atmospheric damage, disrupts traditional ways of living (particularly in the developing world), destroys ecosystems and feeds more and more power into oligopolistic industrial structures. The concept of sustainable development stresses the interdependence between economic growth and environmental quality, but it also goes further in demonstrating that the future is uncertain unless we can deal with issues of equity and inequality throughout the whole world. It is possible to make development and environmental protection compatible and to begin to deal with the problems caused by a lack of consideration of social issues, by following sustainable strategies and by not developing the particular areas of economic activity that are most damaging to the planet and its peoples.

The Brundtland Report, commissioned by the United Nations to examine long term environmental strategies, argued that economic development and environmental protection could be made compatible, but that this would require quite radical changes in economic practices throughout the world. Mass consumption is not possible indefinitely and if society today acts as if all non-renewable resources are plentiful, eventually there will be nothing left for the future. But more importantly than that, mass consumption may cause such irreparable damage that humans may not even be able to live on the planet in the future.

This chapter examines a number of possible ways of defining the sustainable development process by examining six models of sustainability. These are not meant to be definitive strategies for achieving sustainable development, but models which illustrate the complex issues and interrelationships which we must deal with. The chapter goes on to examine how companies might report on progress towards sustainable development using a stakeholder accountability process.

DEFINING THE SUSTAINABLE DEVELOPMENT PROCESS

Business has a central role to play in bringing about a more sustainable future therefore. As a starting point, any environmental strategy must demonstrate a real commitment on the part of the whole organization. This may mean a change in corporate culture and management has an important role to play. In leading that commitment and laying out the organization's corporate objectives with respect to the environment, management has to be the catalyst for change. Moreover, change has to be on-going and management must be ever mindful of the full range of (often competing) objectives to which it is subject. Management has to find compromise between these objectives if they conflict and design corporate strategies which are operational, consistent and achievable. Change will have to be addressed in a systemic way, dealing with the company as a whole rather than in a compartmentalized way and seeing the company as unavoidably interconnected with everything around it.

Moreover, the company needs also to consider its social impact and this involves a range of ethical considerations. Managers are aware of these issues and research (Welford 1994) has indicated that when considering social and environmental impacts on their families they are keen to see a whole range of higher standards being adopted by industry and governments. This concern does not always spill over into the workplace because of competing objectives and other priorities. However, more ethical firms will, in the future, begin to internalize more of the social impacts which it has identified and managers will play a key role in defining these impacts and putting systems in place to improve performance more widely defined.

What businesses need is some guidance as to how to proceed. That guidance has to be more than simply building on continuous environmental improvement as the eco-modernists would have us believe – that is not equivalent to sustainable business practice. Moreover, there can never be a single approach to a complicated issue, universally relevant to every type of business organization. Since we do not have a clear idea of what precisely sustainability looks like in the business context we can never be prescriptive about the measures which must be taken to deliver one particular objective. At best we can only provide pictures and descriptions of the road down which businesses should tread. Anyone who claims to provide more should be treated with much scepticism. Here we provide six alternative (but not mutually exclusive) pictures (there will be many more). They are all compatible with a move towards a sustainable future. Which road a business embarks on will depend on the particular organization, its product profile and the overall aspirations of its leadership. Table 8.1 provides a summary of the six models which follow. The challenge for business is to use these ideas to define its own sustainable development agenda, to put appropriate policies and procedures in place and to report on progress towards a sustainable business operation.

Table 8.1 Alternative models of sustainable development for business

Model number	Model name	Number of Dimensions
1	Environment, equity and futurity	3
2	The social, environmental and economic approach	3
3	The 3 Ps	3
4	The sustainable development values pentagon	5
5	The 6 Es	6
6	Measures of sustainability	7

There is therefore a need for business to encourage a wide range of perspectives within the organization and then to manage the excitement that will be generated by the discussions about the best way to move towards a sustainable future. As the company does move forward it must always bring its workforce with it. If it does not it will find itself alone without the support of the people who are central to the organization. The way to achieve this is to increase the degree of participation in the workplace and to empower groups and individuals to play a full part in the process of change. The models which follow should therefore not be seen as prescriptive, but a set of ideas and approaches which can provide the starting point for a corporate sustainability strategy.

Model 1: Environment, equity and futurity

One of the most basic models of sustainable development is outlined by Welford (1995) and takes as its theme a three dimensional approach seeing sustainable development as being made up of the environment, equity and futurity (Figure 8.1). These are closely connected issues and each element, it is argued, needs to be addressed by industry in the following ways:

Firstly, the environment must be valued as an integral part of the economic process and not treated as a free good. The environmental stock has to be protected and this implies minimal use of non-renewable resources and minimal emission of pollutants. Ecosystems have to be protected so the loss of plant and animal species has to be avoided. This is the realm of corporate environmental management tools.

Secondly there is a need to deal with the issue of equity. One of the biggest threats facing the world is that the developing countries want to grow rapidly to achieve the same standards of living as those in the West. That in itself would cause major environmental degradation if it were modelled on the same sort of growth experienced in post-war Europe. There therefore needs to be a greater degree of equity and the key issue of poverty has to be addressed. But equity applies not only to relationships between the developed and developing worlds, but also within countries between people. A major source of inequality exists between those who are employed and unemployed and this must also be tackled within the context of sustainability.

Figure 8.1 A Simple Model of Sustainable Development

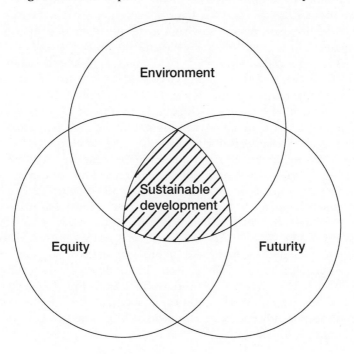

Thirdly, sustainable development requires that society, businesses and individuals operate on a different time scale than currently operates in the economy. This is the issue of futurity. While companies commonly operate under competitive pressures to achieve short run gains, long term environmental protection is often compromised. To ensure that longer term, inter-generational considerations are observed, longer planning horizons need to be adopted and business policy needs to be proactive rather than reactive.

Industry must seek to provide the services demanded by consumers with the minimum environmental impact at all stages. This is a far reaching challenge as it involves a reformulation not only of production processes but of the products themselves. While many consumers may be unwilling to reduce the overall levels of consumption to which they have become accustomed, they have proved willing to select the good which produces a reduced environmental impact. Companies need to focus their environmental strategies and subsequent green marketing campaigns on supplying goods with a sustainable differential advantage. In so doing the producer has to accept the responsibility for the environmental impact of the materials and processes used at the pro- duction stage and for the final product and its disposal. In many ways therefore, industry has to take on a whole range of new responsibilities towards the environment.

Sustainable development is not only about direct impact on the environment however and we have already argued that corporate strategy dealing with narrow environmental performance measures is inadequate. It is argued that a key part of the concept (which is often conveniently ignored by industry) is about equity. The massive inequality in wealth and standards of living displayed across the world makes sustainable development harder to achieve. Those living in the developing world often aspire to the standards of living of the developed world and we know from an environmental stance such aspirations are presently not achievable. But what right does the developed world have to deny other human beings development in the same unsustainable way in which they themselves have developed? Therefore we can see that environmental improvement is inextricably linked to wider issues of global concern which do need to be addressed. Equity has also to be tackled at the level of the firm however. New forms of industrial organization should seek to empower workers and increase their decision-making powers, to increase democracy in the workplace and to share profits with the workforce, alongside improving environmental performance. This demands a more holistic and ethical approach to doing business which values workers as an integral and valuable part of the organization rather than a resource to be hired and fired as external market conditions change.

Model 2: The social, environmental and economic approach

One of the weaknesses of the previous model is that it lacks any consideration of the sustainability of the company more traditionally measured i.e. through profitability and economic efficiency. Thus another way of examining the problem in a three dimensional way is to consider sustainable development as being made up of environmental, social and economic elements (Figure 8.2). The sustainable organization will have a high level of performance on the social, environmental and economic/financial fronts therefore. To neglect any one of these elements is to neglect a fundamental part of the sustainable development agenda.

Figure 8.2 Elements of the Sustainable Organization

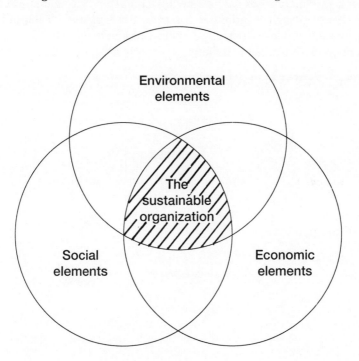

What we have seen to date, of course is a neglect of many of the social elements of sustainability. Figure 8.3 maps out a common approach to the links between environmental performance and economic perform-ance which ignores that social dimension. Here we have divided firms into four broad categories. Those with good economic performance as well as good environmental performance we might see as the ubiquitous eco-efficient firm, wholly in line with the trend of eco-modernism discussed earlier in the book. They are however, certainly not sustainable organizations (even though many commentators try to persuade us otherwise) because they lack the social dimension of sustainability. There will also be what have become know as 'green babies': firms which are environmental innovators but do not yet have the financial stability needed to ensure continuation into the long run. These are the sorts of firms we need to identify for development assistance: they can be helped to develop both their financial and social performance in order to become more sustainable organizations. High levels of economic performance with little regard to environmental issues is represented in Figure 8.3 as 'business as usual'. These firms with their solid financial bases are the ones which can and should grasp the wider social and environmental agendas. Other firms are inherently unstable because they lack any financial or environmental strength. Once again however, these firms must be candidates for carefully targeted development assistance since to lose them altogether would be to lose the jobs which are central to a sustainable society.

Figure 8.3 Environmental and Economic Performance

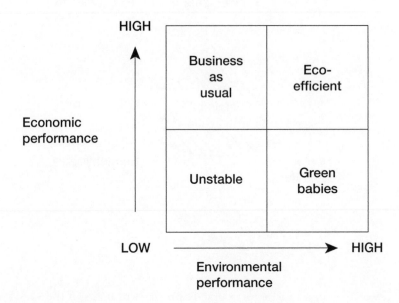

In Figure 8.4 we can do the same sort of exercise ignoring environmental considerations and concentrating on the economic and social elements of sustainability. There are many fewer firms who consider social issues before environmental issues than vice versa, but there are a good number, which commonly because of political or religious principles often fall into this sort of category. The social innovators are those companies who have strong social and financial performances. These are the sorts of companies which have been successful in promoting, for example, fair trade, worker participation and have campaigned against child labour. Unfortunately, many more such companies find themselves with much poorer economic performance even though their social performance is high. These are the alternative organizations such as many worker cooperatives, small collectives and quasi-non-governmental organizations. In part, their poor economic performance is by design since the aim of the organization is often to produce a small surplus rather than to maximize profits. Nevertheless, their poorer economic performance does, sometimes, stifle further development. Similar to the arguments made above, high economic performance with a poor social performance is very much business as usual, whereas poor performance on both counts leads to a very unstable situation.

Figure 8.4 Social and Economic Performance

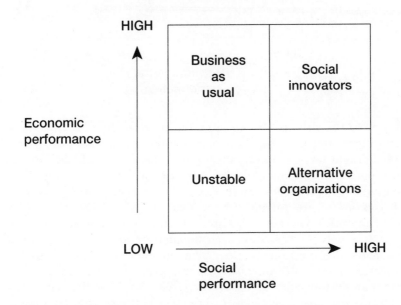

For sake of symmetry, we can also examine a matrix mapping out the relationship between social and environmental performance, ignoring the economic dimension, in Figure 8.5. Once again we find the unstable organization in the bottom left hand quadrant. We also find our alternative organizations and 'green babies' in the figure. They can

become eco-efficient and social innovators as their financial performance improves. The firms with both high environmental and social
performances are our potentially sustainable organizations. Potential,
because they are only sustainable if they last: this requires sound
economic performance as well.

Figure 8.5 Environmental and Social Performance

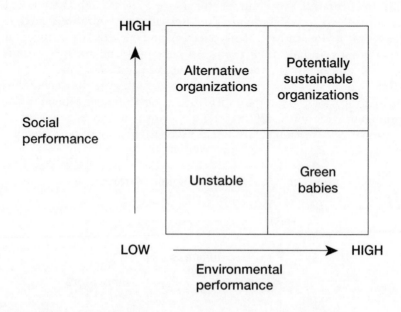

To explore the sustainable organization we must therefore put these
three dimensions together. This is done in Figure 8.6. Here we have a
three dimensional representation illustrating combinations of
environmental, economic and social performance which can bring about
a sustainable organization. Here we can see our social innovators (who
still lack an environmental dimension), our eco-efficient firms or
environmental successes (who are nevertheless still weak on social
aspects) and two categories of sustainable organization. The weak
sustainable organization has poor economic performance and as has
been argued above will only be truly sustainable if it can improve this
economic performance to ensure long term survival. The company
which we are most interested in, however, is the strong sustainable
organization which performs well with respect to all three dimensions.

The argument here is very simple therefore. The sustainable organization must have strong economic, environmental and social elements to
its activities. It must therefore monitor and measure these aspects and
ensure that they improve over time. The fact remains however, that this

Figure 8.6 Social, Environmental and Economic Performance and the Sustainable Organization

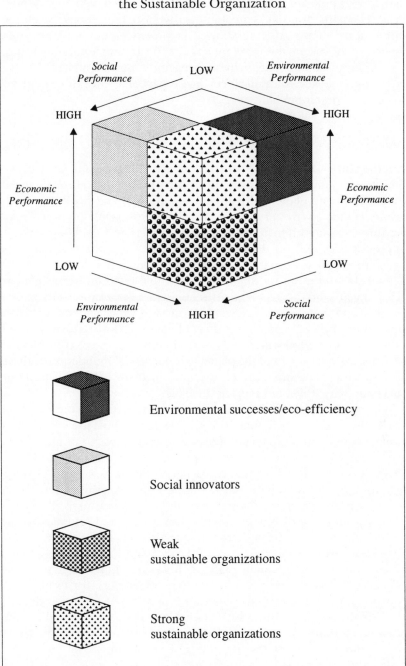

model does not describe exactly what the sustainable organization looks like. It does however point in the general direction in which we should head. The path towards sustainability is therefore represented by a three dimensional vector. Moving along it involves strengthening all three aspects of the sustainable development agenda. In simple auditing terms, the organization might begin by auditing and reporting on its financial, environmental and social performance as part of an overall strategy for sustainable development.

Model 3: The 3 Ps: People, planet and product

Another three dimensional approach to achieving sustainability in the business organization is to examine impacts on people (a broadly social dimension), the planet (broadly environmental) and product (which would include goods, services and profits, all as useful outputs). There are very clear links here to the previous model therefore. However, this approach is capable of defining much more clearly the types of tools which the company can use in achieving sustainability.

As a starting point we might see the whole purpose of business as revolving around the 3 Ps. The main objective of a business is to make a range of goods and/or provide services in a way which generates profits. But it does this in the general context of having to work with a range of people through employment, supply chain linkages and as customers. It uses the basic resources of the planet as the material foundation of these very activities. The aim is therefore to maximize the benefits within this sort of activity whilst minimizing the bads.

As a starting point Table 8.2 outlines the targets for consideration under these three broad dimensions and suggests some tools of analysis which might be used. In terms of product (which we are defining much more widely than just material output) targets are goods produced, services provided and profits (or surpluses) made as a result of these activities. Indeed we can include in this definition anything useful from an economic perspective. Tools such as life cycle assessment allow us to track the impacts of our products more widely and allow us to say something about sources of raw materials and ways in which they themselves were produced. We can easily build in social and ethical considerations here which might include the rights of indigenous populations, fair wages and fair trade arrangements, for example. A functionality assessment takes an even broader view of the product of the firm. In asking questions such as what is this product for? and is there a better alternative to providing the services which this product offers? we are forced to justify the usefulness of our outputs and to consider other alternatives which can provide the same results but at lower environmental, social or financial cost.

In terms of people, the first responsibility of the firm must be to its own employees (particularly with regard to their own health, safety, employment rights and continuity of employment) and then to the whole range of other stakeholders which the company has. Clear employment policies and audits of employment practices are a good starting point internally. Externally there needs to be stakeholder assessment, social audits and dialogue between the company and all interested parties.

More traditional environmental management techniques can be used when considering our third dimension, the planet. Environmental auditing is central here along with strategies such as education of employees, customers and others and where appropriate campaigning in a broader sense to contribute to the change necessary to reverse the environmental degradation of the planet.

One of the benefits of this model is that we can link targets to tools and, in turn, tools to reports. There is nothing here that has not been tried and tested by a number of firms. What only a few firms have done, however, is to put all these aspects together into a reporting framework specifically designed to track sustainability. We return to this issue later in the chapter.

Table 8.2 Operationalising the 3 Ps model of sustainability

Dimension	Targets	Tools
Product	goods	life cycle assessment
	services	functionality assessment
	profits/surpluses	financial indicators/ accounts
People	employment and employment practices	employment policies and audits
	other stakeholders	stakeholder assessment and social audits
Planet	environmental improvement	corporate environmental management tools
	species protection	
		environmental auditing
		education and campaigning

Model 4: The sustainable development values pentagon

The basis of this model can be found in the more general attempts to define sustainable development, typified by the work of Gladwin et al (1995). However it has been expanded here to include elements of sustainability which were lacking in Gladwin's original approach and which we have considered in earlier chapters of this book. This is a much broader approach than that taken in the models up until now but it has the advantage of being applicable not only to the business organization, but to any organization, or indeed, whole societies. It is a more difficult approach to operationalize and implicitly takes a very strong definition of sustainable development. Using this sort of approach the business can nevertheless see, more clearly, its role within the larger agenda. The model is different to the others presented here because it is much less technical in its nature and much more values driven. It is well suited therefore to companies who have been social innovators and where a strong set of values already exists. There are strong parallels with this sort of approach and the culture change and social auditing strategies advocated in Chapter 7. The five elements are illustrated in Figure 8.7, where the pentagon as a whole is a representation of sustainability. Let us deal with each of those elements in turn.

Figure 8.7 The Sustainable Development Values Pentagon

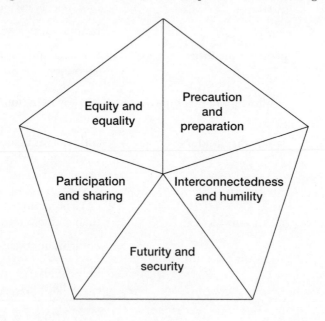

Equity and equality

A fairer distribution of resources and property rights both within and between generations is central to the sustainable development agenda. This is, of course, a very subjective issue and what constitutes fair is open to some debate. Nevertheless it is clear that present situations are not fair and we have argued in previous chapters that present inequities and inequalities are a major source of unsustainable practices. Sustainability means that human activities (or the activities of the firm) should not shift costs onto, or appropriate the property or resources of other human interests without proper compensation. It is up to the firm, therefore to ensure that its own activities do not impinge on the abilities of others to live their lives as they would wish, or to use resources in a way which deprives others, both now and in the future, having the same opportunities to use those resources. Within its own organization too, the firm should deal with equity and equality issues though equal opportunities programmes and more pluralist cultures as discussed in Chapter 7.

Participation and sharing

Sustainable development goes beyond ecological efficiency and needs also to embrace social sufficiency. A very important element in the process is therefore participation. As far as possible decisions need to be shared because better quality decisions, more acceptable to those who must operationalize them will be made. Participation is central to the democratic process and the sustainable organization is likely to have strong elements of industrial democracy: participation, profit sharing, ownership rights, etc. Sustainability is all embracing and must therefore be inclusive, embracing both ecological and human systems. Again, this demands more pluralism within the firm and stronger emphasis put on building strong relationships within the organization and between stakeholders. Social auditing processes will help to spread the idea of participation and sharing more widely.

Interconnectedness and humility

This book has often revisited the idea that sustainability is about understanding the systemic and interconnected nature of the world's problems. There is a need for people (particularly managers in power) to resist pandering to their own egos and recognize their own significance in the wider order of things. This practical (as well as often spiritual) enlightenment enables people to become more humble, to think of others more generously and to make better quality decisions. At the same time managers can be leaders and communicate the sustainable development message. Stronger links along the supply chain, better stakeholder communications and education initiatives are possible ways of achieving this. The business organization must also recognize its own connectedness. It cannot exist in isolation and ultimately its own survival depends on the survival of the whole system in which it operates. It must make the contributions necessary to ensure that this happens.

Precaution and preparation

Precaution is central to any environmentalist's agenda. Given the massive uncertainty and unpredictability of the world in which we exist we must give the benefit of any doubt relating to business activities to people and the planet. This constraint requires us to be well prepared: ensuring that actions are reversible, taking pre-emptive safeguards, increasing margins for error and undertaking contingency planning. This means that we do not seek to achieve traditional business objectives at any cost but that there is a trade-off between such objectives and the operationalization of sustainable development. Here the business must often grasp ethical dilemmas between a new business opportunity and the precautionary principle.

Futurity and security

As a minimum sustainable development requires no net loss of eco-systems into the future, the continued integrity of natural and social systems, the maintenance of natural capital, any pollution held down to local carrying capacities and the protection of human freedoms. These are issues for both now and the future and are essentially about securing a sustainable quality of life for all species, across all generations. The business must adopt longer planning horizons, be prepared to justify its activities and communicate these sorts of values to stakeholders.

Operationalizing this model is, of course much more difficult than earlier models because its aims and objectives are much less precise. In many ways however, this is the nature of sustainable development and business can think carefully about its own impact with respect to these various dimensions and try to contribute to an overall agenda which must be a partnership between individuals, businesses and institutions at a local, national and global level. The starting point has to be to examine the values of the organization and all its employees. Simply shaping those individual values in a way which is consistent with sustainable development values will actually generate many of the desired outcomes within the organization. Spreading those values to stakeholders and the wider public through education initiatives and campaigning is the next step. The social auditing process is central here.

According to Gladwin et al (1995) this sort of approach requires that we develop new management theories as if sustainability matters. We need to concentrate on sufficiency rather than maximization, on equity rather than efficiency and on limitation rather than plenitude. Thinking must be cyclical rather than linear and the frame of reference must be the whole world rather than narrow business as usual objectives. Sustainability will result in the organization shifting from the objective paradigm of positivism to more subjective alternatives: from exterior nuts and bolts to interior hearts and minds. Such changes are truly transformational but many commentators (e.g. Hawken 1994) would argue that business is now the only institution in the modern world powerful enough to foster the changes necessary for ecological and social sustainability.

Model 5: The 6 Es

This model is a combination of many different people's work and has developed over the last couple of years. The six Es consist of the environment, empowerment, economics, ethics, equity and education. We can view these as six areas where the business should have a clear policy and agenda for change. Table 8.3 outlines these policy areas along with suggested tools for operationalizing a change process. The sustainable firm will not only use these tools to achieve its sustainable development objectives in these six areas but will also report on progress. This model is essentially a 'policy in, reporting out' framework where the activities of the firm are transparent. In other words, the business is expected to have a policy in each of these six areas, to operationalize that policy using the indicative tools suggested in Table 8.3 and then to report on progress. Like all the models presented here no firm will be able to produce a perfect profile in all six areas (even if that could be defined). Reports should detail progress in each element and demonstrate a degree of continuous improvement. They should also point to areas which still require attention and produce objectives and targets for the next reporting period.

It is worth briefly reviewing the sorts of idealized outcomes which the business should move towards in each of these six areas:

Environment
The environment is to be protected with minimum use of non-renewable resources. Environmental performance will be monitored and measured and it is likely that there will be an environmental management system in place with regular audit activity. Products will be assessed according to a life cycle assessment and redesigned where practicable to reduce environmental impact. Products will also undergo a functionality assessment to determine whether there is a better way of providing the benefits of the product. There will be strong connections along the

Table 8.3 Policy areas and tools for sustainable development

POLICY IN⌐
↓

Policy area	*Indicative tools*
Environment	life cycle assessment environmental management system and audits functionality assessment resource management
Empowerment	teambuilding participation equal opportunities declaration of rights
Economics	profits/surplus employment quality long term financial stability and investment
Ethics	transparency of objectives openness to concerns honesty values statement
Equity	fair trade policy and activity end price auditing development aid sponsorship
Education	training customer information community involvement campaigning

↓
REPORTING OUT

supply chain to integrate all stages of the product's life. After production, firms will, as far as possible manage the use and disposal of the product through product stewardship procedures. Much emphasis will be placed on local action including close connections with local community initiatives and protection of the health and safety of all employees and neighbours.

Empowerment

Everybody must feel part of the process of improvement and must be empowered to recognize and act on their own obligations as well as work together closely with colleagues. There will be strong participation in the workforce with respect to decision-making, profit-sharing and ownership structures. The organization will be open to new suggestions made by anyone in the workforce and workers will be rewarded on the basis of contribution to this overall ethos as well as work done. Human capital will be valued and workers will not be treated as simple factors of production. There will be enshrined rights within the organization relating to equal opportunities and individual freedoms. Diversity will be encouraged, not stifled.

Economy

The economic performance of the firm will be sustainable in that it will be sufficient to provide for on-going survival, the continued provision of employment, the payment of dividends to shareholders and the payment of fair wages to all concerned in the organization. Financial audits will be extended to a justification of profits made and a demonstration that they have been made though good business practices rather than cost cutting exploitation. There will be periodic new investment in both physical capital as well as human capital (through education and retraining). Business relationships should be mutually advantageous to all parties concerned so that there exists supply chain stability. Jobs are a central part of sustainability and the provision and growth of employment is to be encouraged. Products made will be of good quality, durable and suitable for the purpose for which they were intended.

Ethics

The organization will have a clear set of values which it will publish and which will be periodically reassessed through the social audit process. The firm will at all times be honest and will be open to questions about its ethical stance, providing evidence relating to any activities which are being challenged. It will be a transparent organization and relations with subsidiaries, contractors and agents clearly identified. Ethics are not simply something which the organization simply declares, it must translate them into practice via codes of conduct, education, communication and information. Businesses serve a variety of purposes for different stakeholders. Therefore we might argue that as a necessary condition, business activities are justifiable only in so far as they can be shown to meet the legitimate requirements of stakeholders.

Equity

Issues associated with equity exist both within and outwith the organization. Closely linked with empowerment issues there must be clear statement of rights and equal opportunities within the firm. Trade along the supply chain must be equitable and particularly with regard to international trade there must be assurances for workers in developing countries, for indigenous populations and for human rights. End price audits of goods whereby a product's final price is broken down into an analysis of who gets what share of that price is immensely valuable and can be used to demonstrate that subsistence wages being paid to the poor in developing world countries is not the whole basis of the product's provision. The distribution of the benefits of product (or service) provision must be demonstrated as being just. Where appropriate the firm will be involved in wider development initiatives though technology and know-how transfer, sponsorship, charitable donations and the provision of development aid to partners in developing countries.

Education

Education is at the root of the sustainable development process. We will make little progress without being able to communicate the challenge and to educate people to live in a more sustainable manner. Every business has to accept that it can be an educator because of its close links with both employees and customers and should be providing suitable information and education to anyone working for it or purchasing its products and services. The firm can also be involved in community initiatives, wider public campaigns and be part of the process to raise awareness more generally. It can work closely with campaign groups and non-governmental organizations through general cooperation, more specific sponsorship, the secondment of staff and similar initiatives.

The 6 Es approach therefore provides a set of ideals which the company can work towards. It contains a number of values and issues too commonly ignored in business; in many respects it challenges the business to accept a much wider responsibility for all its actions. The starting point is simply for management to think about these issues and through interaction with the workforce to produce policy statements in each of the six areas. However, that must be followed by concerted action as the business seeks out the road towards sustainability.

Model 6: Measures of sustainability

This model is perhaps one of the most highly developed and defined of all the ones presented here and is based on the work of Welford (1996).

As a result of a consultation exercise the approach advocates the definition of seven broad 'elements of sustainability' within which we need to identify more detailed measures:

1 General principles
2 Equity
3 Futurity
4 Biodiversity and animal protection
5 Human rights
6 Local action and scale
7 Life cycle impacts

This necessarily implies the very broad definition of sustainable development looking at both environmental and wider social issues which we have advocated. It is argued that only by beginning to deal with these dimensions can we really move towards a sustainable future. It is not being argued that every firm has to be perfect in every element identified. Indeed, for some organizations there may be conflict even within an attempt to deal with these issues. It is argued however, that companies must be aware of these issues and should respond to them in a positive way over time. We can then move along a path which leads to performance consistent with sustainable development at the level of the firm.

The implementation of sustainable development objectives discussed above and the preparation of meaningful reports on performance requires the support of appropriate measures of performance and information systems. Figure 8.8 illustrates the process for managing a business according to sustainable development principles. Stakeholders concerns and wishes have to be analysed which feeds into the development of sustainable development policies and in turn into sustainable development objectives. The implementation of these objectives requires measurement of performance and the adoption of appropriate standards. Internal and external reporting on these measures and the ongoing monitoring of performance leads back into communication and further analysis of stakeholders. And so the cycle goes on leading to further development of sustainable development policies and objectives which will take the company further and further along the road towards sustainability. But at the centre of the process has to be a culture change programme which develops the values and associated activities of the organization in line with its sustainable development agenda.

A clear distinction however, needs to be made between measures at the basic eco-efficiency level (which are necessary but not sufficient to attain sustainability) and measures at the wider social and ethical level associated with sustainable development. Clearly, both the wider

Figure 8.8 Managing Sustainable Development in the Business

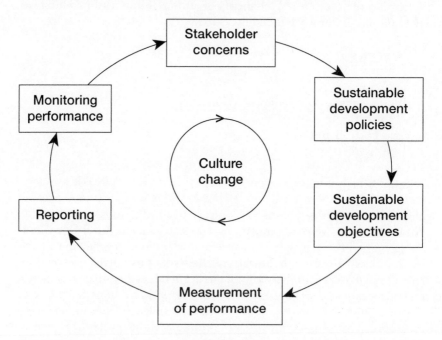

consequences or impacts of a firm's activities, and the narrower environmental performance of the firm need to be considered. Whilst traditional environmental auditing procedures deal with static (short term) and internal performance measures, sustainability criteria demand that we consider longer term internal and external impacts which move beyond narrow environmental criteria towards wider social and ethical criteria.

Given that we have identified the need to move towards sustainability by widening the scope of what we measure we are left with the more difficult task of identifying exactly what to measure. We have identified seven elements associated with sustainability in business and they can be translated into key target areas. Our vector towards sustainability is therefore seven dimensional. In terms of our general principles the firm must demonstrate accountability, transparency, and education and learning.

1 General Principles

a Accountability. The company should demonstrate that it can be held accountable to all its stakeholders. We would expect to see the appointment of non-executive directors and systems put into place which are compatible with the best practice of corporate governance. The internal management structure would be well documented with clear job descriptions, reporting lines and organizational charts. This would be freely available to anyone requesting it. Links would be built up with the local community in order to facilitate consultation and dialogue.

b Transparency/Openness. If a company is transparent, open and honest it is less likely to be able to hide environmentally damaging practices and less likely to be accused of doing so by others. Transparency is likely to begin with a wide range of participation arrangements both within the company and beyond. There will be free access to information which is not of a commercially sensitive nature. This will ensure that the company is capable of proving its environmental claims. Part of this information is likely to include documentation on the effects that the organization has on habitats along with their associated impact mechanisms.

As part of a strategy of openness it is likely that there will exist an explicit ethical framework written in terms of corporate values. We need to consider very carefully how we begin to measure values, but by looking at different firms' sustainable development policies, their values or corporate ethics can be compared in terms of the range of issues that they cover.

Lastly, corporate reporting is central to any company working with these ideas. Internal reporting systems that measure performance with regard to sustainability can have a significant effect on corporate culture. Regular, third party verified reports covering financial, environmental and social measures will identify the company's achievements and any failure to meet targets set. Measures need to be reported and audited in a common, accountable, transparent and accessible style. The concept of transparency is therefore used to reduce the distance between the organization and external participants, so that society can 'see into' the organization, assess what it is doing with the resources that determine future options and react accordingly.

c Education and learning. Information availability will not only be important to the achievement of transparency but it is also likely to be at the centre of a company's attempts to improve education and learning both within and external to the organization. Open communications with all stakeholders should try to impart education about the organization and wider issues which will improve everyone's understanding of the sustainable development process. Within the organization we would expect to see clear training records and strategies aimed at two-way learning so that the organization not only imparts education but is a learning organization as well.

Once again, the existence of consultation frameworks and dialogue must be at the heart of sustainability measures. This will include all stakeholders. Moreover, through such a process, the organization can actually become a facilitator of change.

2 Equity

a Empowerment of all stakeholders. Empowerment strategies must be seen as being at the centre of any measures of sustainability. It is by empowerment that we can begin to challenge and change traditional balances of power. Open institutional structures are required in the firm so that any stakeholder has the ability to challenge and question the organization over any issue. Once again, we are looking for two-way processes here with interaction and dialogue shifting the organization on to a more sustainable path.

b Participation. The logical next step must be to implement participation measures. Most importantly, we would identify the need for participation within the sustainable enterprise and this would be measured in a number of ways. There is likely to be participation in decision-making as well as financial (profit-sharing) participation and other appropriate non-financial rewards. Essentially we are searching for evidence of an equitable distribution of benefits. Management and workers would be seen to cooperate with each other in order to achieve common goals. The sustainable organization is also likely to have a very wide ownership structure with wider share ownership packages available for employees.

c Trading practices. One of the most common criticisms of internationally oriented firms is that they are exploitative of developing world trading partners. The adoption of end price auditing techniques whereby a company declares how the final price of a product is derived (and specifically how much goes to indigenous workers in the developing world) would certainly be in the spirit of achieving increased equity. Moreover we would want to see the company justify that its activities result in an equitable distribution of value added. These issues are clearly linked to the notion of fair trade. Within the issue of international equity the sustainable business needs to put the emphasis on fair trade above free trade. Specifically this will include measures to ensure the maintenance of the welfare of indigenous populations and their lands.

Trading practices in the sustainable organization are also likely to look towards an increase in local sourcing of materials. This will be linked both to a strategy for reducing environmental damage resulting from distribution, but also linked to an attempt to build close links and networks with local communities.

3 Futurity

a Precaution. A sustainable business needs explicit policies and practices which take it beyond the law or beyond simple compliance. This certainly requires the firm to demonstrate due diligence in all its operations and procedures and, again, this must be linked to stakeholder accountability. In effect we require the firm to be anticipative and to have systematic scenario planning and risk assessment procedures. Moreover, this requires the firm to have a long-term planning horizon and to challenge the short-termism so often criticised in business.

b Use of non-renewables. Clearly, the sustainable organization will be involved in the phasing out of non-renewable resources and this will mean a new emphasis placed on research into alternatives. Substitution strategies will be linked to closing the cycle of resource use and an emphasis placed on systems which reduce the use of, repair, reuse and recycle resources.

4 Biodiversity and animal protection

a Habitat and species conservation. The protection of ecosystems and biodiversity is central to sustainable development. Businesses can be involved in habitat regeneration strategies both locally and often internationally. Partnership and local linkage will be important in achieving this goal. As a start, organizations should report on species and habitats at a local level and through the assessment and identification of their own impacts and improve their own performance in this area. For new sites, processes and products we should expect to see the publication of full environmental impact assessments.

b Animal testing. The abandonment of animal testing is part of a wider social ethic for any business. It also reflects an organization's due respect for other living things. As such, businesses should demonstrate that they are in conformance with recognized 'no animal testing' standards and best practice elsewhere.

5 Human rights

a Employment policies and equal opportunities. A sustainable business might be considered as a business run in a better way. The sustainable business has a particular way of treating its employees. Like much good business practice the starting point here is to have a clear policy on equal opportunities which both creates the feeling that equality of opportunity is important and maps out the procedures by which this will be achieved. Compliance with codes of practice and compliance with legal requirements will be important measures. Employee representation in decisions about employment and appropriate training and education will be central to more participative modes of operation.

b Quality of working life. People spend a lot of time at work and part of the wider social ethic of any organization ought to be to try to increase the quality of the time spent at work. This will not only involve the company complying with health and safety legislation but also having wider human resource policies which provide a forum for voicing dissatisfaction without fear of reprisal. Ultimately the sustainable organization will be able to demonstrate that it is moving towards systems which provide for increased levels of industrial democracy.

c Women. Women have been relatively undervalued in the workplace and their absence from positions of authority must be seen as a weakness in many organizations. In line with Agenda 21 we need to see much more dialogue with women and policies which empower them and allow them to play a fuller role in any business. Non-discrimination policies will be important to legitimizing the role of women.

d Minority groups. Again, minority groups are also under-represented within the decision-making structures of most businesses. As with the case of women, we would want to see increased levels of dialogue, empowerment and non-discrimination procedures.

e Indigenous populations. The protection of indigenous populations and their land rights holds a very special place within the ethos of sustainable development. Historically, indigenous populations have been exploited in a number of ways and the sustainable organization will have to demonstrate that it has turned away from any practices which continue this exploitation. In particular, we would expect to see fair wage policies for indigenous workers in place in businesses, an emphasis of purchasing directly from indigenous populations (and not through agencies and third parties who simply extract value added for their own ends) and no use of child labour.

6 Local action and scale

a Community linkage. Close relationships with the community within which a business operates have been identified as important. As well as having the traditional dialogue groups and consultative fora, the company should have clear systems to provide an appropriate response to complaints and requests for information (which would not normally be refused).

b Appropriate scale. The size of business activity is important. Rather than putting an emphasis on optimum size in terms of how big an organization can grow we might also think about optimum smallness as well (Welford 1995). It might be argued that much environmental damage has been caused by large-scale production and mass consumption. A justification of the scale of any activity would be a baseline measure of sustainability in a business. Stakeholder involvement will be central to decisions regarding scale and particularly to the decision over whether to internalize or subcontract some operations. Moreover, close links with stakeholders and particularly with the local community raises the question as to whether a certain level of profits might be distributed locally via the support of appropriate local initiatives and projects.

c Partnership and cooperation strategies. We keep returning to the need for the sustainable organization to have clear linkage and dialogue with all stakeholders. This will involve support for wider initiatives which can help us move towards sustainability. Moreover, such linkage and participative and cooperative strategies can help to cut down on the duplication of some activities, therefore resulting in a saving of resources.

d Appropriate location. The choice over the location of a particular plant or facility can have enormous impacts on the environment. Clearly, inappropriate activities should not take place on or near to sites of environmental importance and, again, there needs to be clear neighbourhood policies and linkages to ensure minimum impact on the local environment. Location will also impact upon distribution networks and sites should be chosen which will minimize the environmental impacts of distribution.

7 Life cycle impacts

a Product stewardship. The life cycle of a product begins with the extraction or farming of raw materials and ends with the disposal or reuse of those same raw materials through waste. At every stage of the life cycle of a product businesses should take responsibility for reducing any negative impacts. There is therefore a clear role for product stewardship policies within the business which commit the organization to the management of the whole life cycle. The ultimate aim ought to be to reduce waste and environmental damage at all stages and, where possible, to close the loops which allow that waste to occur.

b Life cycle analysis. The starting point therefore has to be a full life cycle assessment of all products which not only identifies environmental damage but also other impacts consistent with the elements of sustainability identified above. Such analysis will be most credible when it is linked to third party verification.

c Design. Although an important element within the life cycle assessment, the role of design will be crucial to the sustainable organization. Emphasis should be placed on redesigning products to make them more sustainable and to increase the potential for repair, reuse and recycling through design for disassembly strategies.

d Product durability. In most instances, we should be seeking to have longer durability of products. In some circumstances where technology has improved substantially it may be better to replace products before their natural death, but built in obsolescence and other design factors used to increase sales rather than durability are fundamentally unsustainable. We should expect durability reports for products which give the consumer an expectation about the life of the product and which can be compared with other competing products.

e Product justifiability. A detailed debate over needs and wants in any society has no conclusion and it would clearly be wrong to dictate to people what constitutes their needs as opposed to more frivolous wants. Nevertheless through consultation with all stakeholders we should expect a company to be able to justify the design and other characteristics of a product. Moreover, through detailed life cycle assessment and a consideration of the impact of a product on all the elements of sustainability, it should be possible for businesses to publish sustainability audits for each of its products.

REPORTING PROGRESS TOWARDS SUSTAINABLE DEVELOPMENT

Having identified how we might define the road towards sustainability as described in the six models above (which has given us some ideas about what to record and measure), we must now address the difficult task of how to measure them and subsequently report progress towards sustainable development. Direct environmental impacts such as the emission of chemicals into a local river are relatively easy to measure, although we must also be committed to defining their impact mechanisms and secondary effects. But some of the measures identified above are not capable of being measured in such a direct or quantitative way. We must therefore begin to think about different kinds of measurement techniques, which, nevertheless allow us to record progress towards sustainability and which can be built into a corporate reporting strategy. All we really ask of a business therefore is to track improvements over time.

There are three important principles to bear in mind in the measurement process:

1   The judgement as to how far a company is attaining any particular measure of sustainability must be made by a wide range of stakeholders.
2   Absolute measures are less likely to be practical than qualitative measures based on judgement and, where necessary, supported by evidence.
3   It is the direction of change and the speed of change towards sustainability which we are ultimately interested in. We therefore need to track progress along our road towards sustainability.

We must recognize that different impacts will be measured in different ways and may have completely different consequences. It is therefore unlikely that we could ever achieve an aggregated score of sustainability. Nevertheless, the use of a set of scales rather than scores may move us forward. This approach provides a set of ideal measures of sustainability at one extreme and opposite measures at the other. Such a scale might be used by a range of stakeholders of a business in an assessment of how far a business has moved. It could provide the organization with a tool to analyse shifts in external assessment by its stakeholders.

For example, let us take our general principles from Model 6 and look specifically at accountability. Our 'ideal' measures are on the right hand side of Table 14.2 and 'undesirable' opposites are on the left. A scoring scale would be provided for stakeholders to make a judgement about progress. This would identify areas of best practice as well as areas requiring attention. An aggregate score might be calculated for each target area.

We have therefore begun to identify the direction of sustainability for businesses. We have recognized that measures more associated with the direction and speed of change are more important than absolutes. Some aggregation of the scores awarded on our scales is possible for each of the seven elements of sustainability required but an aggregated score is less relevant. A high score for futurity measures might have to be set against, for example, a low score for equity. Comparison of scores within and between categories will give us an indication of the priorities which the company must examine in its future planning.

The sort of reporting system which is likely to be used by the firm tracking sustainability is presented in Figure 8.9. The starting point must be for the firm to chose the approach it wishes to adopt and to translate

Table 8.4 Suggested measurement scales for target areas

There are no non-executive directors who can be considered as independent	1 2 3 4 5	Independent non-executive directors have been appointed
Corporate governance has been ignored	1 2 3 4 5	Systems compatible with principles of corporate governance are in place
There is no readily available documentation of the internal management structure	1 2 3 4 5	The management structure is documented and available for public scrutiny
There are no links with the local community	1 2 3 4 5	There are clear links and consultative processes with the local community

this into a set of policies which will be published. It is likely that these policies will be determined both as a result of the general activities of the company (because it will want to concentrate on priority areas) and by a broad overarching values statement outlining the organization's purpose, mission and ethics. Policies, systems and procedures then have to be audited. This is likely to include a wide ranging ecological audit detailing more traditional environmental effects as well as secondary impacts and the results of life cycle assessments of products. There will be a broad based stakeholder assessment following the social audit methodology outlined in Chapter 7 and a financial audit covering economic dimensions of sustainability. These three general elements are brought together in a company's sustainability report.

Such a reporting procedure is, of course, expensive but without the discipline which the auditing and reporting framework introduces it is unlikely that real progress can actually be made. Moreover, since progress is mostly relative to broad based policies rather than absolute in terms of quantifiable outcomes, the reporting process also gives firms the opportunity to compare progress with each other. It also gives stakeholders the opportunity to make better judgements about the firm, and it gives the firm a platform on which to build its education initiatives. There is no reason at all why these cannot also be linked to marketing campaigns. For us to move towards sustainability, however, we must

Figure 8.9 Reporting Framework for the Sustainable Organization

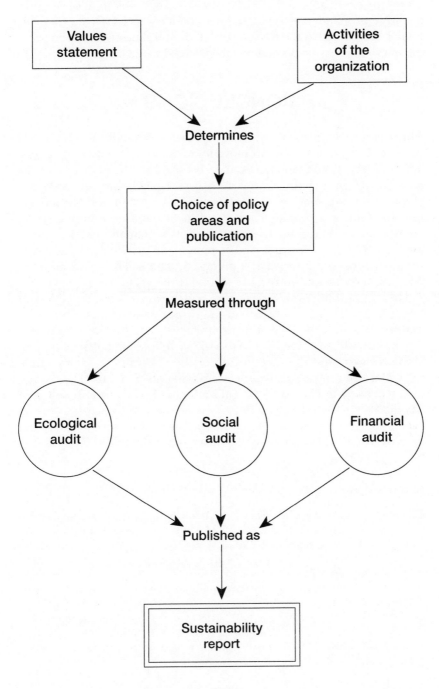

recognize that such reporting should be the norm and not just the realm of the 'alternative' organization. And if companies will not move this far on their own accord there has to be some consideration of whether a degree of mandatory reporting is to be introduced. Given that this book has argued that the track record of most businesses has been poor, mandatory reporting procedures might well be needed.

CONCLUSIONS

This chapter has presented a range of ideas, through the six models presented, relating to ways to move towards sustainability in business. The models should not necessarily be seen as alternatives, but as generalized approaches from which the organization can pick and choose according to its own activities, priorities and values. The models and their integral elements might also be seen as a checklist for companies searching for the road towards sustainability. More than anything though, the reader must remember that the models really define a process rather than a precise outcome. The publication of policies, audit procedures and reporting is central to that process.

There is nothing presented in the models which is not tangible and operational. It is for management to grasp the initiative, to engender enthusiasm for change in the organization and to move forward. Leadership will be crucial but so too will be followership. Participation, empowerment and the recognition of the real value of every single worker are all central to any process. Moving down the road to sustainability is likely to change the organization and its culture. It will be a change for the better both in terms of the internal dimensions of the firm and the external impacts which it has on the environment and society. The world can be a better place – but the business must be a better place first.

References

Gladwin, T N, Kennelly, J J and Krause, T (1995) 'Shifting Paradigms for Sustainable Development: Implications for Management Theory and Research', *Academy of Management Review*, 20, 4

Hawken, P (1994) *The Ecology of Commerce: How Business can Save the Planet*, Weidenfeld and Nicolson, New York

Welford, R J (1994) *Cases in Environmental Management and Business Strategy*, Pitman, 1994

Welford, R J (1995) *Environmental Strategy and Sustainable development: The Corporate Challenge for the 21st Century*, Routledge, London

Welford, R J (1996) *Corporate Environmental Management: Systems and Strategies*, Earthscan, London

9

Rediscovering the Spiritual Dimension of Environmentalism

Richard Welford

Trends towards eco-modernism which have been described on numerous occasions in this book stress objectivity, scientific measurement, technological determinism and eco-efficiency. The rallying cry of the eco-modernists is to link the environment with the economy, linking the greening of industry with market forces. This is how industry and others have hijacked the debate over environmentalism. Yet many would see ecology and spirituality just as inextricably linked as ecology and commerce. And to ignore this is to shut off many centuries of accumulated wisdom about the environment.

Spiritual aspects of our consciousness have nevertheless been progressively and systematically relegated to the domain of the subjective, private, individual or even subconscious. To all but a few, they are not perceived as having direct relevance to society. They have become a set of values subjugated by capitalism, the free market and the laws of supply and demand. They are secondary to the values of wealth creation, security, mobility, comfort, welfare, education and health.

In order to move towards a sustainable future we must go beyond seeing the environment in sterile scientific terms (with a more minor social dimension sometimes tagged on) and come to recognize, appreciate and enjoy the spiritual dimension of ecology. Of course, it is vital that we reduce pollution, plant trees, clean our rivers, maintain biodiversity, recycle our products, and so on. However, we require much more fundamental change if we are really going to reverse the destructive tendencies of the modern world. The most critical change which must take place is a transformation of our very relationship with the Earth.

The Earth does not need to change in order to survive, but we do. We must change our values, our outlook and our behaviour. We must recognize our interconnectedness with the world.

The threatened extinction of species in the rainforests, jungles, mountains, plains, seas and rivers in the world today is the result of abrupt and violent changes wreaked on the environment by human greed and ignorance. Instead of evolving into new forms, species are simply disappearing and it is now apparent that as they disappear we will disappear with them. It is not just the destruction of food chains and ecological balance which will destroy us. When the animals are gone our very humaneness will disappear. We do not exist without the richness of the environment around us. As we kill off one more species then part of us is lost as well. This is all part of the spiritual dimension of ecology which we must try to regain. This chapter makes some suggestions about how we can do just that.

THE DEMISE AND REBIRTH OF SPIRITUALITY

A spiritual force is absent in so much of Western culture. People have a sense of emptiness which they seek to fill by consuming more and looking towards the day when they might just be able to amass all those material comforts which they dream of. We become cocooned in walls of brick and mortar which keep us secure and warm. But that cocoon often prevents us from breaking free from the day to day habits, pressures and norms which would allow us to explore a wider spiritual existence. But more and more people are exploring new spiritual dimensions and are discovering simplicity and humility. Such individuals can be a great force for change as a critical mass of enlightenment builds up. They know that to explore the world outside of bounded rationality is to explore a new dimension of living and life more rewarding than humdrum materialism. It is not difficult to meditate, to escape and ultimately to fly to a new level of consciousness.

But global capitalism represents a force which is hardly compatible with a spiritual dimension. It has come to be such a powerful force that it really does control people. People are subjugated by its systems and values because it is now virtually uncontrollable. Global capitalism drives out spirituality because it cannot cope with it. Indeed, it is perhaps the spiritual dimension which poses the greatest threat to the continuation of business as usual. Governments are unable to control large corporations, nomadic capital and the tendency to treat humanity as a mere factor of production. But individuals who become enlightened, who lead by example and create a wave of consciousness can (and must) transform the way we treat the world. They will be the force that can tame the corporation. We forget that we have the ultimate sanction against unethical business – we simply stop buying their products.

At the heart of the ecological problem is also another great barrier to change. This is the male ego. Ego is connected to power and the wish to control others. Egos have a habit of getting bigger and bigger instilling false consciousness and arrogance in those who become successful. Power allows people to circumvent the normal learning process by offering attractive short cuts. As egos grow they fuel arrogance and we feel that we are simply right and can simply explain things the way they are. So often, I meet successful industrialists who simply tell you what they believe, as if there were and could never be an alternative. Pinned against the wall they expect you to nod in agreement and if you dare to disagree then a patronizing smile and a vague verbal reference to when they were young and naive soon shuts you up. I have given up engaging with such people. Their minds are already shut down. Perhaps their spirits are as well.

Ego and power often allows individuals to manifest their desires with a minimal effort. But those desires are often illusory. Such desires include the latest sporty BMW car with the leather seats, alloy trim and metallic paint – a car which has killed to be made and goes on killing as it is used. But real power does not lie in egos – it is actually to be found within humility and the search for learning and understanding. Such a search is essentially a journey – one which if we all embarked on it now would have profound effects on the shape of the world.

For me, the spiritual path is not connected with organized religion – itself, too often, a tool of control and suppression. Indeed, organized Christian religion has a history of replacing complex, multi-dimensional spiritual beliefs with much more restrictive, ordered and guilt-laden commandments. The arrogance of Christian missionaries has been responsible for the loss of great spiritual and ecological wisdom. The genocide committed in the name of colonization was even more evil. Those of us who live in the West must recognize that we have a history of murderous exploitation. As we wiped out indigenous populations and tribal knowledge we lost much of our own connectedness with the world.

Spirituality is not about a single order or set of decrees. It is about self-enlightenment, about breaking free and about discovering an alternative dimension. Spirituality includes the intuitive, the non-measurable, the aesthetic, the caring and the loving. For me, many answers are to be found within Buddhism and Shamanism, but for others different perspectives have more resonance. But the spiritual dimension can link us together, can put us in contact with tribal beliefs and for many will allow some contact with spirit forces.

What I do see is that spirituality is encircling us and that its power to change is beginning to take root. Business should beware! Spirituality requires little materialism, thrives on simplicity and is very adept at removing institutional power. Spirituality is migrating and moving. Buddhism, Shamanism and the nature-based wisdom of indigenous cultures is mixing to produce a sophisticated ecological teaching which is powerful and appealing. Those embedded in the system will resist the change. They may even fight it, first by belittling it and decrying it, but then by organizing against it. But it is a force which cannot ultimately be resisted. It actually requires relatively few people to be enlightened for major changes to happen in society. We are getting closer to that critical mass.

I find that a number of important considerations paint the sort of picture which can provide turnaround. These tend to mix notions of deep ecology, Buddhism and Shamanism but do not draw on any one paradigm exclusively. As such I cannot separate spirituality from ecology and find it distressing that scientific, technical and corporate approaches to environmentalism try to do just that. The important point is that we recognize a link between ecology and spirituality and not try to dictate what it looks like. However, with regard to environmental issues there is great commonality within many spiritual paths and a starting point might be to recognize six important principles: the living Earth; inter-connectedness; a sense of place; compassion and humility; change and impermanence; and, reawakening. Let us review those principles briefly here.

The living Earth

There have been many attempts made to describe the Earth as a living system in itself. Probably the most recognized of these has been James Lovelock's 'Gaia Hypothesis'. This postulates that the physical and chemical condition of the surface of the earth, of the atmosphere, and of the oceans has and is actively made fit and comfortable by the presence of life itself. This in contrast to the conventional wisdom which held that life adapted to the planetary conditions as it and they evolved their separate ways. The concept of Mother Earth or Gaia, has been widely held throughout history and has been the basis of a belief which still coexists within many religions. The argument is therefore that the biosphere is much more than just the complete range of all living things within their natural habitats.

Lovelock (1979) argues that the entire range of living matter on Earth could be regarded as a single living entity, capable of manipulating the Earth's atmosphere to suit its overall needs and endowed with faculties and power far beyond those of its constituent parts. Compared with the giant sized organism which is the Earth, the human being is small and insignificant in comparison. But if we meddle with the complex parts of that organism, threatening the integrity of the whole, then the offender may be dealt with and removed.

Many tribal cultures also see the world as a whole and living organism often characterized as mother, father, goddess and extended family. Commonly, it is recognized that nothing can be entirely separate from all other things and that the interconnectedness of the whole world is part of us as well as us being a part of it. Stressed at one end the system will respond somewhere else and we cannot be separate from those impacts. Yet we too often fail to recognize our symbiosis and treat the world as our resource: to exploit it for the benefit of the richest one-fifth of human existence. When Gaia does turn on us, it is unfortunately the weakest, poorest and those with least blame who suffer first.

As individuals we can begin by recognizing the Earth as a self-sustaining organic presence. We need to acquaint ourselves with the very medium in which we move, become part of it and not see ourselves as ruling over it. We are a part of a very complex metabolism and by destroying any part of that we are harming ourselves. Because we do not understand the complex workings of that metabolism it would seem sensible to protect every part of it. This forms the basis of the precautionary principle.

Interconnectedness

All that exists, according to Buddhist understanding, has no identity that is self-reliant and distinct or separate. We must therefore recognize that we are all connected to each other in some way and although capitalism tries to break us down into manageable units it can never completely destroy a sense of community. But we too often think of communities in terms of spatial dimensions, particular interests, cultural norms, gender, sexuality and race. For many tribal peoples, community does not stop at these thresholds, nor the threshold of our own species. Community includes other species (plant and animal) as well as environmental features (rivers, mountains, etc) and unseen ancestors and spirits.

Joan Halifax (1990) puts this into context by drawing on the speech made by Chief Sealth in 1854. This Chief was from the Puget Sound area which would now be in Mexico City. However, before the colonization of this area by the white man, this area was abundant with tribal peoples and wildlife. I find this native American view of interconnectedness to have powerful messages about both ecology and the mistakes of the past.

Our dead never forget this beautiful Earth,
for it is the mother of the red man.
We are part of the Earth
and it is part of us.
The perfumed flowers are our sisters;
the deer, the horse, the great eagle,
these are our brothers.
The rocky crests, the juices of the meadows,
the body heat of the pony, and man
all belong to the same family.

The shining water that moves in the streams and rivers
is not just water
but the blood of our ancestors.
If we sell you our land,
you must remember that it is sacred,
and you must teach your children that it is sacred
and that each ghostly reflection in the clear water of the lakes
tells of events and memories
in the life of my people.

The water's murmur
is the voice of my father's father.
The rivers are our brothers,
they quench our thirst.
The rivers carry our canoes,
and feed our children.
If we sell you our land,
you must remember and teach your children,
that the rivers are our brother – and yours,
and you must henceforth give the rivers the kindness
you would give to any brother.

What is clear is that the environment around us is actually part of us. It is no longer removed, separate and disposable but it is intrinsic to our own vitality. When we campaign and argue to save the environment, we are not simply protecting something out there, we are protecting ourselves. If we can convince those who cut down the rainforests, that they are in fact cutting themselves down, then progress might be much quicker. The disconnectedness which we often see is related to the sense of ego which we have already discussed.

Recognizing interconnectedness and acting on it is very much part of an individual's own personal and spiritual development. The challenge is to restore the natural, heartfelt perception of our interdependence.

Too often there is an alienation between our thoughts and our bodies, between our bodies and the Earth and between us and other species. Until this fundamental alienation and division is healed, there may be no lasting solutions to the environmental problems surrounding us. In general terms a good starting point is re-education inspiring a deep sense of interconnectedness with all life and the physical environment.

The process of maturing as a human being involves a widening of one's identification and a process of self-realization. Through a closer connection with the world around us we can actually start to experience ourselves differently. Normally we identify ourselves as located within the mind and body. We too often see ourselves through our possessions and the more material aspects of our lives. Often we can identify with children and other family members but rarely do we connect ourselves with more distant members of the human species, and even more rarely with members of other species. Yet spiritual growth is based in the experience that broader identification is both possible and rewarding.

When we live as if our bodies were isolated objects we lose our connectedness with each other, with other animals and with the Earth itself. We live as if time simply runs from past to future, robbed of the opportunity to rest in the finite richness of the present. We live as if our mind were localized exclusively within the head as if it were the source of all awareness and feelings, and as though interconnectedness with all of nature is simply a nice idea that lacks credibility in the eyes of a limited conventional science.

However, many people are now questioning the validity of some scientific assumptions. Indeed, it is many scientists themselves that question the traditional and sterile division between science, philosophy and spirituality. The objectivist, scientific school of thought is beginning to crack. There is an increasing recognition that we simply cannot explain everything around us in precise, factual terms. This is not to denounce science, which offers great potential to reverse environmental degradation. But it is to suggest that science alone cannot and will not provide us with all the answers. In parallel with this, we cannot rely on technology to dig us out of the environmental crisis.

The natural outcome of these changes is that we cannot simply rely on pure, unbiased observation to provide solutions. In the postmodern world positivism is limited. However, that is not to suggest that a purely subjective view of the world is entirely appropriate. We must mix the objective and the subjective in a world where feelings and emotions are just as important as science and technology.

A Sense of Place

The identification with a sense of place has a key role to play in the resolution of ecological conflicts and this also has an important spiritual dimension. In Zen practice, for example, the development of this sense of place is part of the development of pure expression. The identification with where you live is ultimately a recognition of selflessness in the local ecology. It is, accordingly, our relationship with that local ecology which can bring about a sense of awakening.

The local ecology is the realm in which our day to day activities and experiences intersect with the biological cycles that directly support them. It is here in our daily lives that we can work to reverse environmentally destructive trends. Particularly at home and in the workplace environmental responsibility can be developed and taught to others creating new waves of consciousness.

For bioregionalists the sense of place has a particularly important significance. They have mapped out the practical dimension by describing innovative ways of living, working, building homes and communities and growing food. Life that is congruent with the local ecology and reflective of the unique cultural patterns that have arisen there are celebrated by bioregionalism and Buddhism alike.

By getting to know our local ecology better we will get to know some of nature's myriad of things a little better. Wisdom and compassion naturally flow from this insight and these, in turn, influence a process of character change. As the biological and cultural nuances of the place become increasingly more intimate then ultimately you will see them as part of yourself.

Compassion and Humility

At the philosophical core of deep ecology is biospecies equality, harmony with nature and a recognition that the Earth's physical resources are limited. These three important perspectives are realized not just through the accumulation of scientific facts, but through our direct experience with ourselves, each other, other species and the environment we share. Both Buddhism and Shamanism argue that such realization is based on communion, understanding through experience, and seeing through the eyes of compassion. Both approaches also emphasize simplicity in life. Both use nature as a primary source of inspiration and understanding. They stress interdependence, equilibrium and ceremony as a means of discovery. Within the human community, much of the experience of communion is in terms of love. Love is how self-aware and free beings bond together.

As we begin to explore the world in which we live and start to feel part of a living organism, then we realize that we are a lot less significant than our egos might have us believe. Whilst we might imagine our senses to be well developed, for example, we lack the echo-locating sensory systems of bats and whales, the subtle heat sensors of snakes, the electro-reception of certain fish and the magnetic field sensitivity of migratory birds.

The Lakota Sioux still practise the Native American tradition of vision-quest as a means of exploring the world and developing the self. They prepare for this by fasting (no food or water) for four days. On the eve of the quest they participate in a sweat-lodge ceremony for purification and are given a drink of water to teach them appreciation. Then for up to four days they sit alone within a sacred space marked by a circle of stones, with nothing but a blanket. Sitting through the heat of the day and the cold of the night it is difficult to sleep. The task is to maintain awareness of everything that takes place (including thoughts and dreams) and upon returning to recount all experiences to the elders who interpret the messages.

These conditions and disciplines are designed to remove the ego. It is argued that only in the absence of ego is there a pathway for visions to occur. Through an exploration of the unconscious mind one begins to understand oneself as a part and product of the relationship between Earth and the sky, the primary forces of the universe. It also enables the individual to create a better identity with nature and to have much more intimate and meaningful relationships with other people.

We must therefore come to realize that there is much more to the natural world than one can grasp through studying numbers and abstract scientific concepts. If we are to take our cues from the environment and learn to live in harmony with nature we have to go beyond the linear structure of human language and receive the messages of the elemental world more directly. We receive those messages through our senses and intuition. But we need to attune those senses through open-ness and compassion, and humility within a large, complicated, mystical world. To be humble is to be open to new ideas and new experiences. It is to challenge our existing values and perceptions and make every effort to drive out any sense of ego.

But dwelling in harmony means dwelling as if life in the broadest sense, not just human life, really matters. It means liberating our minds from the shallow, conservative, anthropocentric views and attitudes drilled into us by a consumer culture that rewards the desire to manipulate others for selfish purposes, violence as a way of solving problems, egocentric individualism, discrimination as a way of organizing society and a superiority over nature.

Change and Impermanence

We live in times of great change and we currently inhabit only one very small part of the entire history of the planet. An obvious outcome of this is that all that exists in the physical world is impermanent. Change is inevitable and according to Buddhists any attempt to hold things in their fixed positions creates disharmony and suffering. Life can therefore be seen as arising, interacting, transforming and passing. Indeed there is a cycle of life which we cannot avoid even though we try.

Nothing whatever is permanent. We are born, grow up, go to school, go to work, grow older and sooner or later we will die. Our lives get shorter every moment and there is nothing we can do about it. When death comes all our family and friends, property and possessions will be left behind. All those things we now regard as so important become insignificant. We could become frightened and depressed about this, but that would not be accepting impermanence in a positive way. Instead we should acknowledge change to be inevitable and think about how we can lead our lives in a more worthwhile and compassionate way.

We must also stop imagining that everything around us exists in a solid way. If we try to make things more fixed we will suffer when changes occur. Our fear of change and impermanence makes us behave in ways which are equivalent to holding things in fixed positions. We use cosmetics to hide our ageing and as a result inflict pain and torture on the animals used to ensure that such cosmetics do not harm us.

If we refuse to accept change when it comes and resist it instead, we will simply be fighting a losing battle. Our emotions will go up and down and our inner stability will be affected. The whole point about recognizing change and impermanence is to develop less attachment to what we are doing. It will make us see our careers, material possessions, relationships, aspirations and behaviour in a much wider context. It can help to release us from conventional ways of life based around consumption, materialism and entrapment by stultifying careers.

Reawakening

Western culture has created a dualism between people and nature. Nature is seen as a resource for our use, to be exploited in the name of economic growth and progress. In so doing we have made the grave mistake of depriving nature of respect. This is very much a product of our time and our system – it has not always been like this and a productive way forward is to be aware of alternative perspectives on the environment. To rediscover these alternatives is to reawaken ourselves to ecology and its spiritual dimensions. Let me give a couple of examples.

The reciprocity between humans and the rest of nature was seen as both a great mystery and a basic assumption in many aboriginal cultures. Some regarded the elements and the other creatures of their world as relatives: grandfather, grandmother, father, mother, sister, brother, or at least cousins. Sometimes they were closely linked to ancestors and to damage nature was to threaten one's own acceptance into the spirit world. Nature demanded respect and there was a knowledge that to upset the order of nature was an extremely perilous thing to do. Nature would take its retribution.

Similarly, for many Native Americans nature and the physical environment demanded special care. The stars were regarded as the greatest hunters with the bravest hearts, and they supplicated the stars to take their children's hearts and give them the heart of a hunter. Likewise, their relationships with the sun, moon, lightning, wind and rain, as well as the creatures around them were intensely personal. The elements were immediate presences with which they maintained personal relationships. Such a system acknowledges that humans live within and depend upon the environment around us, which deserves due respect and which imparts a strong spiritual dimension.

Western culture has also cut itself off from and sometimes destroyed its connections with spiritual energies. The archetypal energies which we have see in cave paintings, in Egyptian burial chambers, in pagan worship, in tribal ceremonies and in astrology, to name but a few, have been denied and repressed by our culture for hundreds of years. We have stamped them out as crude, backward, superstitious and anti-God. We have persecuted people associated with these powers in witch hunts of various kinds. But now, as people search for answers our culture is becoming more receptive to alternative approaches to spirituality. The popularity of tribal art, the growth of homoeopathy, interest in the Tarot, meditation, and the use of crystals, all bespeak of a longing much deeper than a mere fad or fascination with the exotic.

The path towards reawakening and ultimately to enlightenment requires increased awareness and understanding and this, in turn, gives us power. Here ecology and spirituality mix as one. Buddhists talk of the need to cultivate awareness and Halifax (1990) shows us how those same roots exist for medicine people:

When the Shaman seeks the power of the eagle, he seeks the power to see; if he seeks the power of the bear, it is to dream awake. The power of the gander is to understand the three realms of past, present and future. The power of the wolf is to find the trackless way. The power of the buffalo, the bison is that of wisdom. All of these qualities are aspects of awareness.

The challenge for Shamans and meditators alike is to find balance. When equilibrium is realized, harmony, beauty and then joy arise. In Buddhism this is the point of meditative stabilization and in shamanism, shamanic equilibrium. It is at this point that clear awareness rises.

The process of reawakening will lead us on the path towards enlightenment. It means being receptive to the new, open to new experiences and new ideas and a recognition of our small but significant part in the way of things. Reawakening brings with it freedom, compassion and love and provides us with a true appreciation of the environment around us. The path is long and we have a lot of learning to do. But to set off down the road of spiritual development is a natural process of development and we should encourage others to do the same.

BUSINESS AS A SPIRITUAL COMMUNITY

When we look at what is happening to our world it becomes clear to me that that turnaround will be difficult. The corporate world is currently not interested in such turnaround and governments are increasingly powerless to act. Unless we have roots in a spirituality that holds life sacred and encourages joyful communion and interconnectedness turnaround will be impossible. The spiritual dimension provides the focus for facing the enormous challenges ahead. It stresses an interdependence so that we treat other people, other species and the physical environment as part of who we are rather than something separate with which we are in constant competition. Therefore, when we talk about the greening of industry, the greening of the self, the greening of the economy and so on, to ignore the spiritual dimensions of that process is to move forward without real passion.

To many it might seem strange to see the business as having a spiritual dimension. But why not? In this book we have argued that business ought to be ethical, honest and an educator and campaigner. So why should it not have a spiritual dimension reflecting its connectedness to the world around it. Spirituality may not be a traditional rallying cry for business but once we recognize that a business's greatest resource has to be the people it connects together to get jobs done then we must recognize that relationships which already exist within the organization will have some sort of spiritual dimension.

As a spiritual community a business does not have a spiritual identity itself. Indeed, if one were to exist it would be most likely to be based around organized religion. There are indeed such organizations, based on strong religious and humanitarian principles. But the sort of spiritual community which a business can create is a much more open and eclectic one. The starting point is simply not to deny the link between the business community and the spiritual community. Work and the workplace are extremely important parts of the individual's spiritual development. It is difficult to embark on a spiritual journey without security in terms of an income. But it can be more than just a support mechanism for individual's own journeys. The organization can actually begin to explore for itself. Culture change, values redefinition and even traditional strategic planning can all involve searching for and exploring the new.

A good starting point for the spiritual organization is the starting point of Buddhist economics. According to Schumacher (1974) this is the recognition that the fundamental source of wealth is human labour. Too often we see labour as a neo-classical factor of production, as nothing more than a cost, and even as a source of inefficiency which if eliminated can increase profitability. The ideal situation for the employer is to have output without employment. In such a hostile work environment, is it any wonder that for so many people their ideal is to have income without employment?

Recognizing and building on spiritual dimensions of work can begin to resolve this impasse. A Buddhist approach, for example, takes the function of work to be at least threefold: to give a person a chance to utilize and develop skills and faculties; to help people overcome their egocentredness by joining with other people in a common and fruitful task; and, to provide the goods and services needed for oneself and others. This is hardly a radical departure from good employment practices, yet too often the emphasis is on the output and not on the human dimension of the workplace. Thus work is often organized in a manner which becomes repetitive, meaningless, boring and depressing. In effect it reduces the human to little more than the ubiquitous cog in an enormous wheel and work becomes soul-destroying.

Businesses can also be the focus for education. At heart, humans are contemplative and caring but we have lost touch with that side of our personalities. This is often because we become little more than part of the overall system and close relationships, trust, loyalty and love are all squeezed out. But it does not have to be like that – we simply need to learn and practise what comes natural enough to us given the space and energy. That process can happen within the family, within the workplace and anywhere else where we are in contact with each other.

The business organization (or any organization for that matter) can make a contribution to the six important principles which were laid out above. By seeing its own existence as part of the living Earth, sharing in interconnectedness, having a strong sense of place, showing compassion and humility, recognizing change and impermanence and contributing to reawakening, the business itself can be a force for positive change.

A business can be seen as a tribe forming part of the living Earth. A tribe because it is, after all, only a collection or coalition of people. Without those people it could not function. Tribal cultures are therefore no less pertinent to the modern industrial organization as they are to many aboriginal groups. We can learn to appreciate each other more and recognize that ours is just a small part of the living Earth. Learning to live in harmony with each other and with the environment around us is simply ancient wisdom brought into a contemporary context.

In turn, the business and people within it must be part of the inter-connectedness of all life. Too often we see the firm as having boundaries in terms of its locations and the products and services it provides and too often it shores up these boundaries as defensive strategies. Yet productive cooperation will always be superior to blind competition and recognizing cooperative opportunities is part of recognizing intercon-nectedness. The concept of interconnectedness also teaches us to value everything around us. When our production relies on raw materials from the developing world, for example, is it really acceptable to pay the lowest possible price for those raw materials ensuring that people who work for us further down the supply chain are maintained in the present poverty of their lives? Is it right that our products should cause direct suffering on animals when we choose to test ingredients on them?

Although we have said that the business should not create boundaries which will remove it from the interconnectedness of nature, it is import-ant for any organization to have a sense of place. Thinking globally and acting locally is not only a powerful strategy, it is a practical tool which can be used by the business to organize its environmental consciousness. Activities to promote local environmental improvement will be powerful if replicated elsewhere. Moves towards more bioregional models of industrial organization, local cooperation between businesses and the development of ecologically sensitive management systems can provide many advantages for both businesses and the environment (Welford 1995).

Communion, compassion and humility have a very important role to play in the business organization. The spiritually aware, environmentally conscious firm is one where there is less emphasis placed on top-down management and more emphasis placed on cooperative, collective strategies. The egos of management are replaced by trust and all members of the organization are valued for their own skills and attributes. A caring work environment can actually enhance the perform-ance of the business and makes it a more humane place to work. The responsible and caring firm can also develop a passion for its own local environment, developing local nature conservation schemes, supporting local wildlife initiatives and being involved in local education pro-grammes. These are practical strategies which the firm can undertake which nevertheless stem from recognizing a wider spiritual dimension to both the environment and the workplace.

The firm must also acknowledge its own change and impermanence and be prepared for changes which are inevitable. Holding on to fixed positions is simply bad business and the firm must be flexible and capable of change. But part of recognizing impermanence is also recognizing how transient things are and how unimportant they can be compared with other aspects of the world. The firm does not exist in isolation, nor should it expect unstinting loyalty from its employees. Indeed, it should encourage a sense of attachment and encourage employees to have other interests. A programme of involving workers in community based projects, helping them with their own further education and ensuring that there is not a culture in the organization which expects managers to work seventy hour weeks is a start.

Finally any organization can be part of a reawakening process. It simply has to follow the people within it and allow them to explore new dimensions of spirituality. But the business must be awake itself to the changes that will occur as a result of a growing tide of spirituality. More will not be seen as better than less. There is likely to be more scrutiny with respect to the environmental and social impacts of products and processes. The company can choose to be a follower but it is much more likely to be successful if it is a leader. To that extent the company should embark on its own reawakening and ethical and spiritual development through strategies associated with honesty, integrity, accountability and transparency (Welford 1996).

FROM FRINGE DWELLERS TO SPIRITUAL CONQUERORS

Until more people, more organizations and the corporate world itself rediscover, embrace and act on the spiritual dimensions of environmentalism some of us will have to accept that we are in a minority seen as somewhat quirky by those living in our mainstream society. We can however, rejoice in the fact that we are not alone and that our numbers are ever increasing. Those many people discovering alterative spiritual dimension to their lives are referred to by Stuart Wilde (1993) as fringe dwellers. He defines the fringe dwellers as people whose spirit (the very core of their being) is leaving or has left the system. They have detached themselves from and projected themselves beyond material dimensions. They find answers in tribal ritual and other spiritual paths. They are often rediscovering a spirituality which organized religion has actively sought to destroy through its own arrogant ego.

But the fringe dwellers are not a few mystics, ascetics and eccentrics. Millions of people all over the world have taken this step forwards and many follow them regularly. They are a force for change, are socially well adjusted and are hugely influential and can provide answers to many of the questions people are constantly posing. They often go through the motions of fitting in to mainstream society, they work, manage, teach and learn. But they inhabit a spiritual dimension which is on the edges of mainstream society, in a dimension of consciousness that is removed from the mainstream.

Wilde (1993, p 84) has some wonderful advice for many of us:

> *If you are a spiritual fringe dweller – or if you are becoming one – the first point of reconciliation is to admit it. You have to understand that you have projected yourself out of this world, so you may never really fit. People will mostly reject your ideas. You may never gain the recognition or acceptance to which your talents may suggest you're entitled. But you don't need recognition, and to crave it fuels the ego and affirms a lack of acceptance of self – so why drive yourself crazy? Just agree that the life of a fringe dweller is a wonderful place to be. At least you are not earth bound.*

Living in harmony with nature means cultivating mindfulness of the multitude of gifts that flow freely to us each day. Freed from the desire for greater worldly wealth or traditional political power, and liberated from the belief in unrestrained economic growth, we can settle more effortlessly into the delightful flow of energy which is nature.

However, Wilde is a little pessimistic in his vision for fringe dwellers. In fact, there is a growing awareness of the spiritual dimensions of life amongst many people. An interest in many alternative paths, new age phenomena, holistic medicines, meditation, spirituality and so on witness the beginnings of a new era. The fringe dwellers of today may be in a minority but we are growing in numbers and influence. Fringe dwellers will become spiritual conquerors: an important part of the sustainable development process.

CONCLUSIONS

Whilst there is much more ecological awareness now than there was a decade or so ago, it has not yet proven to be sufficient to redirect the course of the commercial culture which is laying waste to the natural world. We too often resist the normal grief that should be associated with all that is being lost. Because we cannot control our egos we too often fail to acknowledge the value of diversity. We are a part of the system which is causing the crisis but when challenged to do something about it cannot begin to imagine how we can stop the steamroller of large corporations in capitalism. This is now taking a heavy toll on humanity in terms of helplessness, lethargy and despondency. A few are finding that revitalization is possible by finding and developing the spiritual sides of their lives. The growth of this dimension is going to become a significant force for change.

There is a spiritual path and it and ecological considerations mix as one as we move along it. It is not however, a singular path but a differentiated and multidimensional one. That is its strength; the greater the differentiation, the greater the vitality and perfection of the whole. In this diversity of expression we are forced to challenge positivism and the supremacy of science. Acknowledging the value and power of subjectivity gives us an interior identity, an understanding of our self, our relationship with the environment and a recognition of the more mystical side of existence. The spiritual dimension offers us a way back from our contemporary alienation with the Earth. Through the practice of non-violence, compassion and contemplation we are able to celebrate the awe of nature, the value of every being and intimacy with the physical environment.

Business will have to be a part of this new spiritual wave. Indeed, if it so wishes, it can play a productive and positive role. It may not do that because it will perceive that its power is being threatened and to some extent that is true. But how strange that we talk of an inanimate organization as having power. Ultimately it is the people within the organization with the power: the power to change. As the spiritual wave impacts on their consciousness as well, so the nature of the organization will change in harmony.

References

Halifax, J (1990) 'The Third Body: Buddhism, Shamanism and Deep Ecology' in Badiner, A H (ed.) *Dharma Gaia*, Parallax Press, Berkeley

Lovelock, J E (1979) *Gaia: A New Look at Life on Earth*, Oxford University Press, New York

Schumacher, E F (1974) *Small is Beautiful*, Abacus, London

Welford, R J (1995) *Environmental Strategy and Sustainable Development: The Corporate Challenge for the 21st Century*, Routledge, London

Welford, R J (1996) *Corporate Environmental Management: Systems and Strategies*, Earthscan, London

Wilde, S (1993) *Whispering Winds of Change*, Nacson & Sons, Sydney

10

Towards a More Critical Dimension for Environmental Research

Richard Welford

Chapters in this book have argued repeatedly that the environment is heading towards clear crisis and that businesses and their managers are responsible for much of this. Moreover, whilst businesses have accepted the general need for environmental and social responsibility, the rhetoric has not been translated into meaningful action. Instead through the paradigm of eco-modernism business tells us that there is no alternative to the free market system, that private capital flows in a free trade environment will yield environmental improvement through technology transfer and that they will take on even more environmental responsibility when consumers demand it. They ignore the fact that as powerful social actors, businesses have a duty to create change but prefer to claim that they are the oppressed when they plead for further deregulation.

In most cases, businesses have completely ignored the social aspects of sustainability, even when they have recognized the need for environmental action. As we have seen however, the environmental damage already done is not being reversed, it is getting worse. Eco-modernism and the self-regulatory approach which business heralds is clearly not working. Meanwhile there is a growing unemployment problem, poverty is increasing, repressed groups are still discriminated against, indigenous populations are still losing their livelihoods and the political power of the transnational corporation removes the democratic power of the individual and the democratic accountability of governments.

The conclusions of this book are numerous and summarized in more detail at the end of each chapter. However, it is clear that businesses could and should do more to protect the environment and move to more equitable social arrangements. In many cases this means reversing many of the unsustainable practices which businesses indulge in and challenging the exploitation inherent in the system within which businesses operate. In order to move towards a more sustainable future it is clear, therefore, that we need to know more and to better understand the links between society, social reality, business activity, the environment and sustainable development. This is particularly the case in a world where the major polluters (businesses) are defining these concepts for themselves in a way which, at best, gives us a very weak definition of sustainability. Business must do more but cannot be allowed to do so in isolation. There is both a need to track what businesses are doing and a need to produce proposals for what they ought to be doing. This book has made some tentative suggestions in that respect but there is a need for much more debate and discussion about the way we do business in the future. We therefore need a more critical research agenda and a clear framework for putting the results of that research into a clear programme of action. Research must provide us with new knowledge, a better understanding of social reality and provide us with alternatives so that we can consider how we can begin to make the changes necessary to avoid the mounting crises in our societies.

THE INADEQUACIES AND INEFFECTIVENESS OF CURRENT BUSINESS RESEARCH

To date, research into the links between business activity, the environment and sustainable development has been inadequate in terms of both quantity and quality. There has been too much description on the one hand and on the other, a fixation with trying to prove (using a more scientific method) that eco-efficiency will improve the economic performance of the firm. That is not to suggest that these approaches are flawed – only that they are limited and have, in general, not added significantly to the debate over sustainable development. There is a need for a much more critical perspective which stresses both knowledge and action. We need to see much more normative research which challenges business to do things differently and lays out an agenda for change.

A more critical research agenda must be more able to identify the contradictions and tensions which exist between business, its stakeholders and environmental and social implications. It needs to provide a critique of 'business as usual' and be clearly aware of the consequences of continuing the modernist path. Most importantly, the results of research must be operationalized through better communication strategies and a heightening of awareness and commitment towards sustainable development amongst management.

Increasingly, researchers have been working closely with business and have produced some interesting accounts about how a few 'leading edge' companies have taken account of the social and environmental consequences of their actions. But, in typically positivist mode, researchers have been less willing to engage in a political debate. Too often, for example, academics communicate their research findings only with other academics and their students and fail therefore to grasp the need for change amongst policy-makers and decision-takers. They shy away from translating research findings into a real agenda for change. The results of research should not be judged in terms of publications – that is merely an intermediate indicator of activity. The ultimate measure should be associated with action and change. Unless such research leads to change it is in fact pointless.

Any research agenda covering moves towards sustainable development must be very clear of the demands of sustainable development. We have argued before that we might not be able to precisely define what sustainable development is but we know what it is not. It is not just about eco-efficiency, it is not merely about integrating ecology with economy, and it is certainly not about just putting environmental management systems in place. Sustainable development requires much more systemic thinking and interdisciplinary approaches. It means, for example, including issues such as equity, justice, rights, empowerment, bio-diversity, ethics and a whole raft of social issues. To ignore these aspects might still result in some interesting research about environmental management but we should never equate that with sustainable development. To do so is dishonest and will only go to legitimize the inadequate approaches of the business world which repeatedly tries to equate eco-efficiency with sustainable development. We must nail that lie.

One of the main aims of research must be to provide answers and solutions and help humans move to a position of increased awareness, knowledge and ultimately enlightenment. Human life can be improved but that requires us to recognize interconnectedness and to improve the life of other species with which we share the planet and the environment in general. Ultimately we must ask ourselves what we seek. In other words, what are our terminal goals? These can never be materialistic since 'things' only serve the outer attributes of the inner self. Greek political experience and Greek philosophy provide us with three terminal goals: freedom, justice and reason. To improve the freedom of the individual (and particularly repressed groups), to ensure justice and to give life reason must also be the ultimate goal of the researcher.

However small that contribution might be, it is the only justification for using public money to finance research.

The purpose of this concluding chapter is therefore to lay out a research agenda which is capable of being much more critical of the relationship between business and the environment. It is vital that we move towards a more interdisciplinary approach to research which moves us beyond the narrow subject boundaries which so often dominate our approach to investigations. We require a systematic critique of social conditions which will also point towards a clearer direction of a more sustainable society and which is capable of translating research output into action for change. The approach must therefore be emancipatory, releasing constraints on human rights – including rights to live in a more environmentally sound world. This represents a clear challenge for traditional scientific research which is narrow in its focus, has come to dominate the research agenda and provides little consideration of matters associated with freedom, justice and reason. This approach to research is not particularly new but it has too often been ignored in the past and been over-shadowed by positivism (which has so often let us down). However, it is an innovative and exciting approach which has the potential to produce higher quality research and action. This approach is based on what has become known as critical theory.

COMPARATIVE APPROACHES TO RESEARCH

There are, of course, a number of alternative approaches to research. In Figure 10.1 these are grouped into three alternative approaches to seeking knowledge. This approach (which was adopted in chapter 3) is based on the work of Burrell and Morgan (1979) and positions these alternatives along two continua. The subjective–objective axis focuses on the fundamental assumptions made about the nature of reality. On the one hand, extreme subjectivism argues that social reality is constructed on the basis of the perceptions of individuals (constructivism). On the other hand, extreme objectivism assumes that social reality exists as a concrete entity, which is independent of individual perceptions.

The order–conflict axis focuses on views with respect to social change. On the one hand, we have order, typified by regulation, consensus and shared beliefs. The aim here is to explain how society works, to explain certain stable phenomena and how society tends to hold together. On the other hand, we find conflict, radical change and discontinuity. Conflict approaches stress change and turmoil and focus on how human beings can be emancipated from the dominant structures (such as eco-

Figure 10.1 Comparative Approaches to Research (derived from Murray and Ozanne, 1991)

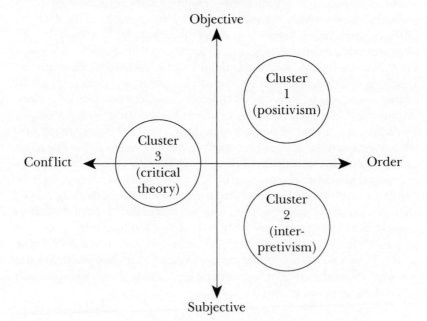

modernism) that limit and repress their development and the development of society.

Business related research has often been dominated by objective–order paradigms (cluster 1 in Figure 10.1). This stresses research into the operation of markets and businesses through the tools of neoclassical economics, behaviourism, cognitive psychology, structuralism and management science. It stresses model building and the use of scientific method with an emphasis on statistical techniques. It has been a powerful movement and because so many academics believe it to be the only way to do research, it has had a self-perpetuating life as younger researchers have been constrained by their mentors. Despite the common calls for interdisciplinary research, this type of scientific approach continues to often adopt traditional, narrow techniques with the aim of explaining and predicting existing social behaviour. We can consider this whole approach as positivism. Positivist social science is based on determining causal relationships between variables and then using this information to manipulate and control the social world. But the approach is sterile with little vision and no underlying ends being identified.

Other approaches to business related research (which have probably grown in importance in the last ten years) have begun to emphasise an approach more consistent with the subjective–order orientation (cluster 2). This has certainly enriched our understanding of the modern business enterprise and its activities. Much of this research has been very descriptive and is often not easily generalizable. Its starting point is to recognize that the world is too complex and diverse to boil down into simplified models. Its qualitative approaches provide much richer accounts of phenomena. However, it tends not to be critical or visionary and its approach is difficult to build into useful models with practical value. This type of research can be considered as interpretivism. In an interpretive social science the main aim is one of clarification, that is, outlining the relationships between key paradigms and associated behaviours with an emphasis on social norms, values and beliefs. This sort of research provides little basis on which to interpret events in society as a whole however.

The third cluster in Figure 10.1 represents critical theory which stresses both the objective and subjective approaches to research but sees the product of its research as aiming to create change. Thus social reality is seen as being full of conflicts and contradictions which need to be exposed. Research stresses the action which needs to be taken to create social change which will improve human life and wider aspects of human existence (including the environment). Its approach is much more generalizable because it examines the conflicts and contradictions between various social actors, institutions and power structures. Its message is a message of identifying problems and then creating awareness, action and change. Since many of us now recognize that there is a need for quite radical change in the way we do business if we are to reverse environmental degradation and social conflict, then the approach to research to be found in critical theory has much to offer.

An approach which aims to be critical and lead to change for the better means adopting a conflict orientation. Here there is much more emphasis on identifying the structures which prevent progress, in other words highlighting those barriers to the improvement of the well-being of the planet. Seeing business as one of these barriers seems a much more productive starting point than simply analysing or describing what businesses are doing as they march forward on the eco-modernist path. Critical theory also emphasizes that knowledge is never independent and neutral but fundamentally tied to the interests of those people and institutions with power (in this context, businesses). The issue becomes not whether an apolitical, positivist approach to research is possible but rather what political stance we should take (and declare). Those who try to undertake apolitical research will, of course, shun this approach. But if we carefully examine what they are doing we usually find that their approaches are incredibly conservative and bounded by a narrow view of both knowledge and its roots. They maintain the status quo without even considering the consequences of so doing. They legitimize business as usual and add very little value to what are very complex issues.

As was discussed in Chapter 3, our starting point for meaningful research must therefore be to accept that knowledge is produced and that it is not neutral information which can be applied in a number of different ways. By separating knowledge (facts) from how it is used (interests), interpretivists and positivists fail to challenge the existing system: indeed, they simply reinforce the status quo. So much research on business and the environment, for example, not only replicates existing structures and functions, it actually makes them even more embedded. Research paper after research paper on environmental management systems or eco-efficiency simply reinforces those approaches as the most valid. Critical theorists, on the other hand believe that science is not an activity far removed from practical and moral action. Thus the emphasis for researchers is on translating their results into actions. Critical theory stresses the need for a political and moral social science, designed to change society for the better (Fuhrman 1979). Research must be capable of generating social change strategies which can be used by policy-makers and public interest groups.

For those committed to improving the environment in which we live and moving towards a situation more consistent with sustainable development, there are a number of general themes which should form the basis of research methodologies:

1 Whatever the subject under study, research should be based on a critique of society and its constituent parts. Thus structures and power relationships should be clearly considered.
2 Approaches need to be interdisciplinary since distinctions between different types of scholarly activity will tend to mask our treatment of interconnectedness. A combination of philosophical, political, economic, structural and psychological perspectives are needed to fully understand authority, culture, behaviour and science.
3 Research should emphasize interrelationships. Findings should not be separated from values, belief systems, spirituality and emotions.
4 The results of our research should emphasize potential improvements to humans, societies and to the world in which we live. In particular, it should focus on improving the quality of life for repressed social groups.
5 Research should have an emancipatory interest in knowledge that enhances the possibility of freedom.
6 Research should unmask social contradictions, revealing how the social structure facilitates and maintains these distortions. In so doing, results should outline alternative social structures which can be a force for change.

7 Part of the research process should be to consider what action can be taken to solve a problem, as a natural part of the whole exercise. In other words, one of the outcomes of research should be an agenda for change.

RESEARCH METHODOLOGY

The starting point for a more critical research agenda is to question the relatively extreme positions of both positivists and interpretivists. Since positivists believe that a single, objective reality exists, they under-estimate the importance of seeing the world as a product of history, culture and institutional structures and fail to show how the results of their research can make a change in the society under consideration. On the other hand, interpretivists believe that all the knowledge in the world is subjective and therefore undervalue the material dimensions of reality which can, if controlled, be harnesses for change as well.

Murray and Ozanne (1991) point out that critical theorists specifically point to and study the tensions and inconsistencies between meaning and structures. These contradictions can be the source of change and part of the research process must be to point towards the direction of change. It is imperative to recognize that reality is socially produced but that the structures making up that reality (e.g. businesses) can become stubborn, entrenched and very powerful. They then resist social change and become constraining. Unless there is room for reflection, the meanings people attribute to social structures change more slowly than the structures themselves. One aim of research must be to make people more aware so that their ideas about reality are not congruent with the structures which dictate that reality. This awareness can serve as an impetus for rational social development and change. Thus as people become more aware of the damage which businesses and their own consumption patterns are doing to the environment and the health of themselves and their children, then they will be better prepared to take hold of the change which is required.

From a critical perspective one cannot separate the social organization of knowledge production from the knowledge itself. Moreover, although reality can be considered a human product, it is often created by power-ful elites of people and therefore behind the backs and against the wills of some individuals (Jay 1973). Thus those who own and manage businesses, finance capital and manage the physical and communi-cations infrastructure, generally have more of an impact on the creation of reality than does the average person. Furthermore, the most powerful may be able to push society in a direction which solidifies their own

Table 10.1 Alternative methodological approaches to research (derived from Murray and Ozanne, 1991)

Research process	Positivism	Interpretivism	Critical theory
General methodology	Scientific method and prediction	Case studies and description	Problem identification, problem solving and change
Preparation stage	Review of existing literature and comparison with other work	Identification of a phenomenon of interest	Identification of a concrete practical problem
	Develop an *a priori* conceptual framework	Subject's boundaries are left open and undelineated	Identification of all parties involved with this problem
General research structure	Develop empirically testable hypothesis	Categorization of prior conceptions	Interpretation: construction of an understanding of each group and interrelationships between groups
	Fix design for the testing of the hypothesis	Immersion in a 'natural' setting	Empirical examination: consideration of historical development and of the development of social structures and processes
	Gather data	Design, questions and sampling strategies evolve as phenomenon is studied	Dialectics: the search for contradictions and inconsistencies in the problem being investigated
	Strict adherence to scientific protocol	Reliance on the human instrument for gathering description	Awareness: discussion of alternative ways of seeing the situation of all groups
	Statistical analysis of data to yield results	Content or textual analysis to yield an interpretation	Change: participate in a theoretically grounded programme of action to change social conditions
Information gathering techniques	Laboratory or controlled experiment	Participant observation	In-depth interviews
	Large scale survey	In-depth interviews	Historical and structural analysis
			Survey of 'interested' parties
Evaluation criteria	Validity and reliability	Creation of thick description	Improvement in quality of human life with an emphasis on repressed groups
	Predictive capability	Comparative case studies	Improvement of social and environmental conditions

dominance. It is therefore difficult to see how a sophisticated researcher can on the one hand claim to be a non-political scientific theorizer (as positivists would wish) and, on the other hand, as an individual, a political participant. Researchers do not and should not inhabit a moral and ethical void.

Research should therefore be emancipatory, designed not only to reveal empirical and interpretive understanding but also to free social actors who are constrained. Researchers should be fully engaged with the subject under study and must move beyond mere observation of subjects or participants and attempt, through dialogue, to reveal barriers and constraints, thereby motivating conscious political action and change. The critical researcher is therefore a liberator, seeking to make us all aware of oppressive structures as a first step towards effective research.

In Table 10.1 derived from Murray and Ozanne (1991) our three generalized approaches to research are outlined and compared. The critical approach is contrasted with positivist and interpretativist approaches in order to provide the reader with a frame of reference. Here, however, we deal in detail only with the critical theory approach. In terms of research methodology the approach is considered in four stages: the preparation stage; the general research structure; information gathering techniques; and, evaluation criteria.

Preparation Stage

The focus of critical theory is problem identification and problem solving (e.g. recycling of waste, ozone depletion, exploitation of indigenous populations). It is not an abstract research methodology but focuses on real problems perceived by the researcher and others. In the initial stage of research the problem is identified and all groups and individuals who are affected by or who are part of the problem are identified. The researcher must prepare him/herself to be fully engaged in the situation under investigation and be prepared for the contribution to change process which will result from the research. It is important to take every step possible not to neglect or forget about certain interest groups since this will result in asymmetrical findings and an incomplete account of and solution to the problem.

General Research Structure

The research structure can be broken down into five generalizable steps as follows:

1 Interpretation

Central to the critical perspective is the view that social problems result from contradictory interests and differences in power. Thus social structures and processes benefit some groups but are detrimental to others. This will be very much related to power structures. The first step is to develop a detailed understanding of each stakeholder's view of a situation, because actions can only be fully understood in relation to an understanding of their particular interests. This requires dialogue between the researcher and interested individuals and groups which will reveal the social, cultural and historical text. The researcher therefore hopes to understand social action of all subjects and interrelationships between subjects. In some ways this is similar to the type of understanding which interpretivists seek. However, for the critical researcher this is just the first step in a more detailed process.

2 Empirical examination

Social reality requires both an understanding of individual groups and interrelationships as well as an understanding of the material forces that can constrain social action (the object). Thus it is important to understand the historical and cultural development of relevant social structures (e.g. capitalism and the market mechanism) and processes (e.g. exchange and employment). The aim is to provide an empirical account of the context in which the ideas of social actors have developed. Once social actors understand that their own social conditions are culturally and historically constructed, then they are able to realize that they are capable of building their own future structures. Thus this understanding is central to any change process which will follow.

The first two stages of the research therefore link closely to systemic thinking which we have identified as important throughout this book. There is a need to fully appreciate the interconnectedness of social structures and the interconnectedness of issues. The researcher needs to think widely about all the links into the social process and involved in the problem being identified. That is not to argue that social actors will be powerless because they are a small part of the problem. Indeed, being clearer of the whole picture and understanding one's traditional place within it helps to more clearly identify the action which can be taken to change it.

3 Dialectics

This part of the research process clearly differentiates critical theory from positivism and interpretivism. By comparing both the social actors' understandings of the situation under study and the perceived interrelationships between different groups, with the more empirical account of the development of structures and processes, the researcher can identify inconsistencies and contradictions which exist in a particular situation. These are likely to arise through a mismatch in power structures between various groups and interests. The revealed contradictions need to be more fully identified and elaborated and any group which is constrained or damaged is identified. The problem becomes more interesting when the same individuals can be identified as having contradictory positions, for example, as both exploited and exploiter. When it comes to corporate environmental issues, men who are both managers and fathers often find themselves in this position.

4 Awareness

Communication is the key here. The researcher needs to engage the social actors in dialogue to help them see their current situation differently, open up alternatives and initiate programmes of action. It is up to the researcher to identify alternative paths and to show social actors alternative ways of behaving (including challenging the traditional vestiges of power). Thus putting together educational programmes, to create pressure group activity and encouraging others to empower themselves is central.

5 Change

The final step is to put the awareness stage into action. A programme of action should be seen as the natural extension of the critical research agenda. Action and application is the natural and ultimate test of a proposition. Not to take action as a result of a research process is to waste the whole process of research in the first place. As part of this, it is up to the researcher to have a clear vision of unconstraining social conditions and to bring them into existence through political action.

Information Gathering Techniques

The critical researcher will use a whole range of techniques for gathering information, evidence and data. Both subjective (e.g. participant observation) and objective (e.g. sampling) methods may be used and results compared. Whilst gathering relevant material from a wide range of sources, the researcher will certainly want to immerse him/herself into the situation under study and is therefore likely to use in-depth interviews to gather a rich and deep account of the situation. What is important in the critical approach is to gather information about structures, cultures and historical events which have shaped the present situation. This naturally leads on to a consideration of competing objectives between different groups through an analysis of power relationships.

Evaluation

The key to evaluating critical research is to determine whether there is evidence of real tangible benefits to people (particularly repressed groups) and the planet. The researcher must demonstrate a real understanding based on the perceptions of people involved in the research, how social conditions are a product of history and culture and show how contradictions impact upon the aspirations of different groups. Most importantly, the researcher should become involved in programmes of change capable of bringing about improvements in the problems identified, making society better. This is the ultimate test of useful research.

A RESEARCH AGENDA FOR ENVIRONMENTAL MANAGEMENT

Since the ultimate aim of the critical approach to research is to bring about change it has an applied, practical focus. It does not exist in a sterile scientific vacuum and it seeks to do much more than simply describe. Application is an integral part of the research process. It is not for others to apply the results of the research when and if it suits them: it is up to the researcher to drive his or her own change process. It is therefore the researcher rather than the practitioner who first decides how results should be used. Moreover, since this type of research cannot be seen as neutral, it is up to the researcher to make political dimensions of the research clear and to reveal who benefits and who loses from the socially constructed contradictory interests. The research should be emancipatory aimed at improving the quality of life for humans and animals which are constrained and damaged by more powerful interests. It should provide for meaningful environmental improvements and a move towards sustainable development.

When it comes to environmental research, where we are faced with enormous problems and contradictions, the focus of research must be on problem solving. We must therefore focus on the conflicts which exist between groups (e.g. between transnational corporations and the indigenous populations who are forced off their land, or between wealthy entrepreneurs and the low wage poor). Academics must therefore be free to pursue their research interests and research methodology and not constrained by the powerful institutions which create inertia. We must be careful about not becoming too close to any one business, no matter how committed to change they claim to be. Moreover, research (or academic positions) funded directly by business must be viewed with considerable suspicion. In the field of the environment, we could benefit greatly from a group of committed researchers who are unattached to external constituencies and who can offer a critique of those groups who control power and influence the direction of society. Such powerful institutions must take on much of the responsibility for the unsustainable practices which we observe today.

One of the most important tools in the analysis of environmental problems is the dialectical step. The researcher needs to be aware of tensions and contradictions which exist between different groups and needs to be able to explain and interpret distortions which exist in any system. In particular, those who benefit from any distortions need to be examined along with their motives. So often we find that the contradictions and tensions between subject and object are the result of social construction by the business world (e.g. the promulgation of the assumption that free trade is important). If this contradiction has a coercive influence (e.g. on indigenous populations, on the sustainability of the planet and on consumers who buy products which they would not normally buy) then the company should be held liable. Most importantly, the researcher should not simply stand back and report these tensions. The next stage must be to engage them and to propose some solutions.

Ultimately, for environmentalists (including researchers with a commitment to environmental improvement) the findings of the research process and the potential solutions highlighted should form the foundations for action. We must disseminate our work to as wide a constituency as possible, and in the case of company liabilities, to legislators, policy makers and consumer groups who can all also be encouraged to take action in their different ways. The ultimate outcome would be to see some action take place which helps to resolve the contradictions (e.g. tighter controls on international trade, better protection for indigenous populations and better public information on the impacts of internationally traded goods).

The focus of research on business and the environment should be to recognize that the role of the business is to bring goods and services to the market in such a way as to satisfy consumer wants whilst achieving the traditional objectives of business (profit maximization or the maximization of shareholder wealth). Central to the dialectic are the contradictions which arise between the private interest (economic efficiency) and the public interest (social efficiency). Moreover, the researcher must recognize that the historical development of capitalism often means that in the market place it is the private interest which is a more powerful force than the public good, and that the contradictions which do exist do so because they benefit businesses and their owners. At the root of these tensions are the power structures which support the corporate elite and their aspirations.

The role of the researcher is to enunciate the contradictions and point to the vested interests which benefit business but which cause social and environmental damage. The practice stage might involve some sort of campaign to put pressure on the business to take account of the whole range of its stakeholders rather than the more narrowly defined interests. But practice may also mean working with the business, convincing them that they can actually benefit by tackling the contradictions which they face. The argument of the researcher might be that although business benefits from present arrangements, it might be possible to change those arrangements and benefit still further by narrowing the gap between the company's own objectives and the aspirations of others. For example, if a company can be encouraged to improve the environmental performance of both its processes and products and to organize its activities to be more socially responsible, then its products can gain added value and this can lead to a competitive advantage which is not so socially disadvantageous. The researcher can help ensure that this competitive advantage can act in both the private and public interest so that contradictions are narrowed. They can, for example, encourage the firm to base their marketing campaigns more around education than the 'hard sell' as some companies have already done. However, if this sort of approach proves fruitless and if companies remain unwilling to shift their positions or take on board their social responsibilities, the researcher should be prepared to take on a more adversarial stance.

CONCLUSIONS

A critical approach to environmental research requires longer time horizons and a deeper commitment to identifying and solving substantive problems. But in so doing it is a much more powerful force for change than more traditional approaches to research (positivism and interpretivism). The researcher must extend his or her involvement beyond merely reporting results into real action for change either through working with businesses who are committed to social and environmental improvements or, alternatively by challenging them head on in a more adversarial manner. My own research has generally found that the latter stance is the natural outcome of the general research structure and this book reflects the sad fact that there is still an enormous gap between business activities and the aspirations of their stakeholder groups.

The critical approach differs from other research methodologies by explicitly acknowledging its emancipatory interests. It seeks to free people from all forms of domination and arrive at some answer to the terminal goals of research (freedom, justice and reason). In so doing it seeks to outline and envision better forms of rational social organization which are more sustainable and better protect the traditionally repressed groups of humans.

References

Burrell, G and Morgan, G (1979) *Sociological Paradigms and Organizational Analysis*, Heinemann, London

Fuhrman, E (1979) 'The Normative Structure of Critical Theory', *Human Studies*, 2, 209–28

Jay, M (1973) *The Dialectical Imagination*, Little Brown, Boston Mass.

Murray, J B and Ozanne, J L (1991) 'The Critical Imagination: Emancipatory Interests in Consumer Research', *Journal of Consumer Research*, 18, 129–43

Note

This chapter recognises its links to the seminal contribution of Murray and Ozanne (1991). In particular, the research methodology suggested here follows their generalised structure.

Index